International Federation of Library Associations and Institutions
Fédération Internationale des Associations de Bibliothécaires et des Bibliothèques
Internationaler Verband der bibliothekarischen Vereine und Institutionen
Международная Федерация Библиотечных Ассоциаций и Учреждений
Federación Internacional de Asociaciones de Bibliotecarios y Bibliotecas
国际图书馆协会与机构联合会

الاتحاد الدولي لجمعيات ومؤسسات المكتبات

About IFLA   www.ifla.org

IFLA (The International Federation of Library Associations and Institutions) is the leading international body representing the interests of library and information services and their users. It is the global voice of the library and information profession.

IFLA provides information specialists throughout the world with a forum for exchanging ideas and promoting international cooperation, research and development in all fields of library activity and information service. IFLA is one of the means through which libraries, information centres, and information professionals worldwide can formulate their goals, exert their influence as a group, protect their interests and find solutions to global problems.

IFLA's aims, objectives, and professional programme can only be fulfilled with the cooperation and active involvement of its members and affiliates. Currently, approximately 1,600 associations, institutions and individuals, from widely divergent cultural back-grounds, are working together to further the goals of the Federation and to promote librarianship on a global level. Through its formal membership, IFLA directly or indirectly represents some 500,000 library and information professionals worldwide.

IFLA pursues its aims through a variety of channels, including the publication of a major journal, as well as guidelines, reports and monographs on a wide range of topics. IFLA organizes workshops and seminars around the world to enhance professional practice and increase awareness of the growing importance of libraries in the digital age. All this is done in collaboration with a number of other non-governmental organizations, funding bodies and international agencies such as UNESCO and WIPO. IFLANET, the Federation's website, is a prime source of information about IFLA, its policies and activities: www.ifla.org

Library and information professionals gather annually at the IFLA World Library and Information Congress, held in August each year in cities around the world.

IFLA was founded in Edinburgh, Scotland, in 1927 at an international conference of national library directors. IFLA was registered in the Netherlands in 1971. The Koninklijke Bibliotheek (Royal Library), the national library of the Netherlands, in The Hague, generously provides the facilities for our headquarters. Regional offices are located in Rio de Janeiro, Brazil; Pretoria, South Africa; and Singapore.

IFLA Publications 157

The Road to Information Literacy

Librarians as Facilitators of Learning

Edited by
Roisin Gwyer, Ruth Stubbings,
and Graham Walton

De Gruyter Saur

IFLA Publications
edited by Louis Takács and Ingeborg Verheul

ISBN 978-3-11-028084-5
e-ISBN 978-3-11-028100-2
ISSN 0344-6891

Library of Congress Cataloging-in-Publication Data
A CIP catalog record for this book has been applied for at the Library of Congress

Bibliographic information published by the Deutsche Nationalibliothek
The Deutsche Nationalbibliothek lists this publication in the Deutsche Nationalbibliografie;
detailed bibliographic data is available in the Internet at http://dnb.dnb.de.

Walter de Gruyter GmbH & Co. KG, Berlin/Boston

∞ Printed on permanent paper
The paper used in this publication meets the minimum requirements of American National
Standard – Permanence of Paper for Publications and Documents in Libraries and Archives
ANSI/NISO Z39.48-1992 (R1997)

Cover Image: Jupiterimages/Brand X Pictures/Thinkstock
Typesetting: Dr. Rainer Ostermann, München
Printing and binding: Strauss GmbH, Mörlenbach

Printed in Germany

www.degruyter.com

Contents

Effective Information Literacy Interventions

Effective Continuing Professional Development

Foreword

This volume contains a selection of papers that were prepared for the Continuing Professional Development & Workplace Learning Section and the Information Literacy Section satellite conference that took place in Tampere, Finland between the 8th-10th August 2012. The satellite conference preceded the World Library and Information Congress of the International Federation of Library Associations and Institutions (IFLA) held in Helsinki from 11th to 17th August 2012. The Tampere satellite conference was a significant event, as it was the first time the two sections (Continuing Professional Development and Workplace Learning Section & Information Literacy Section) had collaborated on a joint event.

The theme of the joint satellite conference, 'The Road to Information Literacy: Librarians as Facilitators of Learning' reflects the concerns of both partners. With the rapid growth of information available, especially digital information, it is imperative that individuals are able to find, evaluate and ethically use information to support their learning, social and work life. In addition, governments across the world are increasingly recognising the importance of information literacy to society, both in terms of economic and social success.

IFLA actively endorses the Alexandria Proclamation on Information Literacy and Lifelong Learning, which states:

> "Information Literacy lies at the core of lifelong learning. It empowers people in all walks of life to seek, evaluate, use and create information effectively to achieve their personal, social, occupational and educational goals. It is a basic human right in a digital world and promotes social inclusion of all nations" (Garner 2006; p. 3).

Librarians have a key role in developing individuals' information literacy capabilities.

The satellite conference explored issues that cut across a variety of organizational structures, library types, different cultures and geographical regions and included:

- How to provide professional development to librarians in all types of libraries, so they can help their user communities become information literate;
- Tools to support and promote information literacy;
- Information literacy in a work context and;

    – The importance of the information literacy concept to the role of library / information professionals regardless of the type of information organization they work in.

In many ways, the ideas and focus for this conference came from the CPDWL's previous IFLA satellite conference in Bologna, Italy. This took place between the 18th and 20th August 2009 and the theme was 'Strategies for regenerating the library and information professions'. Developing workforces that are competent and confident in taking on information literacy activities is one way new roles and approaches can be introduced to the profession. The two Sections have the profile, skills and experience to organise a substantive conference on the theme of 'Road to Information Literacy: Librarians as Facilitators of Learning'.

    The conference showcased examples of best practices in developing a library work force that uses information literacy capabilities to support their readers. These examples have been presented through research based scholarly presentations and experiential, practical stories of successes and lessons learned. The intention has been to cover the following general themes:

    – Strategies for designing and implementing a professional development information literacy program for librarians.
    – Helping librarians to become effective information literacy guides for their community.
    – Fostering librarians own conceptual understandings and practical applications of information literacy in their work.
    – What works best in institutionalizing information literacy in workplace training programs?
    – How do we sell information literacy as a necessary practice to librarians and administrators?
    – What tools and resources are needed to support information literacy development for librarians?
    – What information literacy standards and competencies should be incorporated into a staff development program?
    – The role of library associations and library education programs in preparing librarians for information literacy and education roles.

The papers included in the volume highlight the qualities and skills needed to become information literate and reflect the development of information literacy from finding and accessing information to an increasing emphasis on the evaluation and management of the vast amounts of information now easily available. There is also recognition of new forms of literacy, such as digital literacy. These areas have not always been the province of librarians, but the partnerships and collaborations described in some papers show how librarians are moving out of traditional roles and physical territories to embrace wider skills and environments. Underpinning all this is the need, outlined in the keynote address from Professor Lonka, for the creation of integrated physical, virtual, social and mental learning spaces. The role of librarians in the successful design and delivery of information literacy programmes is considered such as how virtual learning environments in schools and universities can be used to deliver information literacy programmes. Some papers look at using particular social networking tools, such as wikis, or knowledge management tools as a basis for building an information literacy programme. One paper is concerned with developing students of librarianship through a service learning model which helps foster information literacy within a local community. There are also tips on how one can evaluate librarians as facilitators of learning.

The challenges of including information literacy in staff development programmes are described. Papers cover programmes for all staff within large institutions such as national libraries, developing particular teams within an individual institution and also how one person librarians can develop themselves. One paper looks at how succession planning for delivering information literacy can be fostered between individuals in a university setting. The impetus for staff development can come from the implementation within a library service of web-scale discovery tools and there are examples of how these implementations have been used to help develop library-wide information literacy skills which then underpin service to users. How librarians develop a range of skills, including information literacy, teaching and negotiation skills through formal qualifications, CPD events, mentoring and even trial & error are described.

Librarians are collaborative by nature and keen to learn from each others' experiences. Cultural or regional differences in developing information literacy staff development programmes are explored. Papers are included from all five continents and reflect differences, but also similarities. Cross-sectoral and international partnerships can encourage the sharing of effective practice and the development of library staff skills. At least one international collaboration is described between African and European partners learning from each other, as well as partnerships across sectors such as public and university libraries working together to promote literacy across a whole country.

Another crucial element was for the papers to look at the challenging questions posed such as how we promote modelling of good information literacy practices in libraries, strategies for teaching librarians to be excellent communicators and the types of feedback most helpful to librarians implementing an information literacy program.

The Conference Planning Team was fortunate to have more than 80 proposals submitted. From this encouraging response, about 50 were developed into conference presentations and over 20 were selected for this publication. Papers have been received from across the world and they were all submitted to an international reviewing process. It is a real privilege to be able to publish the 2012 Elizabeth W. Stone lecture given by Professor Kirsti Lonka. She is Vice Dean of the Faculty of Behavioural Sciences and Professor of Educational Psychology at University of Helsinki, Finland.

The Editors would like to thank a wide range of people who made this collection of papers such a success. Gratitude is expressed to the authors who have captured their innovative and creative ideas so well on paper. The reviewing panel are very much appreciated for their commitment and timely work. It is also recognised that the Sections' committee members displayed foresight in realising the need for a conference around this theme. De Gruyter Saur have long supported CPDWL's conferences and their continued input is valued, as is the help received from IFLA in the person of Louis Takacs.

Roisin Gwyer, University of Portsmouth Library, United Kingdom
roisin.gwyer@port.ac.uk

Ruth Stubbings, Nottingham Trent University Library, United Kingdom
ruth.stubbings@ntu.ac.uk

Graham Walton, Loughborough University Library, United Kingdom
j.g.walton@lboro.ac.uk

Garner, S. D. (Ed.) (2006). High-Level Colloquium on Information Literacy and Lifelong Learning Bibliotheca Alexandrina, Alexandria, Egypt November 6-9, 2005. Report of a Meeting Sponsored by the United Nations Education, Scientific, and Cultural Organisation (UNESCO), National Forum on Information Literacy (NFIL) and the International Federation of Library Associations and Institutions (IFLA). UNESCO & IFLA. Retrieved from the IFLA website: archive.ifla.org/III/ wsis/High-Level-Colloquium.pdf.

The Road to Information Literacy: Librarians as Facilitators of Learning

8-10 August 2012, Tampere, Finland
Organised by the Continuing Professional Development and Workplace Learning Section (CPDWL) and the Information Literacy Section (IL)

Susan Schnuer, CPDWL and Leena Toivonen, IL Co-Convenors

Welcome to the Ninth Satellite Conference of IFLA's Continuing Professional Development and Workplace Learning Section in Tampere, Finland. We are pleased to follow a pattern that CPDWL initiated with the last Satellite meeting in Bologna, Italy by co-sponsoring this event with another IFLA section, Information Literacy. The two sections have set high standards for the quality of the Satellite meeting and the planning committee has worked tirelessly and collaboratively to organize, what we hope will be a fruitful meeting for all participants.

We want to take a minute to thank our sponsors who have so generously supported this event – City of Tampere, Tampere University Library, Tampere University Press, and Emerald Group Publishing Limited.

Plans began for this meeting at the last World Congress conference in Puerto Rico. CPDWL was looking forward to holding its next satellite meeting in Finland but also wanted to partner with another IFLA section. Within the first few minutes of discussion the Information Literacy section was mentioned as a possible partner. They were enthusiastic about the idea and a theme for the conference soon emerged from our joint discussions.

Together we determined that the satellite meeting would provide a platform for exploring issues such as providing professional development to librarians so that they could help their user communities become information literate. We also wanted to focus on information literacy in the work context and the importance of information literacy to the role of library and information professionals. Our desire is that these proceedings will convey the richness of the interactions and the complexity of the topics that were presented.

We hope that you will find the papers in this volume help you in your voyage of navigating the roads of Continuing Professional Development and Information Literacy in your library.

Engaging Learning Environments for the Future
The 2012 Elizabeth W. Stone Lecture

Professor Kirsti Lonka
University of Helsinki
kirsti.lonka@helsinki.fi

Abstract

New requirements for skills, competencies, and knowledge emerge from the innovation-driven knowledge society. This paper explores the possibilities and challenges for developing new integrated physical, virtual, social and mental learning spaces that promote knowledge creation and collaboration. My main claim is that it is vital to take into account modern theories of learning when designing physical learning environments. Especially, this is important in the context of universities which have maintained their basic forms of knowledge practices for centuries. Now it appears to be time for profound changes, due to the changes in societies, technologies and the demands of working life. This paper introduces projects that aim to change the design of future learning environments in higher education.

Introduction: Changing ideas of learning and studying

Learning always takes place in a context (Biggs, 1996; Bruner, 1996; Lave and Wenger, 1991). This context is not only situational, but it relies on culturally and historically developed structures (Vygotsky, 1978). Human beings have evolved in such a way that their normal cognitive development depends on a certain kind of cultural environment for its realization (Tomasello, 1999).

Bruner (1996), accordingly, emphasized that the human mind or brain does not simply 'grow up' biologically, according to a predestined timetable, but it is opportunistic to nurturing in a human-like environment. Bruner emphasized that it is imperative to learn to understand the subtle interplay of biology and culture. His intention was not to deny the biological constraints on human functioning, but to recognize the power of culture to shape the human mind and to increase our efforts to bring this power under control. One way of promoting human functioning is to recognize the power of learning environments in shaping our intellectual efforts. Here, it is quite impossible to avoid looking at changes in technologies and social media from the perspective of education.

In order to understand student learning in higher education, we must look at how it evolves in the dynamic interplay between the learner and the learning environment (Lindblom-Ylänne and Lonka, 1999; 2000). Learning environments consist of the practices of teaching, learning, and assessment (Biggs, 1996) as well as the physical learning environment. Now this very context of higher education is radically and rapidly changing. Education never takes place in a vacuum, but the societal and cultural changes should be reflected in the practices of institutional learning. Are higher education institutions following the signals of the global innovation economy?

Modern theories of learning see the learner as central in the creation of meaning, not the teacher, as the transmitter of knowledge (Biggs, 1996). In general, learning is viewed as an active, constructive process rather than a passive, reproductive process (Bruner, 1996; Lonka, Joram and Bryson, 1996). While such a socio-constructivist approach to learning and knowledge has become dominant in educational research, the current pedagogical practices in higher education still very much rely on teacher-centered methods, where students have a passive role (see Lonka, 1997). Classroom learning and teacher education appear quite immune to changes as well. There are attempts, for instance, to change the practices of teacher education towards inquiry-based and student-centered forms of learning (Litmanen et al., in press; Lipponen and Kumpulainen, 2011), but such changes still appear to be more the exception than the rule.

Nevertheless, methods and practices of higher education as well as professional training have cultivated innovative inquiry-based collaborative methods that intellectually socialize students to participate in solving problems, posing explanations, and developing their conceptions through problem-based learning and collaborative inquiry processes (Loyens and Gijbels, 2008; Muukkonen, 2011). This process is driven by the urge to pose questions and to seek explanations, aiming at working toward more thorough and complete understanding (Bereiter and Scardamalia, 2003; Hakkarainen, 2009; Lonka, Hakkarainen and Sintonen, 2000). The new technology-mediated learning environments allow extending these inquiry practices across a wide variety of learning environments. Not enough innovative effort, however, has been put to integrate architectural and pedagogical design with the new technological tools.

In Finland, student activating and inquiry-based methods have become increasingly popular during the last two decades (Hakkarainen, Lonka and Lipponen, 2004; Lonka and Ahola, 1995; Muukkonen, 2011). Such methods have been applied to change teacher-centered lectures that sometimes involve hundreds of students into reflective inquiry and collaborative experiences (Lonka, 1998; Lonka and Ketonen, in press). New technological tools shall make this easier to accomplish.

An integrative model of innovative learning and instruction (Lonka and Ketonen, in press) depicts learning as an iterative and cyclic knowledge advancement process (see Figure 1). It involves an iterative process of 1) diagnosing current knowledge and activating a meaningful context to guide and direct learning, 2) going through and facilitating various inquiries in which new knowledge and understanding is produced, and 3) assessing learning gains and knowledge produced so as to engage the participants in a deepening learning and inquiry cycle (Lonka and Ahola, 1995: Lonka, Hakkarainen and Sintonen, 2000; Lonka and Ketonen, in press). Such activities characterize equally well the activities of teachers, students, professionals and researchers.

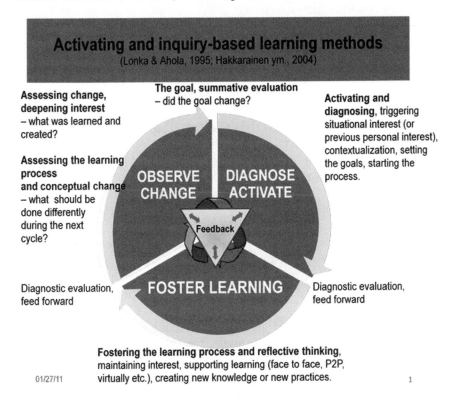

Figure 1: A general model of student-activating and inquiry-based learning methods

In higher education, the subject of active learning may be as typical for an individual as a team or a community that is evaluating its own knowledge, carrying out investigations, and assessing the results of such collaborative knowledge building (Scardamalia and Bereiter, 2003). Even though the teacher, project or curriculum may define many goals and activities, it is still possible to give the active role to the participants. The core principles of the present model assist in facilitating genuine inquiry by making practices of undergraduate education closer to inquiry involved in research or learning in the professions.

Epistemic agency and emotional challenge

Epistemic agency (Scardamalia, 2002) indicates that students deal with problems of goals, motivation, evaluation, and long-range planning that are normally left to teachers or managers. Instead of studying for isolated courses and credit units, students themselves engage in *personally meaningful study projects* (Muukkonen, 2011). They take charge of their collaborative knowledge advancement by using new technologies, interact with communities external to the university, and bring about a real-world change. Students themselves should jointly plan and organize, as well as pursue activities that are personally relevant, and take cognitive responsibility for their own inquiry. Our previous research indicates that such a process is not only intellectually, but also emotionally challenging even for highly selected groups of university students (Litmanen et al., in press)

Student activating learning methods are thus not only intellectually stimulating, but also, emotionally and motivationally engaging (Tsai et al., 2008). It is important to engage and motivate the learners, and make them active participants and agents of their own learning. It is very important to trigger situational interest, maintain it, and help students to turn it into personal interest (Hidi and Renninger, 2006). Self-regulatory skills are also essential building blocks for life-long learning (Heikkilä et al., 2011; in press). This involves not only individual level, but the so called social metacognition entails interpersonal skills, such as perspective taking, empathy, and mutual understanding (Jost et al., 1998).

Heikkilä and Lonka (2006) showed that motivational factors are crucial in terms of successful higher education study. The study by Heikkilä et al. (2011) further demonstrated that it was useful to combine cognitive and emotional aspects for investigations of students' learning. Heikkilä et al. (2011) discussed the possibility that "self-directed students", who had the best academic results and who did not suffer from emotional exhaustion, experienced a positive, fulfilling state of mind, referred to as "study engagement". The concept of study engagement is defined as vigour, dedication, and absorption (Schaufeli et al., 2002). Heikkilä et al. (in press) even showed that motivational factors were not only related to study success, but were also connected with the general well-being of teacher students

Study engagement is very close to the concept of "flow" introduced by Csikszentmihalyi (1988). He proposed that people may experience intense feelings of enjoyment and creativity during their daily activities, called *the op-*

timal experience or *flow experience*. The universal precondition for flow, according to Csikszentmihalyi (1988), is the reasonably high *challenge of the task* as well as the feeling of *competence*. If the challenge is high, and the feeling of competence is high, there is a possibility of experiencing flow. In contrast, if the challenge is high, but the person feels inadequate, this results in anxiety. A low level of challenge combined with a higher sense of competence results in boredom or relaxation. Apathy indicates that both competency and challenge are perceived to be low.

Our research group has developed new contextual ways of measuring flow and the academic emotions (Pekrun, 2005) related to it. For instance, we measured academic emotions, interest (Hidi and Renninger, 2006), sense of competence and challenge using the Contextually Activated Sampling System (CASS) method, which has proven to be a valuable tool for contextual data collection (Litmanen et al., in press; Muukkonen et al., 2007; 2008; Tolvanen et al., 2011). With CASS, it is possible to follow the daily dynamics of emotions and motivation. This innovation helps to trace real-time learning activities and motivational states by frequent sampling during periods of intensive follow-up. It also makes it possible to take pictures or videotape the current learning environment.

We are also interested in making mass education more engaging. In our study (Lonka and Ketonen, in press), the students were highly engaged and interested during a student-activating lecture course. Interest, enthusiasm, sense of competence, and self-study time correlated positively with the grade awarded for the course. Three clusters (emotional profiles) were identified: *engaged* (36 %), *unstressed* (25 %), and *anxious* (39 %) student groups. *Engaged students* spent the most hours in self-study and received the best grades. *Unstressed students* were the least active in self-study and also achieved the lowest grades. Thus, the activities that take place in lecture halls may have an impact on the self-study activities in libraries or outside university. In the future, the value of educational activities may be measured in terms of how they promote engagement and self-regulated learning.

Muukkonen et al. (2008) looked at optimal first-year students (n = 55) motivational experiences (flow) using CASS. The students reported on experiences in cafeterias, lecture halls, libraries and small groups. For each student, an average for challenge and competence was calculated, and further, the averages were used to create a measure of above (high) and below average (low) challenge and competence. Four combinations (e.g., low challenge and low competence) were then mapped against the reported working or studying related contexts: cafe, lecture, library, and small group. Typical for a cafe was that students reported low challenge but high competence compared to their average values (relaxation). At lecture, the proportion of high challenge with low competence grew larger (anxiety). At library, high challenge combined with either low or high competence were the most frequent (anxiety or flow). In small group activities, high challenge with high competence became more prevalent suggesting more frequent flow feelings in these situations. It is also worth noticing that at the library or in a small group students hardly felt apathy. Overall, we found a significant effect for the location.

It thus appeared that it was easiest for the participants of our study to experience flow in small groups or in libraries (Muukkonen et al., 2008). The fact that the students experienced either anxiety or flow in libraries may be an indication of focused and engaged learning. Previously, we have shown that group functioning in problem-based learning groups in medicine had an impact on learning outcomes (Nieminen, Sauri and Lonka, 2006). The modern libraries may promote both small group studying and individual flow experience. What makes these environments so engaging as compared to lectures? The answer may lie in the social and knowledge practices.

Knowledge practices that guide our learning

It is not enough to only look at changing ideas of learning or to look at developing pedagogical innovations. Such activities are always embedded in the larger cultural and historical context (Bruner, 1996; Tomasello, 1999; Vygotsky, 1978). Collectively cultivated knowledge practices, even more than personal dispositions or beliefs, determine the nature of learning. "Knowledge practices' are social practices related to working with knowledge, i.e., personal, collaborative, and institutional routines; these include repeated procedures for carrying out learning tasks, solving problems, completing assignments, and creating epistemic artifacts, such as essays and research reports (Hakkarainen, 2009; Muukkonen, 2011) Our study by Muukkonen et al., (2008) indicated that knowledge practices taking place in a library may be related to engaging motivational experiences.

Besides an *acquisition approach* which concentrates on individual's learning and conceptual knowledge structures we need a *participation approach* which highlights processes of participation in various cultural practices and shared processes of learning; and one does well to supplement both with a *knowledge-creation approach,* according to which students should learn to orchestrate their individual and social efforts through developing shared objects of activity (Hakkarainen, Palonen, Paavola and Lehtinen 2004; Paavola, Lipponen, and Hakkarainen, K., 2004). Such forms of collective co-regulated activities are increasingly important in higher education. We think that it is possible to see co-evolution between developing new social practices, new ways of studying, and developing epistemic agency in our students.

It is important to understand the complex knowledge practices related to learning. Students have to learn how to deal with hyper complex systems, such as gene technology or logistical systems. This poses heavy challenges for learning, since solving complex problems requires new ways of learning (Lonka, 1997). In some cases, the goal is to enhance the development of expertise at a personal level, but often the target is to promote collective knowledge-creation practices. In scientific or professional work, it is essential to work with shared knowledge objects, tools, or systems to be developed. For instance, at the individual level the target may be the understanding of a theoretical scientific concept. At the social level, we need to learn the multi-disciplinary practices of a research group. Sometimes technological tools are essential in mediating the learning process, for instance, when using high-fidelity simulations, laboratory equipment or Computer-Supported Collaborative Learning (CSCL). Technological and social innovations, however, are interdependent: "technology enhances learning only through transformed social practices" (Hakkarainen, 2009).

In CSCL Bereiter and Scardamalia (2003) were among pioneers with their radical ideas of putting the learner in the centre of collaborative knowledge-building. Hakkarainen (2009) develops their ideas even further by pointing out certain limitations in the CSCL movement. Although many conceptual problems were solved in the research literature, the empirical results of using CSCL were confusing. It appeared to be up to the teacher whether the students really were engaged in collaborative knowledge building and made considerable conceptual progress, or whether they remained at the level of only posing fact-seeking questions and fragmentary knowledge construction (Lipponen and Hakkarainen, 1997). This demonstrates that if the ideas of learning and social practices do not change, the added value of educational technology is limited.

The main problem in CSCL appeared to be that it was too much focused on computers and software. Hakkarainen (2009) pointed out the need to expand the theories towards participatory aspects of learning. Learning takes place in communities of practice (Lave and Wenger, 1991) that guide or constrain the students' knowledge-advancing activities. Bereiter and Scardamalia (2003) were also keen on developing new cultures of learning in the classroom.

Libraries cannot avoid the changes in knowledge practices, either. The practices of informatics have drastically changed during the last decade. Bryant, Matthews and Walton (2009) carried out an ethnographic study to explore new ways of using libraries. Their results showed that Loughborough University Library's Open3 was a popular area, supporting a range of student activities in a flexible learning environment. They emphasized the unique contribution that the library's physical space provided to the student learning experience as well as allowing a level of social interaction. The study further showed the value of ongoing and varied evaluation of the social practices of using university library space.

Corrall and Keates (2011) further stated that the function of the academic library has significantly changed. Libraries used to act as centres in which physical collections of resources were managed. Since knowledge practices have changed library use has become different. Corrall and Keates (2011) showed that the most important functions of libraries are now related to delivering important services, and there is an increasing focus on technologies that support this goal. I would say that one example is the use of peer-refereed scientific journals: very few people physically visit libraries in order to read the latest articles. New scientific knowledge practices include the possibility of loading the readings on one's own computer.

The knowledge practices of digital natives

Technology, in particular, co-evolves rapidly with novel learning practices (Lonka and Ketonen, in press). Learning becomes increasingly blended, which means that face-to-face instruction is often combined with computer-mediated learning environments (Bonk and Graham, 2006). Instead of talking about 'learning environments' or 'technological tools', we should rather talk about *knowledge building environments* (KBE) that enhance collaborative efforts to create and continually improve ideas (Scardamalia and Bereiter, 2003).

The generation of young people, who were born around 1990s, may be called "digital natives", since they were born together with the Internet and mobile technologies (Prensky, 2005; 2012). Typical knowledge practices for this generation are multi-tasking, that is, carrying out several simultaneous activities. They are also reading from the screen, fond of computer games, using social media extensively, and online chatting. Young people outsource many cognitive functions to different technological tools. The concept of "digital native" is still a somewhat controversial idea, and more evidence is needed (Bennet, Maton and Kervin, 2008). Regardless, at least we can say that the knowledge practices of young people have drastically changed during the last decade, whereas educational practices have largely remained the same. Prensky (2012) pointed out that "today's students are no longer the people our educational system was designed to teach" (p. 68).

So called "back-up education" (Prensky, 2008) refers to knowledge practices that ignore the existence of technologies. Digital natives are taught by "digital immigrants". Worried that the Internet or electricity would fail (or for economic reasons) teachers entertain conventional learning tools such as blackboards. Most schools continue applying a paper-and-pencil culture in spite of new technologies. In Finland, for instance, the high school matriculation examination calls for a six-hour session of handwriting.

There is no reason to assume that new technologies would automatically have a beneficial impact on learning and development. Carr (2010) pointed out that constant interruptions associated with the Internet, shallow surfing from one website to another, and a tendency to work with relatively short fragments of text produce "grass-hopper minds", unable to undertake coherent and disciplined thought; minds for whom knowledge is a matter of 'cut and paste.' Without the support of parents and teachers some groups of students may not achieve the advanced skills and practices of using new technological tools. Although social media provides a strong sense of belonging to a community, it may also elicit self-presentation, virtual bullying, and exclusion of those without socially desirable characteristics (Nadkarni and Hoffman, 2012).

The changes in libraries reflect the needs of the new generations of learners and, also, the new knowledge practices that were developed as a result of technological tools. We still do not even understand the impact of social media in all this. These transformations are further reflected in social practices and ways of interaction.

The importance of redesigning our physical learning environment

All the changes described above provide challenges that radically change the needs of users of our physical learning environments. Our latest research projects are especially focused on designing universities where teachers, researchers, and students work and study. In order to respond to these challenges, the Finnish RYM Indoor Environment project (2011-2015) aims at developing an aligned national, pedagogical model for designing such physical and virtual learning environments in contexts of blended learning that elicit in-depth learning through student-activating and inquiry-based collaborative methods.

After the Finnish university reforms in 2011universities became the owners of their own material goods that had been previously owned by the state. As a result real estate forms a central part of Finnish universities' property. At the same time, the facilities and buildings form the main places for learning and knowledge creation. Optimizing and tailoring the facilities according to users' needs is crucial. Investments in renovations and building projects must be based on the owner's and users' needs. For instance, in designing libraries, we have to be aware of the current practices and ways people use these spaces, and further be able to see in which direction the practices are developing. It is therefore imperative to carry out intensive research and find out the human perspective, before making big investments for designing something that will not be useful.

New ways of building should be based on knowledge about organizational psychology and pedagogical understanding. Furthermore, the challenge is to design spaces that are functional for everybody in the scientific community: undergraduates, graduates, PhD students, and faculty. New technologies open new possibilities for organizing learning and research at the workplace. This is not only a challenge, but provides new business opportunities for technology, industry, construction, design and pedagogical innovations.

The RYM Indoor Environment[1] project aims at creatively transforming the prevailing learning environments starting from elementary level and ending up in knowledge creation in top-level research teams, by relying on a shared set of principles (Figure 1) that can be customized to fit the need of the whole university community. The present project aims at transforming learning spaces across universities by relying on the combined strength of innovative pedagogical methods and novel ICT-based instruments of learning that create dynamic spaces for facilitating learning. In order to facilitate knowledge-creating activity (Hakkarainen et al., 2004) it is essential to integrate the physical space of learning with novel technology-mediated learning tools (virtual space) that elicit the participants' personal learning activity (mental space) as well as their collaborative learning activity (social space).

The RYM Indoor Environment project aims at developing learning environments targeted by augmenting various university spaces such as lecture halls, seminar rooms, laboratory spaces with sophisticated technology-mediated tools (e.g., interactive blackboards, wireless mobile devices, and learning management systems). These tools will be tailored and customized according to the most advanced student-activating and inquiry based pedagogical methods to elicit in-depth personal and collaborative learning. An integrated approach to developing the spaces of learning and knowledge creation separates the present project from many other ones.

Our World Design Capital Helsinki 2012 (WDC2012) project Engaging Learning Environments (ELE) in teacher education (PI, Kirsti Lonka) aims at creating integrated learning environments of the future, with a variety of spaces and services, contact teaching and digital tools, as well as internet- and mobile-based working and learning platforms dovetailing together. The seamless fusion of pedagogic and psychological know-how and technology supporting active learning and inclusive methodology is important. The project aims to develop learning spaces and technologies for use in teacher training. The ELE Living Lab creates not only new understanding and learning, but also new knowledge practices and pedagogic solutions.

The biggest WDC2012 project of the University of Helsinki, directed by Inkeri Salonharju, is Smart Design – the service design project in Helsinki University Library. The purpose is to create a coherent, user-oriented and flexible service concept with the help of a web-based developer community. The new service concept and involvement of users enable the reform of traditional library services, the probing and implementation of new technologies and work processes as well as the long-term development of library services also in the future. The service design project will improve the Library's on-site and online services aimed at its user base of nearly 100,000. Together with the new City Centre Campus Library building, i.e. the Kaisa building, the high quality expe-

---

1   www.indoorenvironment.org

riential services offer the World Design Capital 2012 an impressive design product and an interesting venue in the monumental centre of Helsinki[2],

The two WDC2012 projects are intertwined in an interesting way, since the library is partially leaving the Faculty of Behavioural Sciences into the new Kaisa building. This emptying room actually forms the physical spaces for the ELE project. This is a concrete example of how changing knowledge practices physically change our universities, and give possibilities for new design and innovation.

The aim is that we would no longer need to activate anybody, but that all students and academics would learn to enjoy learning and create new knowledge throughout their whole careers. These projects aim at making university environments places where people collaboratively create new knowledge, new practices, and new innovations.

Conclusions

In order to facilitate the development of skills and competencies required in the future, environments of teacher education have to be substantially transformed in a way that elicits productive participation in collaborative learning and knowledge-creating inquiry. In order to keep up the positive development regarding PISA-results in Finland, we have to put more emphasis on using technology innovatively in education in order to foster collaborative learning and inquiry. The development of such social competences as communication and interaction takes place in authentic and engaging learning situations and processes that need to be deliberately cultivated. Further, the wellbeing of students is a challenge also for the development of learning environments.

The methods used in education in universities are in transformation towards activating and student-centered methods. This challenges the learning processes, curriculums and learning environments. Additionally, the development of technology sets new requirements for the learning landscape. Learning takes place in both formal and informal environments, locally and globally, both virtually and socially, in successive cycles of personal and collaborative learning efforts.

We must develop new ways of learning that are both intellectually activating and make students enjoy going to an educational institution. The new generation, which is from the beginning intellectually socialized to use various collaborative productivity tools will not be satisfied in a passive role of the listener and receiver of information (Prensky, 2012). We propose that the new generation requires more engaging, experiential and creative learning methods, including games, simulations, social media, knowledge-creation projects, and

---

2   http://blogs.helsinki.fi/wdc-2012/alyllista-designia-eng/

so on. Future teachers are also part of this new generation, and they should learn how to help their own students to become life-long learners by using current and appropriate learning methods and sophisticated personal and collaborative learning tools.

It is important to make efficient use of those physical environments and tools that each university has, especially in teacher education. Even though Finland is very good in terms of PISA results, it is dangerous to think that this position will remain without constant transformation and betterment. A national effort is needed in order to modernize teacher education at all levels, starting from class teacher and subject teacher education. The learning environments in schools and universities should foster active learning, collaborative scientific inquiry, problem-solving skills, and systematic creation of new knowledge. Current research suggests that this not enough. We should educate a new generation of learners who truly enjoy learning and who can tolerate increasing amounts of uncertainty and complexity. They should be able to regulate their own learning and also support other people's learning. Our knowledge practices should therefore also facilitate motivation, engagement, and well-being. Those nations who manage to meet all these challenges are probably going to be the ones that flourish in a sustainable way.

References

Bennett, S., Maton, K., & Kervin, L. (2008). The 'digital natives' debate : a critical review of the evidence. *British Journal of Educational Technology, 39*(5), 775–786.

Bereiter, C., & Scardamalia, M. (2003). Learning to work creatively with knowledge. In E. De Corte, L. Verschaffel, N. Entwistle, & J. van Merriënboer (Eds.), *Powerful learning environments: unraveling basic components and dimensions* (pp. 55-68). (Advances in Learning and Instruction Series). Oxford, UK: Elsevier Science.

Biggs, J.B. (1996). Enhancing teaching through constructive alignment. *Higher Education, 32*(3), 347-364.

Bonk, C.J., & Graham, C.R. (2006). *The handbook of blended learning : global perspectives, local designs.* San Francisco, CA: Wiley.

Bruner, J. (1996). *The culture of education.* Cambridge, MA: Harvard University Press.

Bryant, J., Matthews, G., & Walton, G. (2009). Academic libraries and social and learning space : a case study of Loughborough University Library, UK. *Journal of Librarianship and Information Science, 41*(1), 7-18.

Carr, N. (2010). *The shallows: how the Internet is changing the way we think, read, and remember.* London: Atlantic.

Corrall, S., & Keates, J. (2011). The subject librarian and the virtual learning environment: a study of UK universities. *Program: electronic library and information systems, 45*(1), 29-49.

Csikszentmihalyi, M. (1988). The flow experience and its significance for human psychology. In M. Csikszentmihalyi & I.S. Csikszentmihalyi (Eds.), *Optimal experience. Psy-*

chological studies of flow in consciousness (pp 15-30). Cambridge, MA: Cambridge University Press.

Hakkarainen, K. (2009). A knowledge-practice perspective on technology-mediated learning. *Computer-Supported Collaborative Learning,* 4(2), 213-231

Hakkarainen, K., Lonka, K., & Lipponen, L. (2004). *Tutkiva oppiminen. Järki, tunteet ja kulttuuri oppimisen sytyttäjinä.* (Progressive Inquiry-based learning: reason, emotions and culture triggering the learning. (In Finnish). Helsinki : WSOY.

Hakkarainen, K., Lonka, K., & Paavola, S. (2004). *Networked intelligence: how artifacts and communities expand intellectual resources.* A paper presented at the Scandinavian Summer Cruise at the Baltic Sea, June 18-21, 2004 (Organized by Karoliniska Institutet, EARLI SIG Higher Education, and IKIT) .

Hakkarainen, K., Palonen, T., Paavola, S., & Lehtinen, E. (2004). *Communities of networked expertise: professional and educational perspectives.* Amsterdam: Pergamon.

Heikkilä, A., & Lonka, K. (2006). Studying in higher education: students' approaches to learning, self-regulation, and cognitive strategies. *Studies in Higher Education,* 31(1), 99-117.

Heikkilä, A., Lonka, K., Nieminen, J., & Niemivirta, M. (in press). Relations between teacher students' approaches to learning, cognitive and attributional strategies, well-being, and study success. *Higher Education.*

Heikkilä, A., Niemivirta, M., Nieminen J., & Lonka, K. (2011). Interrelations among university students' approaches to learning, regulation of learning, and cognitive and attributional strategies: a person oriented approach. *Higher Education, 61*(5), 513-529.

Hidi, S., & Renninger, K.A. (2006). The four-phase model of interest development. *Educational Psychologist,* 41(2), 111-127.

Jost, J.T., Kruglanski, A.W., & Nelson, T.O. (1998). Social metacognition: an expansionist review. *Personality and Social Psychology Review,* 2(2), 137-154.

Lave, J., & Wenger, E. (1991). *Situated learning: legitimate peripheral participation.* Cambridge: Cambridge University Press.

Lindblom-Ylänne, S., & Lonka, K. (2000). Interaction between learning environment and expert learning. *Lifelong Learning in Europe, 5*(2), 90–97.

Lipponen, L., & Hakkarainen, K. (1997). Developing culture of inquiry in computer-supported collaborative learning. In R. Hall, N. Miyake, & N. Enyedy (Eds.), *Proceedings of CSCL '97: The Second International Conference on Computer Support for Collaborative Learning* (pp. 164-168). Mahweh, NJ: Lawrence Erlbaum Associates.

Lipponen, L., & Kumpulainen, K. (2011). Acting as accountable authors: creating interactional spaces for agency work in teacher education. *Teaching & Teacher Education, 27*(5), 812-819.

Litmanen, T., Lonka, K., Inkinen, M., Lipponen, L., & Hakkarainen, K. (In press). Capturing teacher students' emotional experiences in context: does inquiry-based learning make a difference? *Instructional Science.*

Lonka, K. (1997). *Explorations of constructive processes in student learning.* A doctoral dissertation. Helsinki: University Press.

Lonka, K. (1998). The 21st century student – an active learner? An invited theme session keynote lecture. *Proceedings of the 23rd International Conference "Improving University Teaching and Learning",* pp 63-79.

Lonka, K., & Ahola, K. (1995). Activating instruction: how to foster study and thinking skills in higher education? *European Journal of Psychology of Education,* 10(4), 351–368.

Lonka, K., Hakkarainen, K., & Sintonen, M. (2000). Progressive inquiry learning for children – experiences, possibilities, limitations. *European Early Childhood Education Research Journal,* 8(1), 7–23.

Lonka, K., Joram, E., & Bryson, M. (1996). Conceptions of learning and knowledge – does training make a difference? *Contemporary Educational Psychology,* 21, 240-260.

Lonka, K. & Ketonen, E. (in press). How to make a lecture course an engaging learning experience? *Studies for the Learning Society.*

Loyens, S. M. M., & Gijbels, D. (2008). Understanding the effects of constructivist learning environments: introducing a multi-directional approach. *Instructional Science,* 36(5), 351–357.

Muukkonen- van der Meer, H. (2011). Perspective on knowledge creating inquiry in higher education. Doctoral dissertation. Institute of Behavioural Sciences. University of Helsinki, Finland.

Muukkonen, H., Hakkarainen, K., Inkinen, M., Lonka, K., Salmela-Aro, K. (2008). CASS-methods and tools for investigating higher education knowledge practices. In G. Kanselaar, V. Jonker, P. Kirschner, & F. Prins (Eds.), *International Perspectives in the Learning Sciences: Cre8ing a Learning World, Proceedings of the Eight International Conference for the Learning Sciences* (ICLS 2008), Vol. 2 (pp. 107-115). Utrecht, The Netherlands: ICLS.

Muukkonen, H., Hakkarainen, K., Jalonen, S., Kosonen, K., Heikkilä, A., Lonka, K., Inkinen, M., Salmela-Aro, K., Linnanen, J., & Salo, K. (2007). *Process-and context-sensitive research on academic knowledge practices: Developing ASS-tools and methods.* Proceedings of the Computer Supported Collaborative Learning Conference, Rutgers University, New Jersey, USA, July 16-21, 2007.

Nadkarni, A., & Hofmann, S. (2012). Why do people use Facebook? *Personality and Individual Differences,* 52(3), 243- 249.

Nieminen, J., Sauri, P., & Lonka, K. (2006). On the relationship between group functioning and study success in problem based learning. *Medical Education,* 40(1), 64-71.

Paavola, S., Lipponen, L., & Hakkarainen, K. (2004). Modeling innovative knowledge communities: a knowledge-creation approach to learning. *Review of Educational Research,* 74, 557-576.

Pekrun, R. (2005). Progress and open problems in educational emotion research. *Learning and Instruction,* 15(5), 497-506.

Prensky, M. (2005). Listen to the natives. Learning in the digital age. *Educational Leadership,* 63 (4), 8-13.

Prensky, M. (2008). Backup education? Too many teachers see education as preparing kids for the past, not the future. *Educational Technology,* 48(1), 1-3.

Prensky, M. (2012). From digital natives to digital wisdom. Hopeful essays for 21st century learning. Thousand Oaks, CA: Sage.

Scardamalia, M. (2002). Collective cognitive responsibility for the advancement of knowledge. In B. Smith (Ed.), *Liberal Education in a Knowledge Society* (pp. 67-98). Chicago: Open Court.

Scardamalia, M., & Bereiter, C. (2003). Knowledge building environments: extending the limits of the possible in education and knowledge work. In A. DiStefano, K.E. Rudestam, & R. Silverman (Eds.), *Encyclopedia of distributed learning.* Thousand Oaks, CA: Sage Publications.

Schaufeli, W.B., Martínez, I.M., Pinto, A.M., Salanova, M., & Bakker, A.B. (2002). Burn-out and engagement in university students : a cross-national study. *Journal of Cross-cultural Psychology*, 33(5), 464-481

Tolvanen, A., Kiuru, N., Leskinen, E., Hakkarainen, K., Lonka, K., Inkinen, M., & Salmela-Aro, K. (2011). A new approach for estimating a nonlinear growth component in multi-level modelling. *International Journal of Behavioral Development, 35*(4), 370-379.

Tomasello, M. (1999). *The cultural origins of human cognition*. Cambridge, MA : Harvard University Press.

Tsai, Y.-M., Kunter, M., Ludtke, O., Trautwein, U., & Ryan, R.M. (2008). What makes les-sons interesting? The role of situational and individual factors in three school subjects. *Journal of Educational Psychology, 100*(2), 460-472.

Vygotsky, L. S. (1978). *Mind in society: the development of higher psychological pro-cesses*. Cambridge, MA: Harvard University Press.

EFFECTIVE CONTINUING PROFESSIONAL DEVELOPMENT FOR EFFECTIVE INFORMATION LITERACY

Integrating Service Learning into Teaching Information Literacy: The Librarian as Designer and Facilitator for Information Literacy Instruction

Chi-Lung Chang
Librarian, Ching-Yun University, Taiwan
cgangchilung@gmail.com
and
Mei-Mei Wu (corresponding author)
Professor, Graduate Institute of Library and Information Studies,
National Taiwan Normal University, Taiwan
meiwu@ntnu.edu.tw

Abstract

Service-learning is a newly developed pedagogical approach that enhances teaching, learning and reflecting, of which the purpose is to integrate meaningful community service with instruction and reflection to enrich students' learning experiences. This current project is to design and deploy an Information Literacy course taught by a librarian faculty that includes digital learning materials funded and developed by the Ministry of Education (MOE) in Taiwan and Service-Learning approach for the students to serve in a community library. The aims of the study are to understand the role of the librarian as the designer and facilitator in the delivery of information literacy courses, and assess the impact of digital learning materials developed from a service-learning approach on the students' performance in terms of their cognitive, affective (civic responsibility) and library instruction skills. Action research method is applied for the course design, deployment and evaluation. The service-learning approach is taken for the course design that students are required to serve in a community library. Digital learning materials developed by MOE are used as teaching materials. The course which is entitled "Network Information Organization and Retrieval" with a total of 24 students from Ching-Yun University in northern Taiwan participated in the course. The major research instruments include a questionnaire and students' service journals. Quantitative as well as qualitative data are collected and analyzed. The results of the action research are reported and possible implications are discussed.

Background and problem statements

Former Harvard University President Bok (2005) has said that university education be directed to several goals: learning to communicate; learning to think; building character; preparation for citizenship; living with diversity; preparing for a global society; acquiring broader interests and preparing for a career which indicates that course design of university education contains the above objectives to cultivate the students in cognitive, affective (civic responsibility) as well as skills development. Beginning in the 21st century, the Ministry of Education (MOE) in Taiwan actively promotes digital learning, information literacy, and service learning, encouraging faculty to use multiple teaching methods aimed at helping students with information literacy skills and community services awareness.

To improve library information literacy skills and e-learning ability for the college students, the Computer Center of the Ministry of Education (MOE) in Taiwan brought up "Library and Information Application (LIA) for Digital Learning Materials in Higher Education Program" (2008-2011). The plan has been developed in two phases, firstly, development of the digital learning materials, and secondly implementation and promotion of the digital learning materials in colleges and universities. The purpose of which is to provide the students with more self-learning space, and both teachers and students could enhance information literacy skills through using the digital learning materials (Wu, 2010).

In order to support the schools to offer service-learning programs as formal curriculum, the MOE issued the "Reference Manual on Service-Learning Courses and Activities for Universities and Colleges" in 2007. The MOE also established the "MOE Subsidy Guidelines for Offering Service-learning Courses in Universities and Colleges" to persuade schools to operate relevant practices and actually implement service-learning courses. By the 2009 academic year, 125 universities and colleges have established units specifically responsible for service-learning programs, and 120 schools have added service-learning courses into their formal curricula (MOE, 2011). Service-learning as an instructional design and teaching approach is adopted because it is anticipated that students could apply their professional knowledge while carrying out the civic responsibilities to improve self-growth, to accomplish holistic education, and to experience the actual social problems and maybe to resolve them.

Librarians have always been considered educators and promoters of information literacy. The transmission and instruction of the significance of information literacy to students is an essential practice. Based on Dewey's theory of "learning by doing" (Dewey, 1938), this study designs an information literacy course by using digital learning materials and deploying the service-learning approach to allow students to perform in their community services. The objectives of the course design are to promote and to enrich the students' learning experiences through service-learning instruction and encouraging reflection. Digital learning materials developed by MOE are utilized and the students are requested to participate regularly in a community library as part of the service-learning course requirement.

This study intends to explore the role of librarians as designers and promoters in the information literacy course, and to evaluate how digital materials and the service-learning method influence students' learning outcomes in terms of self-growth, civic responsibility, and library instruction skills. Three research questions are:

1. How to design and deliver an information literacy course with digital learning materials and service-learning approach?
2. What is the role of the librarian as the course designer and facilitator?
3. What are the students' learning outcomes with such a course design?

Literature review

Digital learning materials

Although there are different views on using digital learning materials (such as video, audio, animations, games, etc.) for teaching, there are supportive voices for effective teaching (such as Kubey, 2004; Kiili, 2005; Lan, Hung, & Hsu, 2011). As such, Ministry of Education (MOE) in Taiwan launched a digital learning materials project to selectively design Liberal Art courses with digital learning materials. Courses that have been considered the most important courses for college students, such as Environmental Education, Life Education, and Library Information Literacy were selected for the digital course design project.

The digital learning materials for Library and Information Application[1] (LIA) have been developed by using the framework of FILIP (Focus, Information, Location, Integration, and Presentation), with a total 18 units of digital learning materials. They include: (1) library and information application and research process, (2) selecting research topics, (3) establishing knowledge background, (4) recognizing information resources, (5) library introduction, (6) searching library resources, (7) searching internet resources, (8) searching journals, (9) searching newspapers, (10) searching dissertations, (11) information evaluation, (12) becoming a good reader, (13) writing notes, (14) information ethics, (15) making a proposal, (16) writing reports, (17) learning how to cite, (18) making a good presentation (Wu, 2010).

---

1   This is the course title named by MOE to teach library information literacy.

Service-learning approach

Dewey's famous quote of "learning by doing" makes him the pioneer and the advocator of experiential education. Dewey (1938) believes that learning coexists with life experiences. With the accumulation of experiences, learners continuously reorganize and reconstruct their knowledge through action and activities. Dewey believes that broader social environment makes better learning places. Sigmon (1979) defines service-learning as originated from the idea of volunteer service, and is a type of experiential education that builds upon reciprocal learning. For example, Bounous (1997, p5) illustrates community service-learning as "a form of experiential learning whereby students and faculty collaborate with communities to address problems and issues, simultaneously gaining knowledge and skills and advancing self-growth" .

Furco (1996, p.12) distinguishes service-learning from volunteer and community service, and he stresses that "service-learning programs are distinct from other approaches to experiential education in their intention to equally benefit the provider and the recipient of the service, and to ensure equal focus on both the service being provided and the learning that occurs." Implementing the idea in service-learning, students could integrate their service experiences with learning objectives through the activities of service and reflection (Hsu & Lin, 2008).

The U.S. seems to be the first country to integrate a service-learning program into practice. Beginning with higher education, the U.S. has been widely promoting and implementing service-learning through relevant acts and plans (Gretchen, 2011). Since 1985, over 1,100 universities and colleges have participated as members of "Campus Compact" with the mission to fulfill the civic responsibility of institutes of higher education. Campus Compact is a national organization for higher education dedicated to the tasks including: (1)Encouraging students of institutes of higher education to participate in public and community services that develop their citizenship skills; (2)Assisting campuses to form effective community partnerships, and provide resources and services; and (3)Training teachers to integrate the concept of service-learning into their curriculum (e.g. NCASL–SEANet[2], NSLC[3], National Service-Learning Partnership[4]). The United States has been successfully promoting service-learning policies and providing novel course contents and services; it has also implemented the idea of service-learning into the educational policies of primary and secondary schools. The efforts of the U.S. make it a good model for other countries in terms of promoting service-learning (Zlotkowski, 1998).

---

2   National Coalition for Academic Service-Learning – The State Education Agency K-12 Service-Learning Network www.ncasl.org/index.html
3   National Service-Learning Clearinghouse www.servicelearning.org
4   www.service-learningpartnership.org/site/PageServer

In 1993, the U.S. Federal government passed The National and Community Service Trust Act of 1993, and officially established the principles and applications of service-learning (Corporation for National & Community Service, 2011). Since then, higher education in the states has been devoted to blending service-learning into academic fields. Many plans and organizations other than Campus Compact are assisting with the improvement and advancement of combining service-learning with professional fields, in the hopes of developing student civic responsibility while connecting campuses with social issues (Campus Compact, 2011).

Huang (2000) suggests that to effectively implement service-learning based teaching, students need to hold five characteristics of service-learning: (1) collaboration to make the interests, needs, and expectations of both parties satisfied, (2) reciprocity that both parties learn and benefit from each other regardless of class prejudice, (3) diversity, (4) learning-based, and (5) social justice focus to make social changes and to achieve social justice and to solve the problems. Fertnam, White, and White (1996) have proposed four phases for planning service-learning courses: preparation, service, reflection and celebration. When a course is carried out in these four phases, students are able to clearly identify the process of service-learning and its purpose.

According to MOE's statement (MOE, 2011), "multi participation, integration, innovative transformation, and sharing and encouraging" are the major principles for implementing service-learning programs. It is expected that with the implementation of these four major principles, students learning outcomes in terms of cognition, emotion, will, and behavior will be fully improved with the curriculum, which is composed of professional knowledge and the concept of learning by doing, and by internalizing the experiences of service provision

Action research design

It is assumed that with the teaching of the digital learning units, the students will gain knowledge for information literacy and thus would apply their knowledge in helping library community users with literacy skills. The curriculum integrated with the digital learning materials developed by MOE and service-learning aiming to improve the students' ability in terms of self-growth, civic responsibility, and library instruction skills. Service-learning could be a useful tool to reflect the learning outcomes of the digital learning materials on information literacy. The study is based on an information literacy instruction project lead by one of the researchers and a course entitled "Network Information Organization and Retrieval" offered by General Education Center at Ching-Yun University taught by the other researcher, who is a librarian and the instructor of the course, participates the process of providing services with the students. Knowing that local public libraries are generally short on manpower, the utilization of internet resources and reader services is typically not widely available to the local residents. Therefore, the instructor and a local library established a common objective to create a partnership under mutual trust and reciprocity to provide library instruction and collection to the local residents of the public library.

An action research approach has been applied to integrate digital learning materials for teaching informational literacy developed by MOE into service-learning curriculum. The course design is composed of two concepts: the delivery of information literacy and the implementation of service-learning. The first concept focuses on the integration of the teaching materials and the digital learning materials, and its purpose is to train the students' learning knowledge and skills. The second concept centers on the exercises that are designed to accomplish the task of service-learning by learning activities, with the objective of developing students' self-growth and civic responsibility. The concept of course design is displayed in Figure 1:

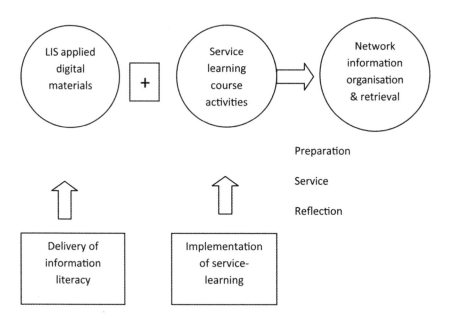

Figure 1: Conceptual Model of Service-Learning Course Design

The action research is designed based on the four phases for planning service-learning courses developed by Fertnam and colleagues (1996). The four phases include (A) *Preparation* – instructors propose plans for service-learning courses, learn about students' backgrounds, study relevant reference information, and design and prepare teaching materials. Furthermore, to communicate with the targeted organization to work with, provide proposals for service-learning activities, and project the beneficial results and possible methods for evaluation, such as the student's service learning journal and the questionnaire are developed; (B) *Service* – course design is executed based on the spirit of "collaboration" and "reciprocity" and the students are required to serve the community library for 12 hours in a semester base. Students need to do the individual study, including (a) studying the designated digital learning materials individually; (b) reading textbooks on service learning; and (c) serve the community library; (C) *Reflection* – after each session and service, students are required to: (a) write the service-learning journal based on the course guidance; (b) discuss and reflect their service experiences with peers and the instructor. And finally, (D) *Celebration* – in this phase, service providers and recipients share their thoughts and opinions to understand whether it is necessary to make adjustments to the service, modify the digital learning materials, or develop learning content with more diverse components to better satisfy the needs of both students' learning and the serving institutes.

There are three major tasks at the preparation stage:

Task 1: Developing the objectives, service activities and the syllabus for the course

a. Objectives: (1) To improve information literacy for students and the library community; (2) To alleviate the lack of human resources in a public library; (3) To enrich students' learning experiences and civic responsibility.
b. Service activities: Library and information services, including look up library resources, book circulation, shelving books etc.
c. Developing a syllabus: The digital learning materials designed for library and information utilization include 18 units; the course in this study selected units 4 to 9, 15, and 18 as the content for the Network Information Organization and Retrieval course. The course begins with an introduction and an online search for resources, and ends with applications and presentations of online resources with service-learning activities carried out in between. The syllabus is presented in Appendix A.

Task 2: Searching for partnership and developing an agreement

By consulting the library directory published by the Public Library Committee of the Library Association of the Republic of China, LAROC (Taiwan), the course has established a cooperative relationship with PingZhen City Public Library for service-learning curriculum purposes. An agreement called "Equality and Mutual Benefit" is developed by the two parties that include the students' duty and obligation, the target for students' learning experiences, how students would conduct the community service, and how to complete the service reflection forms, etc.

Task 3: Designing the research instruments

Developing the questionnaire
A questionnaire was designed based on FIPSE's (The Fund for the Improvement of Postsecondary Education) integrating information literacy and service-learning into courses (Eyler & Giles, 1999) for understanding the students' perception and performance of the learning outcomes. The questionnaire is composed of 26 questions with the five-point Likert scale which is divided into three parts: digital learning material, self-growth and civic responsibility.

Developing the format and guidance of the reflection journal
The reflection journal was designed based on Bloom's Taxonomy (1956) to identify students' cognition and reflection before, during and after the processes of service-learning including (1) why choose to serve, (2) expected goal, (3) working tasks, (4) procedures, (5) reflection, and (6) future illumination. Students are required to complete the reflection journal after each serving-learning session.

Course implementation and data collection

Beginning from the fourth week, students are required to study the assigned digital learning materials to support their knowledge in information literacy. Three topics from units 4 to 6 have been assigned, including "aspects of information resources," "library introduction," and "looking up library resources." To effectively go through the three units and implement service-learning sessions, a few steps are applied. Firstly, a summary of the three units is delivered in a classroom-based environment. Secondly, a visit to the recipient library is arranged so that students learn about the resources and the operation in the recipient library. Thirdly, the students are required to study the contents of each digital learning material unit and are required to complete a four-hour basic internship in the campus library before going out to the community library. Then, with knowledge of information literacy and some work experience, the students go and serve the community public library and write the reflection journal after completing each service.

At the end of the semester, the students were asked to fill out the questionnaire which elicits information regarding the perception and performance of using digital learning material, self-growth, and civic responsibility, with a completion rate of approximately 62%. Qualitative data were also collected from the students' reflection journals writing after completing activities of each service-learning session. The instructor provided instructions for writing reflection journal at the beginning of the semester so that the students could follow the process of service-learning clearly.

As for data analysis, Regression Analysis and Pearson Product Correlation for digital learning materials with students' perception of civic responsibility are applied. And content analysis is used for analyzing students' reflection journals.

Results

A total of 39 students enrolled, with 24 students (16 males and 8 females) accomplishing the whole processes of the service-learning activities, record the reflection journals and complete the final questionnaire.

Students were asked to fulfill the four-hour internship in the Ching-Yun University Library before they could begin the required eight-hour service-learning sessions. According to the students' reflection journals, some students ask to service for more hours to gain better knowledge to be able to assist the recipient library. This phenomenon illustrates that some students improve in terms of self-growth and civic responsibility, and maybe find enjoyment in the processes of service learning.

The following are the results from quantitative data analysis:

Students are satisfied with the "Network Information Organization and Retrieval" course

The average value for student satisfaction in the dimension of digital learning material is 3.94. The students are especially satisfied with the design (4.16), the arrangement of the course (4.16), and the peer cooperation (4.20). The average value of student satisfaction with the dimension of self-growth is 3.90. For the dimension of civic responsibility, the average value of students' satisfaction is 3.94.

Digital learning material has a significant and positive relation with the student's self-growth

A hierarchical regression analysis is applied to derive the influence of digital learning material on students' self-growth. A demographic variable (gender) is placed in the model as a control variable, and the dimension of digital learning material is added as an independent variable. The result of the regression model reveals a significant and positive correlation between digital learning material and students' self-growth ($\beta = 0.709$, $t = 5.268$, $p < 0.05$). The R^2

value obtained from the model of 0.634 indicates that the digital learning material is able to explain as much as 63.4 % of the variance in students' self-growth. In other words, course design is helpful to enrich the student's self-growth.

Digital learning material has a significant and positive relationship with the student's perception of civic responsibility

The results from a hierarchical regression analysis between the digital learning material and the students' civic responsibility reveal that the influence of the digital learning material is significantly and positively correlated with students' civic responsibility ($\beta = 0.614$, $t = 3.907$, $p < 0.05$). The R^2 value is 0.500, which indicates the digital learning material is able to explain as much as 50% of the variance in students' civic responsibility. The digital learning material has a significant and positive influence on students' perception of civic responsibility.

		digital learning material	self-growth	civic responsibility
digital learning material	Pearson correlation	1		
self-growth	Pearson correlation	.758**	1	
civic responsibility	Pearson correlation	.664**	.697**	1

N=24, **= p<0.001

Table 1: Pearson correlation: digital learning material and service activities

Digital learning material is significantly correlated with service activities in self-growth and civic responsibility

The results from Pearson correlation show that the digital learning material and self-growth and the perception of civic responsibility are positively correlated in pairs (see Table 1). The correlation coefficient for digital learning material and self-growth is 0.758, and 0.664 between digital learning material and civic responsibility. The correlation coefficient between self-growth and civic responsibility is 0.697.

Students' reflection journals are also analyzed to understand their perception change for service learning. The results of the qualitative data support the quantitative analysis that students reflect a positive self-growth in the service learning processes. The results are displayed below. The evidence is listed with student code and date of the reflection journal in parenthesis, for example, (Student 15_ Journal_20110108).

The stereotypes of library perception changed through service-learning

Most students in this course reported that library was a place that only provided circulation and reading services. They did not know the purposes of the library and were lack of the knowledge of the operating procedures. They thought working in the library is an easy task without special knowledge. Through the experiences of service-learning, the students reported that they had a better understanding of the objectives and missions of a library. As a result, they changed the stereotype of libraries and began to make better use of library resources.

> "After the process of service-learning, I knew the functions of the library that can be used by everyone for free".
> (Student 15_ Journal_20110108)

Empathy aroused by working and serving people

The students reported that they gained happiness from helping people during the process of service-learning. Their empathy and care for people had been stimulated. The reflection journals reveal that the students' willingness to selflessly help satisfy the needs of others makes the course and the learning more positive and meaningful. Most students reported that they were willing to cooperate with others. As they considered other people while working with them, their empathy is aroused, and their sense of empathy won the approval of the public library.

> "I learned the spirit of service. It must continue to deliver the service to everyone, and I felt that the service-learning course made me growth and reflection". (Student 21_Journal_ 20101224)

New knowledge learned by doing

The students reported that they do not only expect to complete the required hours of service-learning but also look forward to acquiring knowledge and experiences.

> "By the service-learning, I thought the school should release more the opportunities of service-learning course. And students can be exposed

to different experiences and understanding for knowledge and mind-set". (Student 11_Journal_20101224)

"Although shelving book was my service activity, by service-learning, I found the order and location of the books that was very important for saving user's time. And the book number is the express of the knowledge. These things I did not know before".
(Student 07_Journal_ 20101224)

Perception of social responsibility grows

The students' reflection journal reported that service-learning motivated them to continue providing services and giving back to the society, and further helping guide the society in a positive direction. It seems that the service-learning course activates the students' perception of civic responsibility. The action research for the instructional design for digital learning materials and service learning indeed arose the students' civic awareness and action.

"I will participate in the serving activities in the future, it inspires me and impressed me". (Student 24_Jouranl_20110108)

Conclusion

The action research supports the design of the course successfully by cultivating the students' informational literacy and their competence in service-learning in terms of self-growing and gaining the perception of civic responsibility. That is, the students not only have the opportunity to work in a library, but also develop their civic spirit, the perception of civic responsibility.

By implementing the digital learning materials designed for library and information utilization to the service-learning course, this study examines the interrelationships between the digital learning material, student self-growth, and student civic responsibility. The results show that the digital learning material has a statistically significant and positive relationship with both student self-growth and civic responsibility. Although the limitation of the study has been the relatively small sample size for the application of quantitative technique, the qualitative data from students' reflection journals also support their satisfaction with learning experiences.

In this study, the librarian successfully plays the role of the course designer who follows Fertnam, White, and White's (1996) four phases to design the content and activities of the course by combining information literacy with service-learning, an instructor who delivers the knowledge of information literacy to the students and the community residents with the understanding of the needs of a public library, and a facilitator to support learning activities. Fertnam, White, and White's (1996) four phases of preparation, service, reflection and celebration seem to be a successful model for designing and teaching information literacy in integrating MOE's digital learning materials with servce-learning activities.

The results of the questionnaire and the content analyses demonstrated that the instructor guided the students through exploring the motivation, clarifying the missions, and realizing the process and enjoyment of service-learning, and activating the application of informational literacy and skills. Through the continuous guidance of this course, the students were able to internally reflect on the changes to their external behavior, and integrate their information literacy skills with the development of social responsibility.

A number of issues require further consideration for future implementation:

Student participation and background understanding

Student participation is the key to a successful service-learning course. To encourage participation, instructors are suggested to provide a detailed description of the course before students enroll. Instructors are also encourage to survey the students prior volunteer experiences During the course, instructors also need to frequently communicate with students and service recipients to understand the progress and possible problems, so an adjustment can be made if needed. Attractive course features could be used to bring students in and connect them with service-learning by fine course design. It is hoped that students could walk out of the class with a motivation for serving people as volunteers and implementing civic responsibility.

Good relationship with the community libraries

Successful service-learning activities require not only the learning and service of the students, but good cooperative relationships with service recipients (Lin & Lin, 2011). In this study, the service recipient is able to take advantage of the students' service-learning to compensate for its lack of manpower, and have assignments completed. Before students begin their service, they are required to be trained and get familiarized with the working environment, so that they have the basic knowledge to offer their services and thus to learn. To reduce the time that the community library might spend on training the students and to multiply the quality of the students' service are one of the ways to maintain a good relationship with the cooperative libraries.

More administrative support

Due to the time constraint and budget, this study only focuses on the library resources training and did not implement all the 18 units of digital learning materials into service learning. It would be better to plan earlier and request more funding and credit support to encourage the participative desire of the service-learning.

This has been a small scale research. It would be useful if the same action research can be applied in a broader context, that is, more librarian faculty and more students from more institutes in different areas taking the same approach for teaching information literacy through service-learning course design.

Acknowledgements

This research has been partially granted by MOE. The authors would like to thank Ministry of Education for supporting Library Information Literacy Instruction projects.

References

Bloom, B. S. (1956). *Taxonomy of education objectives: the classification of educational goals*. New York: Longman .

Bok, D. (2005). *Our underachieving colleges: a candid look at how much students learn and why they should be learning more*. New Jersey: Princeton University Press.

Bounous, R. M. (1997). Working papers series on service-learning: Vol. 1. *New directions: teaching and research*. Retrieved from the Cornell University website:
http://psc.ilr.cornell.edu/downloads/workingpapers/Working_Papers_1997.pdf

Campus Compact www.compact.org/about/history-mission-vision/

Corporation for National & Community Service (2011). *About the corporation: our history and legislation*. Retrieved from:
www.nationalservice.gov/about/role_impact/history.asp

Dewey, J. (1938). *Experience and education*. New York: Macmillan.

Eyler, J., & Giles, D. E. (1999). *Where's the learning in service-learning?* San Francisco, CA: Josser-Boss.

Fertman, C. I., White, G. P., & White, L. J. (1996). *Service learning in middle school: building a culture of service*. Columbus, Ohio: National Middle School Association.

Furco, A. (1996). Service-learning: a balanced approach to experiential education (pp. 12). Retrieved from:
www.urmia.org/library/docs/regional/2008_northeast/Service_Learning_Balanced_Approach.pdf

Gretchen, J. (2011). *How service-learning can counter cultural narcissism* (Master's thesis). Retrieved from: www.library.umaine.edu/theses/pdf/JordanG2011.pdf

Hsu, M., & Lin, J. S. (2008). Service-learning the basic concepts and theoretical basis. In M. Hsu (Ed.), *Learning through servicing: theories and practices of service-learning across the discipline* (pp19-55).Taipei: HungYeh Publishing Co. (in Chinese)

Huang, Y. (2000). Service learning : actual practice for civic education. *Newsletter for Teaching the Humanities and Social Sciences*, 12(3), 20-42 (in Chinese)

Kiili, K. (2005). Digital game-based learning: toward an experiential gaming model. *The Internet and Higher Education, 8*(1), 13-24.

Kubey, R. (2004). Media literacy and the teaching of civics and social studies at the dawn of the21stcentury.*The American Behavioral Scientist, 48*(1), 69-77.

Lan, Y. F., Hung, C. L., & Hsu, H. J. (2011). Effects of guided writing strategies on students' writing attitudes on media richness theory. *The Turkish Online Journal of Education Technology, 10*(4), 148-164.

Lin, Y. T., & Lin, L. J. (2011). Reflection on the service learning of library and information science majors. *Journal of Librarianship and Information Studies, 77*, 33-51. (in Chinese)

MOE (2011). *MOE service-learning website.* Retrieved from the Ministry of Education website: english.moe.gov.tw/mp.asp?mp=10000 (in Chinese)

Wu, M. M. (2010). MOE Promoting Library Information Instruction as Liberal Art Course. Retrieved from: http://lia.glis.ntnu.edu.tw/a-01.php (in Chinese)

Sigmon, R. L. (1979). Service-learning: three principles. Synergist. National Center for Service-Learning, *ACTION, 8*(1), 9-11.

Zlotkowski, E. (1998). *Successful service-learning programs: new models of excellence in higher education.* Bolton, MA: Anker.

Appendix 1 : Syllabus and arrangement of course

Week	Topic	Reading assignment/digital learning materials	Service learning/location
1	Introduction		
2	Service learning: concept		Description of plan
3	Service learning: case		Film discussion
4	Library visit	Unit 5: Understanding library	PingZhen City Public Library
5	Keyword: concept & application	Unit 4: Aspects of information resources	
6	Library & information 1: management & application	Unit 6: Looking up library resources Unit 8: Find journals	Service-learning start
7	Athletic meet	Self-learning at home	
8	Library & information 2: management & application	Unit 7: search internet resources Unit 9: Find newspapers & media	Experience report: film or reflection
9	Midterm		
10	How to write the report	Unit 15: Planning experts	
11	Network information: Humanity Society 1		
12	Network information: Humanity Society 2		
13	Network information: Travelling 1	Unit 18: easily presentation	
14	Network information: Travelling 2		Service-learning end
15	Presentation 1		
16	Presentation 2		
17	New Year	Self-learning at home	
18	Presentation 3		Celebration: report & discussion

A Catalogue Revolution: The British Library, Primo and the Information Literate Librarian

Louise Doolan
British Library, UK
louise.doolan@bl.uk

Abstract

From 2012 the 'traditional' OPAC will be switched off and the Primo interface of 'Explore the British Library' will be the search, discovery and access portal of the British Library. Before any training programme for our readers could be considered, a substantial and long term development programme needed to be developed, reviewed, regularly updated and initially delivered to 75 front line staff. It was then expanded to include all 1,700 staff across 3 UK locations. Explore the British Library' is the search, discovery and access portal which over the past 3 years has morphed from a beta catalogue, to the discovery and access resource it is today. Underlying this minor technological revolution has been a growing cultural change within. The search experience for the user is through an 'Amazon-style' interface with social networking capabilities but the search refinement functionality of a traditional library catalogue is maintained. This paper will explore the options considered and solutions identified to deliver a focused staff training programme. It will also cover the production of a set of professional competencies identified for a 21st Century Librarian. The challenge of fostering a sense of ownership of the service and adjusting to the change of service delivery in The British Library will be addressed.

Introduction

Three years ago the British Library decided to change one of its fundamental services, its catalogue. The 'traditional' OPAC, the integrated catalogue, had been the main catalogue interface since 2004 and provided access to 13 million collection items, just a fraction of the collections of The British Library; the Library has a number of specialist catalogues for manuscripts, sound recordings and other media as well as a number of card catalogues. Providing multiple catalogues to users and readers caused complications to their research journey, as well as being an inefficient manner to operate a service. In addition, as the use of Web 2.0 technology becomes embedded into the behaviour of the academic researcher, users have come to expect that they will able to use these tools when they work with the content from the British Library.

In response to these user expectations, starting in 2008 the British Library has been developing 'Explore the British Library', its new search, discovery and access portal. The portal, using the Ex-Libris Primo system, provides an interface to enable British Library users the opportunity to discover and access over 56 million collection items, including digitised and born digital resources, through a single interface. Users benefit from an 'Amazon' like experience to search across collections and multiple formats of material simultaneously and order the items for delivery into the preferred St Pancras Reading Room.

Changes in technology and the speed of implementation of these changes is a challenge every librarian faces on a very regular basis. The implications of these technological changes impact on the service the organisation delivers, its users and, always, on its staff. The British Library faces these challenges as frequently as any other library. Where the British Library differs from so many other libraries, is the scale and the impact these changes have. The British Library currently employs 1,700 staff; it has 170 million collection items, 125,000 registered readers. In 2011, 1.2 million items were delivered to readers and the library's Reference Services answered 300,000 face to face enquiries and 60,000 remote enquiries.

Theory behind the transition strategy

A key task for the project team was to develop a communication and training plan for the implementation of the 'Explore the British Library' portal. This was informed by an understanding of information literacy theory and the SCONUL 7 pillars. The professional competencies of the British Library for front line staff was a requirement, to ensure key aspects were covered in the training.

The project team recognised the importance of gaining staff understanding of the reasons for this minor technological revolution, and their support for it. The change project was structured around the principles behind a number of theories of researcher behaviour and invoked professional competencies of library staff and British Library strategies; it was felt that this would ease the acceptance of the change from staff. The sense of pride of the brand of the British Library is high compared to other UK public sector organisations, in the 2011 staff survey, brand pride as well as engagement were recorded at 70%. Often overcoming staff resistance to change can be achieved by clearly demonstrating the advantages and positive impact the change has on the customers, readers and users of the Library. Once an understanding of the concept has been achieved, seeing it in practice often confirms to staff that the benefits have been achieved. In this case, throughout the staff training and communication plans, teams who had limited or no contact with the readers in the Reading Room, were invited to shadow the Reference Services teams and talk to the users of the numerous versions of Search our Catalogue. This included the Primo Technical Team, who gained an insight into a number of the negative comments first hand. Many colleagues have returned several times to the Reading Rooms to engage with the readers, as the changes and new releases of the catalogue have been developed.

Information Literacy

One constant theme running throughout the communication and training programmes for the library staff is the positive impact the changes to front line services will have on the behaviour of the user (whatever their background). The British Library has a duty to support all types of researchers, whatever their age or experience of a library or research. This includes dealing with people who have wide variances in information literacy skills. Information Literacy is evidenced through:

> "Understanding the ways in which information and data is created and handled, learning skills in its management and use and modifying learning attributes, habits and behaviours to appreciate the role of information literacy in learning and research. In this context learning is understood as the constant search for meaning by the acquisition of information, reflection, engagement and active application in multiple contexts" (NASPA, 2004).

The same could be said for some of the staff of the British Library. They may not necessarily understand 'Information Literacy' as a concept/theory or be aware of the extensive programmes and projects throughout educational establishments in the UK. They should have a firm understanding of the research process as they see first hand the research journey individuals make using the British Library services.

SCONUL Seven Pillars

Of the SCONUL 7 pillars, the 'Explore the British Library' training project team concluded there were five out of the seven pillars that would be key foundations to the training plans for all staff throughout the library, to support and enable the researcher on their journey:

- Identify: a researcher is able to identify a need for information to address the research question.

- Scope: a researcher can assess their current knowledge and identify gaps.
- Plan: a researcher can construct strategies for locating information and data.
- Gather: a researcher can locate and access the information and data they need.
- Manage: a researcher can organise information professionally and ethically.

The researcher may not be aware of these five pillars, but the role of the librarian is able to provide the support to assist and enable the researcher to achieve them.

The other two pillars are:

- Evaluate: a researcher can review the research process and compare and evaluate information and data.
- Present: a researcher can apply the knowledge gained: presenting the results of their research, synthesising new and old information and data to create new knowledge, disseminating it in a variety of ways.

These two are subjective and reflective, and whilst the librarian can be a sounding board to the researcher on the path of achieving these skills and knowledge, they are not able to directly provide them for the researcher.

Within the details of the SCONUL 7 pillars (SCONUL, 2011) the competencies are divided into understanding and ability, for example, understanding 'what types of information are available' and ability 'to identify any information gaps'. For the training project team, the focus was changed from 'the researcher is able to', to 'the librarian is able to'. From this starting point the team was able to prepare for the stages of the overarching programme as a number of small online catalogues were merged with the Search our Catalogue. Based on the first training sessions feedback from the Reference Services staff contributed to the 'bugs' to be fixed and assisted in identifying the priorities.

Researcher Development Framework

Significant work has been undertaken on the Researcher Development Framework (RDF) (Vitae, 2010). The framework describes the knowledge, skills, behaviours and personal qualities of researchers at different stages of their careers and encourages them to aspire to excellence. Members of the Search our Catalogue training team used the RDF framework and the SCONUL 7 pillars to examine which parts of the framework were applicable to the staff training programme. RDF has four domains:

- Knowledge and intellectual abilities – the knowledge, intellectual abilities and techniques to do research (Domain A).
- Research governance and organisation – the knowledge of the standards, requirements and professionalism to do research (Domain B).
- Personal effectiveness – the personal qualities and approach to be an effective researcher (Domain C).
- Engagement, influence and impact – the knowledge and skills to work with others and ensure the wider impact of research (Domain D).

Each domain has 12 sub-domains, and within those there are 63 descriptors, all of which encompass 'the knowledge, intellectual abilities, techniques and professional standards' (Vitae, 2010). As with the SCONUL 7 pillars, the project team felt that the more subjective elements of the RDF were less relevant to the project, and they therefore focused on Domain A, the first phase of the framework, to help the Reference Services team support the researcher on their journey.

Professional Competencies

Professional competencies are requirements in both the job profiles and appraisal measurements at the British Library. Out of the ten professional competencies for Reference Services staff the project team identified the following seven competencies relevant to the project for:

- An understanding of how knowledge can be organised, managed and made accessible to on-site and remote users in line with current trends and resources.
- A good understanding of the British Library's collections and the infrastructure that underpins them, including the cataloguing systems and classification methodology.
- A good understanding of the Library's catalogues, and Aleph, and the ability to interpret catalogues and indexes in order to help readers identify and trace items relevant to their research.
- Understanding of developments and trends in the wider library and information world, and their specialist area, that might impact on own area of work, particularly new trends in the delivery of Reference Services and proactively shares this information.
- Excellent knowledge of research methodology and the impact technology has on the research process.
- Good presentation skills.
- An awareness of current and future trends within the library profession, including Web 2.0 & 3.0. An understanding of the relevance of social networking media in disseminating information amongst the library

community, to colleagues within the British Library and to remote and on-site users of Reference Services.

Not all of the principles of these theories were relevant to every member of British Library staff affected by the project. However, when theories were presented as part of the introduction to the training and as part of the reasoning behind this major systems change, staff were able to understand the principles in terms of their roles to support the researcher journey. The staff of the British Library appreciate that many of the readers will already have received information literacy training from their academic institution, either as a student or researcher. Despite this it is not essential that readers have this background knowledge of the theories and principles of information literacy to be successful in their research. What is essential and important to the readers is that staff dealing with their face to face or remote enquiry are trained accordingly and qualified to assist them on their research journey. Part of the Explore project introduced the theories of information literacy to some of the staff for the first time, however the practice and mechanisms of supporting the researchers journey was not new. Training the staff on the theories of information literacy and the practical applications of it with regards to Explore has supported their continuing professional development. A possible future project for Reference Services is developing information literacy training for readers via the Reader Workshop Programme.

In the summer of 2011 the technical project team set the date for the switch off of the integrated catalogue for mid January 2012. This initiated planning for how to scale up the successful training for the Reference Services Team and other front line teams to training for all other British Library staff. At that stage the staff training programme was updated to include the new RDF alongside the relevant principles of the SCONUL 7 pillars and the appropriate British Library professional competencies. The British Library updated its strategic priorities for 2011-2015 and the five strategic priorities were added to the purpose of the training and the underlying principles for the changes in the service:

- Guarantee access for future generations.
- Enable access to everyone who wants to do research.
- Support research communities in key areas for social and economic benefit.
- Enrich the cultural life of the nation.
- Lead and collaborate to grow the world's knowledge base.

Initial training, planning and delivery

Introducing such a new and technologically different service required the development of a complex and detailed communication plan for both staff and readers. There was also a need for an equally long and complex training plan in order to ensure that all front line staff were expert users. This had to take place long before the integrated catalogue service was switched off and 'Explore the British Library' became the main search discovery tool. In preparation for this change in 2008 an early version of the new portal was made publicly available to staff and readers as 'Search our Catalogue'. Users and readers could still access the same content via the established integrated catalogue. The Reference Services Team was then responsible for introducing readers to Search our Catalogue and encouraging them to test the system and provide feedback to the technical Primo project team.

An initial 'hands on' training programme covering the basics of the system was created by the senior user representative on the technical project team. The training was delivered to nine volunteers, with a representative from each reference team. The objective of the training, once attendees had an understanding of the system, was to cascade the training throughout the relevant reference teams.

The other aspect of the training that needed to be considered was just how the initial training of the nine volunteers was to be scaled up to train 75 reference staff to be experts, to support all types of readers and enquirers and the other staff who have front line interaction with readers, users and customers. These staff included the Document Supply Team, Customer Services, the Reading Room Issue Desk Teams, and the Welcome Team. The Welcome Team provides the Reader Registration Service and is the first point of contact a visitor to the library has when applying for a Reader's Pass and to make their first step to commencing research.

In creating training plans the team also had to take account of the ultimate outcome of the Primo programme which was that the current integrated catalogue would cease to exist in the first quarter of 2012. This would require every member of staff within the Library to be able to use the new Explore the British Library service. There had to be assurance that they continued to have a fundamental skill to enable them to carry out their role within the library as effectively and efficiently as possible.

Implementing the staff training programme

In February 2009 requesting functionality was added to Search our Catalogue via the integrated catalogue. This was by no means a perfect solution and an amendment to the current training programme had to be made. This would allow the key trainers within the Reference Services Team to cover the changed functionality but the training took the same format as before. A presentation from a member of the training project team demonstrated the changes to the catalogue, reinforcing the positive impact these changes would have on the researcher's journey. There were also a number of hands-on practice examples, to include all the changes and updates. Duplicate copies of the worksheets were available to the key trainers to enable them to cascade the training to their Reference Team colleagues. Providing the training materials directly to the key trainers enabled the project team to ensure the essential messages of the updates to the catalogue and their accompanying changes to practices were all being communicated to all stakeholders. When appropriate this new knowledge could be passed on to the readers.

Following feedback from the key trainers and the other reference services staff, the number of key trainers was increased. Some reference teams consist of four members of staff and, in other teams, there were 12 staff. In consultation with the teams the project team decided that each key trainer would be responsible for training no more than five members of their team. This change ensured, and continues to ensure, that all key trainers are able to balance their primary roles and responsibilities with their additional training role. The creation of a wider pool of key trainers proved to be a positive amendment to the training programme and had the support of everyone within Reference Services. This became the principle on which all training would now be based for library staff, as the programme for Search our Catalogue now included three updates a year.

As the pool of key trainers expanded and the technical team were able to update the catalogue with greater frequency a number of additional training techniques were explored to ensure the consistency of the training to the key trainers. They cascaded the training and the level of knowledge throughout the department was consistently maintained and updated accordingly. Initially a Virtual Learning Environment (VLE) using the open software of Moodle was considered to be an effective and efficient way to complement the face to face and hands on training. Unfortunately using open software was not permitted due to the number of necessary security controls and restrictions of Information Systems within the British Library. Screen casting with step by step instructions was an option that appealed to the training project team, and proved to be a useful and successful aide memoire to the key trainers.

The key trainers were all given refresher training for trainers. Since commencing this project, the concept of training the trainer within libraries and information literacy has undergone some changes and the emphasis is now on teaching the teacher rather than training. To ensure the reader workshops were suitable for any reader, regardless of their skills and knowledge of using a library or the nature of their research project, the training project team provided all the key trainers with a standard script and presentation with relevant screen shots. Not only did this ensure the uniformity of each workshop, it reduced the additional work expected of the key trainers. It also enabled the project team to update the workshop materials with ease. All the material relating to the workshops and the most up to date versions of the workshop script were stored in the Reference Services relevant SharePoint file. The reader workshops provided an opportunity for other front line team managers to send staff in small groups to the training, without having a negative effect on staffing levels. This pre-empted the staff training programmes but proved to be a useful promotion of the changes by word of mouth. The approach also created a more relaxed atmosphere for the staff to learn in, rather than formal hands on workshop. It was also better that staff were volunteering to attend, rather than it being a formal appraisal objective. Three months after the reader workshops began, over half of the Reading Room and Reader Registration teams had attended a training session.

Whilst the project was still in beta stage the most problematic function remained the requesting via the integrated catalogue. This issue was not to be overcome until late 2011. It was essential in the meantime for the library to encourage more staff and readers to use the catalogue and provide both positive and negative feedback for the technical team. A paper (Packham & Kirk, 2010) has been published covering the training programme for the key trainers and the drop in sessions for readers wishing to use Search our Catalogue. The paper highlighted the successes and issues of the training project to be conquered in the future and the next steps. The paper was not only a useful tool to promote the continuing works of the training project team internally and externally, it was also a good opportunity to review the progress of the project.

The original project plan was scheduled from the second quarter of 2008 when Search our Catalogue was introduced until the third quarter of 2010, when the integrated catalogue was planned to be switched off, and Search our Catalogue became the primary catalogue of the British Library. Unfortunately due to a number of technical and software issues, as well as a staffing resource issue, the project was delayed and the integrated catalogue was switched off on 23 January 2012. The extension of the project had both positive and negative impacts on the team.

The delay to any project will obviously have an impact on morale; the delay also had an impact on the testing and the delivery of updated and new Reading Room services. The project team collectively decided that the delays in fact could be used as an advantage. The option of developing and using a VLE for training the key trainers was revisited. The security issues with the Moodle open software had not been resolved so the project team decided to use the additional time available to research the potential to create in-house aspects of a VLE, using the software available.

VLE software, such as Blackboard, WebCT and Moodle, allows for the creation of content to be learnt and understood. It is also possible to follow up with quizzes to test the learning and ensure it has started to become knowledge, as well as providing a community forum for the participants. The training project team agreed the content of workshops was understood by the key trainers, but other Reference Service staff may not have been as confident in their skills and knowledge. The project team thought it would be a useful exercise to test the search skills and knowledge of the wider Reference Services Team. The project team wanted a mechanism of testing the Reference Services Team without creating a 'back to school' environment or the need to mark 75 tests scripts. Reference Services were already using SurveyMonkey for an online feedback questionnaire on the reader workshops.

The project team decided to trial the use of SurveyMonkey for a staff quiz. It would still require the project to review the responses but the results would be collated at a question level for all respondents and the project team were confident they would be able to review the answers and spot any mistakes that were made. The quiz was labelled a refresher training quiz, and as an incentive to encourage staff to complete it, a number of chocolate prizes were offered. The quiz had 20 questions, all of which were compulsory and all the answers used the free text response option. At the end of the quiz, staff were required to give their name, this allowed the project team to assess the knowledge of the respondents and address any problems the individuals may have been encountering as well as recording the information for the prize draw. The staff were also asked to identify any questions that were difficult or confusing as well as being encouraged to provide any further comments.

The project team were encouraged by the results; almost all of the 75 Reference Services staff completed the quiz, and 95% of the answers provided were correct. The project team were able to identify a lack of knowledge of some of the Web 2.0 functions, such as tagging records. As a result of the quiz the project team amended the staff training programme with an increased emphasis on the Web 2.0 content and its benefits to the researcher. The comments at the end of the quiz were also very useful. Some of the staff were honest in expressing the areas they felt their skills were lacking. The project team were able to appoint the appropriate key trainer to work with these individuals to improve their knowledge and skills. Other comments were reassuringly positive to the project team to reassure them that the quiz was a positive and fun tool to test and increase staff's knowledge. SurveyMonkey does not permit the saving of the quiz, completion needs to be achieved once the survey has been opened otherwise the results are lost. This is not a perfect solution for staff that spend at least 60% of their working week in a Reading Room on a reference desk where they are required to interact with readers. Dedicated back room time was required to give staff the uninterrupted time to complete the quiz.

In summer 2010 'Search our Catalogue', changed its name to 'Explore the British Library'. The service now included searching of the British Library's website content and the websites the library had archived as part of a digital content ingest project. This new and additional content again created a change in the training programme of the Reference Services staff and the content of the presentations and scripts used in the reader and staff workshops.

Evaluation of the success of the training was not just limited to ensuring front line staff use could Explore, but also sought to ensure they were able to explain to readers why such a fundamental change was occurring. In addition they needed to be able to train others: colleagues, new staff and, most importantly, readers. Each reference team delivers reader workshops, many of which focus on aspects of Explore, and are delivered by every member of the reference team.

Project completion

The closure of the integrated catalogue and the training dates for all staff were advertised on the intranet and in the British Library in-house journal 'Shelf Life'. As with the reader workshops, the training sessions were drop-in sessions, but due to limitation on room occupancy a booking system was introduced. Frequently asked questions were also available, based on the questions the key trainers had been asked throughout the last two years of training readers. The staff workshops ran for three months, during which time approximately over half of the staff of the British Library attended. The training project team celebrated this rate of attendance; however there were concerns that could be groups of staff who were not attending the workshops. The project team decided to do some attendance analysis of the staff workshops and contacted some staff from the groups that were under represented. The analysis highlighted low to zero attendance from the departments of Human Resources, Security, Estates and Finance. In conversation with colleagues from these departments, the project team learnt the members of these departments were unlikely to use the integrated catalogue and therefore were not likely to use 'Explore the British Library'. If these teams were to require access to collection items or to undertake research, they would speak to the most appropriate reference service for support and assistance at the time of need.

As the technical and training projects draw to a close and the integrated catalogue had been switched off for a week, the training project team had started to consider when the reader workshops will cease and the delivery of 'Explore the British Library' training becomes part of the business as usual workshop program. The project team will also review the lessons learnt from the project and whether the objectives of delivering an information literate program of training to British Library staff has been achieved. It is not possible to reflect on that entirely at this time as staff training is continuing for the moment. The project team had decided to try and repeat the success of the staff quiz on SurveyMonkey. One of the lessons learned from the quiz is to create two quizzes of ten questions each. It is hoped that this will overcome the lack of saving function and allow for the quiz to be pitched at different levels of users. For example a library assistant at the issue desk would probably not need to know the same level of in-depth functionality as a curator. Further developments to Explore are planned for late 2012 and early 2013, and as these changes are introduced it will be both useful and interesting to test the staff who were trained in 2011 to establish the longer term success of the training, preferably using a VLE. The VLE would also be used to provide further online training and testing as well as automatic scoring of the tests, all of which would help to ensure the knowledge learnt was understood and had become a long term skill. This is being reinforced with further management buy-in and support from the professional competencies of the staff appraisal.

The project team benefited from having been members of the group. They not only worked well together but all believed in the benefits of the new catalogue and were enthusiastic about the changes to the service. During the three years of the project there was only one change of membership to the project team, and this was due to a change in role and promotion within the British Library. The team feels the stability of the membership was a benefit to the delivery of the objectives of the project. When the project team needed perspective and input this was available from a number of colleagues who were not as close to the project.

Conclusion

It would be difficult to conclude that the staff of the British Library are now more information literate than they were at the start of the project. As this was not intended to be an academic project, the staff were not tested prior to the training as to what their understanding of the theories of information literacy were, or whether they would consider themselves to be information literate. This would be a part of the project to be considered for the future. It would be time and resources dependent but it could prove advantageous to test staff now on their understanding of information literacy theories as well as their understanding of Explore. However, by the end of the project staff do have a better understanding of the main theories and how these can be applied to the work they do in supporting the researcher's journey of discovery. While most of them would never claim they are or are not information literate, they are librarians doing a job they have been trained to do, which gives them satisfaction and pleasure.

References

British Library. (2011). *Growing knowledge: the British Library's strategy 2011-2015*. Retrieved from the British Library website:
www.bl.uk/aboutus/stratpolprog/strategy1115/strategy1115.pdf

NASPA: National Association of Student Personnel Administrators. (2004). *Learning reconsidered 2*. Retrieved from the American College Personnel Association website:
www.myacpa.org/pub/documents/LearningReconsidered2.pdf

Packham, C. & Kirk, T. (2010). *Changing the catalogue: training the users at the British Library*. Paper presented at LILAC 2010 Conference, Strand Hotel Limerick, on 31st March 2010. Retrieved from the LILAC website:
www.lilacconference.com/dw/programme/Presentations/Wednesday/Wogan_Suite/Kirk-Packham_changing_the_catalogue.pdf

SCONUL: Society of Colleges, National and University Libraries. (2011). *The SCONUL seven pillars of information literacy: a research lens for higher education*. Retrieved from the SCONUL website:
www.sconul.ac.uk/groups/information_literacy/seven_pillars.html

Vitae. (2010). *The Researcher Development Framework*. Retrieved from the Vitae website:
www.vitae.ac.uk/CMS/files/upload/Introducing%20the%20RDF%20presentation.ppt

Leading Change: Developing Information Literacy Frameworks for Students and Library Staff

Greta Friggens
Faculty Librarian, Creative and Cultural Industries, University of Portsmouth, UK
greta.friggens@port.ac.uk
and
Lisa White
Staff Development Adviser, University Library, University of Portsmouth, UK
lisa.white@port.ac.uk

Abstract

The focus of the paper is to share how the University of Portsmouth Library in the UK updated and developed its information literacy framework to provide support and guidance not only for the development of students but also, in an adapted format, to support the development of Library staff. A staff development focus group built on the recommendations of the Enquiry Services Review Group and the Staffing Review Group. It aimed to identify and articulate key skills and knowledge in a framework, drawing from it a programme of events to support staff development. Careful consideration was given to how this would be introduced. Its purpose was to both facilitate and support a cultural change as well as ensuring sessions would be attended by all staff. The paper takes a practical approach, presenting how each stage of the process impacted on the outcome. The success of the staff development framework and programme of events will be examined. Reference will be made to feedback from staff that have both attended and led sessions or worked with the framework. Consideration will be given to how feedback, in these early stages of the delivery of the programme, might impinge upon its future development.

How did the idea originate?

The idea of developing information literacy frameworks for students and Library staff, originated in response to a series of internal and external pressures on the Library service. Externally, higher education libraries in the UK are undergoing a period of change and uncertainty. After a time of relative stability, they now face considerable pressure to re-examine services and processes in the face of budget cuts and demand from users to offer more personalised services (SCONUL, 2007). At the University of Portsmouth this period of change coincided with the appointment of a new University Librarian. The opportunity was taken to review processes and realign them to the University's mission. A significant influence was Research Information Network's report on UK research information provision which considered 'how academic librarians are experiencing and responding to financial cuts in the current economic climate' (Research Information Network, 2010). The Service Plan for the University Library, for Spring 2009 – Spring 2011 acknowledges that whilst there are economies to be made, there may be opportunities to benefit users. Opportunities resulting from the loss of staff due to retirement and a voluntary severance scheme were timely in facilitating the development of more efficient processes and services to meet user demands. Two Groups were established: the Staffing Review Group and, to feed into that, the Enquiry Services Review Group.

In the same year, the University responded to staffs' desire for more help with managing change. A programme called Leading Change was introduced to recruit staff from all grades to be ambassadors for helping colleagues through such periods. The idea of basing a staff development framework on the Library's information literacy framework (ILF) developed in stages, beginning with the revision of the already well established student ILF. This was established some seven years previously, based on SCONUL's (1999) 'Seven pillars of information literacy'. The next stage offered a solution to the Enquiry Group's idea to develop a competencies framework on which to base the Library staff development programme. Why not align it with the student ILF? If students are expected to accomplish these skills, then Library staff should be competent and confident to help. With ever-changing technologies it was important to invest resources to refresh and update knowledge.

What did the review groups contribute to the programme?

Enquiry Services Review Group

This Group was convened in January 2010 and initiated the programme. Its aim was to advise the Staffing Review Group on the future direction of Enquiry services within the University Library. Its recommendations included the need to train and develop all public-facing staff according to competencies, aligned to the ILF. As all staff spend some time in a public facing role, this meant everybody.

Data from Enquiry surveys carried out in 2007 and 2009 was used as a starting point, enabling the Group to see that, at Portsmouth, the number of enquiries was rising. This reflected the growing student population. Data was recorded across all front-facing Enquiry points and telephone points. An extra survey, convened by the Group in 2010, showed that the number of enquiries was continuing to rise (See Table 1)

Academic year	Number of enquiries	Percentage increase on previous year	Full-time equivalent student numbers	Percentage increase on previous year
2006/2007	3,549	-	16,258	-
2008/2009	4,352	23%	18,273	12%
2009/2010	4,583	5%	19,574	7%

Table 1 : Growth in the number of enquiries and student numbers

The number of both short and more detailed enquiries (those over ten minutes) had risen, suggesting that a combination of both professional and non-professional staff were required for the Enquiry service to operate efficiently. The Reception and Ground Floor information Desks often referred enquiries on to relevant subject teams. A change of culture was necessary to improve the user experience, and training and equipping staff with the skills in order to limit those referrals was essential.

In reaching its recommendations, the Enquiry Services Review Group considered a range of competency frameworks and training programmes. Amongst the examples consulted was that developed by the Council of Australian University Librarians (Rice and Burke, 2004). One of the skills and knowledge suggestions ("Demonstrate an awareness of the information literacy goals and objectives... and the contribution of ad hoc instruction to achieving these") led to the realisation that the ILF would be an excellent basis for reasonable and achievable competencies. The principles of the ILF were easily adapted to suit the skills requirements of staff, for example, the most basic competency in the student framework is to be able to 'Locate the main areas of book stock for your subject'. The staff framework suggests that all staff should know the 'subject layout of the Library including the floor split and location of reference collections. Know how to use floor directories and maps, how Dewey works, including prefixes and suffixes.'

Further to this, the Group's recommendations stated that the framework should support 'all public-facing staff with further competencies for help desk staff. More training, geared to the level of responsibility, is required. Key training should be mandatory. It recognised the role that *all* public-facing staff have in supporting the University's mission and, therefore that training should be 'mandatory' – a cultural change for the Library. These recommendations later formed the basis of a series of meetings of a focus group convened by the Library's Staff Development Group, a standing group of staff from across the Library.

Staffing Review Group

This Group fully supported the recommendations of the Enquiry Services Review Group. It was established at the end of 2009 to create a structure with greater flexibility and better suited to supporting the University's changing profile. The voluntary severance scheme and staff retirements had left key posts vacant, providing an opportunity to make changes to a structure that had been static for the previous ten years. During that period roles changed, particularly with the opening of the new Library extension in 2007. However, this was not reflected in the staffing structure. For instance, the extension changed the nature of the Library Reception Desk fundamentally. Activity there increased making it the busiest Enquiry point in the Library as it became a reception for the whole building, which includes not only the Library, but an IT suite and shared teaching space. Because of its accessible location on a city-centre campus, it has become an Enquiry point for the whole University. Other factors were considered:

- pressure on budgets meant service priorities needed to be defined
- some developing services, e.g. the institutional research repository, were not being given the priority they deserved because the Library did not have the capacity (and sometimes the skills)
- the proposed transfer to a new academic year structure in 2012 suggests that peaks of pressure on Library services will change, for example, opening hours will need revision.

These pressures are likely to be heightened as the UK Government White Paper asks institutions to put students at the heart of the system (Department of Business, Innovation and Skills, 2011) and that those students will become more demanding as fees are raised. With so many changes happening at once after such a long period of stability, the Staffing Review Group acknowledged that staff need to be more flexible and adaptable, particularly as they will be directly affected as Library teams and roles change. The Library structure has moved from subject floor teams to function-focused teams, i.e. User Services, Academic Liaison, Procurement and Metadata, Systems and Business Support.

With movement of staff into new roles, the Group was keen to ensure that all staff are up-to-date with current technology, skills and knowledge.

Why was it important to develop the student information literacy framework?

Soon after the Enquiry Services Review Group reported its recommendations, an opportunity arose for a member of the Group to apply for a University initiative that would enable the revision and development of the student ILF. A University staff survey in 2009 suggested that it could do more to help staff prepare for change. In response to this, an initiative called Leading Change was launched. Staff at all levels were encouraged to submit an application to join the programme and fourteen colleagues, including two members of Library staff, were selected.

This personal and professional development opportunity included a series of seminars and the provision of a coach or mentor to assist with the development of a project that could help bring about change. The project chosen was to develop the ILF into an interactive learning object. It brought together a wide range of guides, reusable learning objects and other information to support the information literacy development of students at all levels. Guides were incorporated into the ILF so that both tutors and students could see what they should be able to achieve, and how to do it, at each level of study. A self-test facility was incorporated so that students could see whether they had acquired that skill. The ILF is flexible and can be used in different contexts:

- for self-directed learning or for tutors to select particular elements to incorporate into units within a virtual learning environment
- by enquiries staff to promote information literacy skills, supporting the work of the faculty librarians
- Librarians at Portsmouth's associate colleges can use the framework to provide equality of access to those studying remotely.

It was also important that the skills included in the original ILF could be updated to feed appropriately into the Enquiry Services Review Group's suggestion of a staff competencies framework. The desirability of the project and its proposed changes were supported by the Library's vision, 'To help develop information literate graduates well able to exploit information for employment, citizenship as well as academic work.' (Professional Service Strategic Summary for the University Library, March 2011–March 2013). The ILF will ensure equitable access to the tools to achieve this. Students with good information literacy skills will understand that they do not need just to rely on set text books to find information; that there is a much wider information landscape to facilitate this. Potentially the interactive ILF could impact on how students view learning resources when they complete the National Student Survey (NSS). The NSS is an opportunity for final year undergraduates in UK publicly funded further and higher education institutions to feedback on their academic experience. Comparative data is then made available online to help future students decide where to study. *UPLift! Library Information Tips* the new name, for the ILF went live, as work in progress in June 2010 (University Library, 2012). The ILF will continue to develop in light of SCONUL's (2011a, 2011 b) revised seven pillars model and in turn, will feed into the staff development framework.

How was the ILF adapted to the staff development framework?

The process of adapting the model to a) provide a framework of skills and knowledge required for all customer-facing staff and b) develop that framework into a programme of training events to support this, was logical. The Enquiry Services Review Group had sketched out a version of the framework which identified the skills that all customer-facing staff should be familiar with and those which all Enquiry staff, with more specialised skills, should know. Currently, 69 potential enquiry types or skills have been identified in the document. These will change and develop according to the introduction of new literacies to the student framework, e.g. new technologies supporting information handling (See Figure 1).

Students do not differentiate between enquiries staff and staff responsible for other functions; they often just need help with getting started. Enquiry staff are expected to know more about the advanced search skills, in order to support what librarians are teaching students in the classroom. Skills for all staff and enquiries staff have been colour coded and mapped in the same document to encourage staff to observe their own development and aspire to moving up to the next grade should opportunities arise.

A staff development focus group was convened to take forward recommendations by providing Library skills sessions to support the new staffing structure. This was chaired by the Library's Staff Development Adviser who also has a post in the Human Resources Department and who has previous experience with customer-focused services in the private sector. The focus group drew representatives from different teams across the Library, including both academic and front line support experience, including a faculty librarian as ILF specialist, Enquiry staff and user services staff with more general knowledge. The mix of experience, grades and roles helped to shape a framework that addressed the gaps in the Group's varied knowledge and so, it was believed, that it could be confidently applied across the Library team.

The framework was used as a benchmark to start mapping knowledge that all staff were expected to have, under the same headings as the student ILF:

- Using the Library
- Using Library resources effectively
- Searching for information using databases
- Using the internet for academic purposes.

This later helped to construct tailored training sessions along the same themes.

How was the staff development programme developed?

The Chair adapted a template used within the wider University for developing events and training sessions.

Eight separate skills training sessions were identified. The first five were applicable and relevant to all customer facing staff, with the remaining three aimed (not exclusively) at staff on Enquiry Desks requiring more specialist knowledge. The Wiki Way was deliberately chosen as the first session. The Library established a wiki to encourage information sharing about its services and processes, so familiarity with its content and navigation was essential. Staff would also use it to sign up for the skills sessions, read the session plans and find any additional material relating to them. Figure 2 shows the plan for the Wiki Way, but each session follows a similar template.

The focus group established that each session would last an hour. With over 80 staff in the Library, each session would need to be run six times over a period of three weeks on different days and times. This would provide flexibility for different working patterns and enable all members of staff to attend. Sessions would be led by Library staff 'experts', working to a session outline, devised by the focus group. Session plans and details are posted on the staff wiki for future reference and to assist with induction of new starters or staff moving into new roles in the future.

Having identified the sessions' detailed content and structure, it was essential to ensure maximum engagement and participation from staff. The Library had moved from a series of optional to more focused sessions where staff are required to attend as part of their role. It is important that longer-serving staff refresh their skills and knowledge and also recognise the importance of sharing their experience to help others gain confidence. Some might have been reluctant to engage so it was important to sell the value of the programme. The sessions were marketed by pre-empting questions such as 'Why bother with the wiki – where is its value for my work?' Broady-Preston and Cossham (2010) explored the importance of mandatory professional development in motivating

Using the library	Using library resources effectively	Searching for information using databases	Using the internet for academic purposes
Subject layout of the Library including the floor split and location of reference collections. Know how to use floor directories and maps, how Dewey works, including filing prefixes and suffixes	Consider the user – campus based students. distance learners, students with disabilities, mature students, students on collaborative programmes, staff and visiting academics	Access an electronic resource using Shibboleth (access management system)	Understand the nature of the web as an information and communication source – knowing how the library website can be used as a gateway to appropriate academic sources
Special collections – location, understanding of the contents and procedures for accessing archives, reserve stock, theses, rare books and Map Library	**Access the library catalogue** from on and off campus	Access information about **web proxy and the off-campus passwords page** on the Library website	**Confidently navigate the Library website** with different user groups in mind, e.g. distance learners or academic staff
Photocopiers, printers and scanners – location, including large format options in Map Library, basics of using, costs	**Search and navigate the Library catalogue** – using keywords, refining by resource type, e.g. DVD, e-book or by subject	**Help with access and login problems**, e.g. 'Help yourself' section of Library website, out of hours support, elibrary team	**Be aware of the different features of Google** and how they can help users to search more effectively, including Advanced search, Google books, Scholar
Group study rooms – locations and procedures for booking and accessing	**Locate a reading list** using Talis Aspire and link to Library Catalogue to check availability of stock	**Recognise how search results are presented** and know how to change the order or refine the results	**Explain the importance of evaluating information from the web** – and recognise parts of a URL that might aid evaluation

IT Open Access area, Postgraduate Suite and 3rd Space – location, content and access	**Identify key resources on a reading list** including book, book chapter, journal title, journal article and know how to search for each on the Library Catalogue	**Be aware of index features such as thesauri** and when it might be useful to use them	**Evaluate a webpage using academic criteria**, e.g. purpose, bias, currency
Photocopiers, printers and scanners – basics of how to use, troubleshooting strategies	**Help users find other good quality resources**, e.g. via 'My subject' and Databases pages on Library website	**Recognise how to print, save and email search results**	
	Understand the Information Landscape – knowing when and why it is appropriate to recommend different sources of information, e.g. audiovisual, and that some are more authoritative than others	**Be aware of additional database features**, such as signing in to save search histories, create RSS feeds or email alerts	
	Understand the principles of referencing why it is an important academic skill and the primacy of departmental guidance over Library advice	**Recognise when you have done your best** and know how to refer user to a Faculty Librarian	

Figure 1: Section from the staff development framework (shaded boxes indicate skills for enquiry staff only)

Session Title: THE WIKI WAY
Presenters: Wiki working Group
   Who the session is aimed at: All Library staff
   Maximum number of participants: 15
   Outline of session:
- To use and understand how to use the wiki more efficiently
- To access information, perhaps not within your department
- To input ideas on searching and navigating this resource

The aims of the session are:
   To cover the following areas and update our working knowledge about how the wiki works within the Library and how it will support the new structure:

WHY BOTHER WITH THE WIKI – WHERE IS ITS VALUE IN MY WORK?

- Why we use the wiki and what the benefits of it are – giving examples of how departments currently use it and its value
- Understanding the structure and where we can input ideas/suggestions
- Navigating the wiki – sharing top tips – also user recommendations to improve its functionality
- Updating the wiki – how to do this or whom to refer it to and how
- A few practical examples of this for frequent/infrequent users
- Sharing experience of using the wiki – likes and dislikes
- Identify what is missing – what did you hope to find but could not?
- Understand where you can access and update key resources, e.g. Library guides and handouts, also teaching materials
- Using this to share good practice and top tips for Enquiry Desks, also share teaching tools and templates
- Have the time to explore this resource and feel more confident in using it
  Learning outcomes:
- For Library staff to develop their skills and feel confident and capable in knowing when and how to make best use of the wiki
- To know how & where to access information across floors and departments

Pre-session preparation (if applicable)
Presenters: Materials used for the wiki session to be included on the wiki for future reference and amendments
Participants: Staff attending this session will need to ensure they have access to the wiki beforehand and log in.

Figure 2: Wiki Way session outline following the established template

the profession. The mandatory element was felt to be applicable to both professional and non-professional staff within the University Library team.

How was the framework and staff development programme introduced to library staff?

As a result of the re-structure, two secondment opportunities had arisen which enabled the framework to be trialled and tested. It allowed the seconded staff members to identify gaps in their knowledge and acted as a driver in order to bridge those gaps. The Staff Development Adviser regularly reviewed their progress and sought critical feedback on the value of the framework. Feedback showed that it helped individuals quickly prioritise areas of knowledge to develop in order to successfully do their job and gave a clear description of how they might achieve it. They also recognised its value as a tool to which they could cross-refer in mapping progress.

At the start of the new academic year, the University Librarian introduced the new staff development programme, including the framework, to all staff. It was timely in that staff felt reassured that they would be supported in adapting to the resulting changes. One of the first informal Library information briefings showcased work on the student and staff frameworks, helping staff to see the correlation of skills for both students and staff. The session was well attended and initial feedback showed that it was well received.

How successful has the framework been in supporting staff moving into new roles?

An opportunity afforded by the staffing review, was for faculty librarians to lead on strategic functional areas. A member of the Enquiry Group, responsible for leading on the development of the ILF, was successful in acquiring the functional responsibility for Enquiry services. This provided an excellent opportunity to continue working with the Staff Development Adviser in utilising the staff development framework to support the movement of three staff into new enquiries roles, one of whom had previously utilised the framework in a secondment.

A new Team Leader and several new staff provided the opportunity to encourage staff to consider it a new Enquiries Team. This was intended to have a new culture where the users' needs were first, as the Enquiry Group had recommended. They were keen to move towards working across the three floors of the Library, rather than being on one floor as had been the pattern previously, recognising that they would be fully supported by the new training programme.

Existing staff were pleased that their need for continual staff development was acknowledged; limited formal enquiries training had taken place for a number of years. Their own contribution to the training sessions, through sharing of experience with the new team members, was well received. In reviewing the feedback from the sessions, consideration will be given as to whether presenters did enough to facilitate this.

What are the development plans?

Along with the ILF and staff development programme of events, development plans were introduced to staff in secondments and new roles. The plans will be introduced more widely as a toolkit for managers and individuals and include the following:

- A skills portfolio for all Library roles mapping the knowledge specifications for each and showing the varied requirements across all grades and jobs. The intention is transparency, so that staff can be clear about the expectations of different roles and where they may need to develop additional skills or expertise to facilitate promotion (e.g. when progressing into a first professional role, skills such as the ability to lead small projects and give staff regular and constructive feedback on performance is essential, but not expected in the non-professional grade)
- A training portfolio, mapping training provided by the Library and University to support development of the required skills, enabling staff to establish their own route towards development (e.g. when progressing into a professional role, effective time management and project management skills are essential, but are not necessarily expected in a non-professional role.

Feedback to date has shown that individuals have found this has helped considerably in placing their work and highlighting future aspirations.

How successful has the staff development programme been so far?

With the programme just four months underway, success may be difficult to measure, although evaluation is in process. The initial aim was to identify and develop staffs' information literacy skills and to increase confidence and ensure maximum flexibility within existing roles. Engagement was essential to acquire maximum feedback. Volunteers from each session collected feedback from their Group, answering a few short questions relating to the session's aims. Feedback was collated and shared across the Library. Had the sessions achieved their aims? Did staff recognise their value? Figure 3 shows the method of recording feedback.

The first session met its aim and, as expected, highlighted some ways a) to make the wiki more engaging (sharing of experience) and b) to identify some training on how to make it so. Each of the eight skills sessions will be evaluated in the same way. Figure 4 outlines the aims of each session, against which, each will be evaluated. At the time of writing, three sessions have been delivered and evaluation is in process.

Initial feedback has shown that staff value the opportunity to take time out to refresh their skills and knowledge. With a variety of roles represented at each session it has encouraged collaboration and cross-sharing of information as intended.

Although in the early stages of evaluation, some questions have emerged:

- Was it correct to expect all staff to attend all of the basic sessions? Early findings suggest that the majority of staff found this beneficial and learnt something new. Senior staff attendance has helped embed the cultural change of a more mandatory approach and has facilitated the sharing of information across roles. Their supportive role in attendance could have been made more explicit
- Should some of the sessions have been tailored for different Groups of staff? Whilst this may be to the advantage of more experienced staff, those with less experience reported benefitting from more knowledgeable colleagues. More tailored sessions would have increased the level of timetabling and organisation. Part of the programme's success is the multiple scheduling enabling all staff to attend
- Did presenters always keep to the session plans? Whilst the aims and objectives of the first sessions were made explicit, on occasion, the full plan was not seen as a priority by presenters who had their own agenda. In hindsight this could have been averted by pairing presenters from different roles
- Were there sufficient presenters to share the workload? To date, well structured timetabling and organisation has meant that the initial sessions were well covered. The second half of the programme focuses on more specialised Enquiry skills. There is an expectation that more members of professional staff will lead them in order to share the workload
- Did all staff attend all of the sessions as expected? Initial results show that the majority of staff did attend. However, this will be monitored over a longer period to see trends in absences or non-engagement
- If sessions have outcomes that need to be actioned, who should take responsibility? Results from the first two sessions show areas for im-

---

The main aim of this session was:
  To use and understand how to use the wiki more efficiently and effectively
  General feedback showed:
  - The session helped staff to use the wiki and enabled users to browse and not just search.
  - Staff found tips in the session about finding information and navigating the wiki very useful. Regular 'wiki tips' are now circulated to all staff.
  - Having time set aside to explore it in more detail was welcomed.
  - This was a useful refresher and enabled staff to pick up on things previously missed, e.g. starred pages and creating PDF versions of pages.
  - Showed different ways people put information on the wiki (structured versus unstructured) helping with knowing how to look for it.

Some of the things we need to improve:
Where does the Library store its shared information?
  - Still unclear what it's for, lots of duplication. Need for a decision about what goes where, wiki, website, shared computer drive, and overall editorial control.

Content
  - Too wordy and not easy to navigate around site.
  - It would be easier if it was more uniform.
  - Getting a clear structure right or templates would help.
  - More précised and concise information.

  Future sessions
  - A session on designing attractive well thought out pages.
  - A more detailed session on creating and editing wiki pages.

Figure 3 : Example of feedback – Wiki Way

provement or identify where further training might be considered. Prioritising this is important to ensure staff feel that their suggestions have been listened to. Timely decision-making and communication is key to maintaining engagement

- Is one hour long enough for delivery of the sessions? On reflection, session content has been ambitious and would either benefit from being simplified or adding 30 minutes, to more fully enable discussion and sharing of experience
- The evaluation is the most ambitious undertaken by the Library and sets a new precedent. The Staff Development Adviser has taken on the large, administrative workload of setting up and monitoring the programme. By introducing a human resources perspective it has enabled a more holistic approach to its development and documentation (e.g. the formal recording of *all* internal learning and development on the University HR system). The programme is exemplary in the University, demonstrating a commitment to investing time and resource in continuous skills development for all Library staff to better support students.

Library Skills Sessions 1-8	
Session Title 1: The Wiki Way	**Session Outline:** • To use and understand how to use the wiki more efficiently • To access information, perhaps not within your department • To input ideas on searching and navigating this resource
Session Title 2: The Library Website	**Session Outline:** • For staff to become more familiar with the Library website in order to support all Library users • For all staff to use the Library website more effectively
Session Title 3: 'Using The Library'	**Session Outline:** • To update Library staff on current procedures in the student areas of the Library and the location of key functions
Session Title 4: 'Using Key Library Resources Effectively'	**Session Outline:** • To update Library staff on using key resources effectively in order to support students and staff
Session Title 5: Beyond Books – What Else Is There?	**Session Outline:** • To consider the ever-increasing range of information sources available to students • To acknowledge that the way students look for information is evolving from using Library catalogues and printed books towards online resources
Session Title 6: Using The Internet Successfully	**Session Outline:** • To showcase a variety of internet resources which may be useful in academic situations • To share knowledge of various Google resources, key social networking sites and audio-visual sources • To highlight the importance of evaluating information from the web and an awareness of copyright and referencing issues
Session Title 7: The Reference Enquiry: What do our users really want?	**Session Outline:** • To explore the importance of the reference Enquiry; what users initially ask for is not always what they want • To facilitate a consistent approach to enquiries across all Enquiry points
Session Title 8: Using Google Scholar and Library Databases Effectively	**Session Outline:** This session will be delivered in two parts Session 1 (1 hour) • To explore Google Scholar and understand how it can help Library users to locate and access journal information, which may link to Library databases • To offer some troubleshooting solutions, in particular for off-campus access Session 2 (1 ½ hours) • To acknowledge the wide variety of database types, but focus on journal databases • To explore some characteristics and common features which will help to develop confidence in using such resources

Figure 4 : Library skills sessions planned for the academic year 2011-2012

What are the future plans for developing the staff development framework and programme of events?

The aim is to promote the framework and programme more widely as part of a toolkit to support both managers and individual members of staff. This is particularly important for annual personal development review and will help individuals with career planning and the Library with succession planning. These documents will also be used at induction, as training guides, and to enable teams, where appropriate, to review work processes and set priorities. The staff framework will continue to develop, mirroring the student framework as new digital literacies are incorporated, thus dictating the need to continue developing the suite of skills training sessions. In the longer term, the framework has the potential to be broadened further to encompass the more specialist Library roles. However, for the moment, the programme will be rolled out as identified, after which a full review will be undertaken, examining feedback from both presenters and participants, before being developed further.

Regular discussion with Enquiry staff confirms that they feel positive and supported by the new staff development programme and that time set aside for training has re-energised their work. The commitment of all Library staff to the new programme is demonstrated by attendance at the sessions and willingness to engage and share experience. Likewise, the development of future sessions seems important to them as their willingness to both collate and offer feedback has been noted. The timeliness of the programme, coinciding with the report of the Staffing Review Group, was undoubtedly beneficial. It demonstrated that the Library was prepared to invest resources to ensure that staff would be supported through this period of change. In return, staff have engaged with the programme, realising that they are part of this changing higher education landscape.

References

Broady-Preston, J., & Cossham, A. (2010). Mandatory CPD and professional re-validation schemes and their role in motivating and re-energising information professionals: the UK and New Zealand experiences. *World Library and Information Congress. 76th IFLA General Conference and Assembly, 128*. Retrieved from the IFLA website: http://conference.ifla.org/conference/past/ifla76/

Department for Business, Innovation and Skills. (2011). *Putting students at the heart of higher education*. Retrieved from the British Government website: http://bis.gov.uk/news/topstories/2011/Jun/he-white-paper-students-at-the-heart-of-the-system

Rice, B & Burke, J. (2004). *QUT Library reference and information enquiry services competencies*. Retrieved from the Council of Australian Librarians website:

www.caul.edu.au/content/upload/files/best-practice/qut2004competencies-reference.doc

Research Information Network. (2010). *Challenges for academic libraries in difficult economic times: a guide for senior institutional managers and policy makers.* Retrieved from the RIN website: www.rin.ac.uk/challenges-for-libraries

Society of College, National and University Libraries. (1999). *Briefing paper: Information skills in Higher Education.* Retrieved from the SCONUL website: www.sconul.ac.uk/groups/information_literacy/papers/Seven_pillars2.pdf

Society of College, National and University Libraries. (2007) *Sconul vision: academic information services in the year 2010.* Retrieved from the SCONUL website: www.sconul.ac.uk/publications/pubs/vision%202010

Society of College, National and University Libraries. (2011a). The *SCONUL seven pillars of information literacy: core model for Higher Education.* Retrieved from the SCONUL website: www.sconul.ac.uk/groups/information_literacy/publications/coremodel.pdf

Society of College, National and University Libraries. (2011b). *The SCONUL seven pillars of information literacy: a research lens for Higher Education.* Retrieved from the SCONUL website: www.sconul.ac.uk/groups/information_literacy/publications/researchlens.pdf

University Library. (2012). *UPLift! Library Information Tips.* Retrieved from the University of Portsmouth Library website: www.port.ac.uk/library/helpyourself/skills/UPLift/

The Two Way Street of Learning: How the Professional Development of Solo Librarians Influences their Role as Information Literacy Guides

Dr. Eva Hornung
Information School, The University of Sheffield, UK
hornunge@tcd.ie

Abstract

Helping patrons to become information literate is a key task for librarians. In order to do that, however, they themselves need to be up to date with their own information skills. Continuing professional development (CPD) is therefore a tool for delivering good information literacy provision. The paper will present some of the findings derived from a recently completed PhD. By exploring the qualitatively different ways in which solo librarians in Ireland understand the notion of CPD, this phenomenographic study aimed at providing an insight into people's perceptions of that term and experiences of different methods of formal and informal learning. Based on an analysis of 30 semi-structured interviews five qualitatively distinct categories emerged ranging from up keeping for organisational goals only to a holistic lifelong learning view. These conceptions in turn informed librarians' opinions on which types of CPD were seen as being successful and effective. In this context the One-Person Librarians (OPLs) discovered how CPD was linked to the information literacy support they gave in the workplace. These findings will be shared here in the hope that other librarians will find new ideas for their IL practice.

Introduction

This paper reports on a recently completed part-time PhD project. Its aim was to understand One-Person Librarians' (OPLs) perceptions of continuing professional development (CPD). Five qualitatively different categories were found and four dimensions of variation within each. This will briefly be outlined below. One unexpected outcome of the research, was how some librarians equated CPD with their role as Information Literacy (IL) providers. OPLs discovered that they were not only receiving, but also providing CPD to others. This link between IL and CPD will be explored in the context of phenomenography. Since readers might not be familiar with this research approach, a short overview will also be given. The discussion will then make some recommendations on ways in which librarians can approach CPD to develop their own IL skills and facilitate their patrons' IL learning.

IL and CPD have been linked in the past. The then President of the International Federation of Library Associations and Institutions (IFLA), Kay Raseroka, made 'lifelong literacy' the presidential theme for her term in 2003 to 2005. She felt that this concept "...recognises that users and librarians need to work at their ability to be information literate over a lifetime" (Raseroka, 2003, p. 110). IFLA recently recommended including media and information literacy into the initial education and the professional development of information professionals (IFLA, 2012). This vision ties in with Webber and Johnston's (2004) idea of the information literate university, where IL informs everything from management, research, the curriculum and students to staff development. This happens in a continuous cycle. Not only librarians at universities, however, will be confronted with IL as an integral part of their work, as a content analysis of LIS job advertisements by Clyde (2005) showed. The majority of posts studied in this survey required some form of education or training duty by the librarian. Clyde recommended the inclusion of IL modules into the LIS curriculum and into CPD programmes. Andretta (2008, p. 150) reported on such a hybrid IL course, which delivered a CPD course within a postgraduate environment:

> "The participants' CPD targets are necessarily linked to the information literacy profiles of the users they support and highlight the challenges brought about by user diversity, while the articulation of effective learning strategies helps them see the connection between these and their information literacy practice".

Bruce's (1999) research into workplace experiences of IL firmly placed IL at the core of the learning organisation and its promotion of lifelong learners. What is more, a current review on research into IL in the workplace and job-related lifelong learning highlighted the need for more studies in this area (Weiner, 2011). Librarians themselves have been well aware of their on-going development needs in a digital information world. In a survey of practitioners by Long and Applegate (2008) respondents ranked "website design/information architecture" and "information retrieval" as the two topics which attracted the highest level of participation.

In Ireland there have been efforts by several organisations to establish IL policies. The Library Association of Ireland (LAI) created a working group (WGIL) in 2006 which investigated IL standards in all types of libraries. To date most of the sharing of experience and resources in IL happens on an informal level with little collaboration within the library sector (Russell and

O'Brien, 2009), which is why WGIL recommended "IL to be made a key strategic training and [sic!] priority for all in the LIS sector" (ibid., p.104). One notable exception to this overall lack of cooperation is CONUL, the Consortium of National & University Libraries in Ireland, which has produced a booklet on integrating IL into the curriculum (CONUL Advisory Committee on Information Literacy, [2011]). None of these initiatives, however, looked specifically at OPLs. Indeed, what has been published on OPLs and IL to date tends to consist of personal experiences in the academic sector (see e.g. Wheeler, 2007). Although not the main focus of the PhD, the present paper reports on some of its findings in relation to OPLs and how they approach their own CPD in order to become more information literate. It will also briefly outline how OPLs can address the CDP needs of their patrons in their role as IL providers.

Research methodology

Development of research questions

The researcher found several definitions of OPLs in the literature. For the purpose of this project she defined them as:

> "a qualified librarian/information professional working on his/her own without any professional help in the immediate organisation other than clerical/administrative".

OPLs are rarely the focus of research in LIS despite estimates that one in three professional librarians worldwide is a solo librarian (Siess, 2003). Their participation in and needs of CPD have been investigated in a few studies (e.g. Shuter, 1974; Slater, 1988; Williamson, 1990), but these tended to be of a quantitative nature employing questionnaires and surveys with pre-defined categories. They also had provided definitions of CPD, thus limiting participants' input. While providing a valid insight into the more technical aspects of CPD, they omitted the more fundamental questions, such as "what do people actually mean when they talk about 'CPD'?" and "how do they experience it?"

This study argues that these need to be understood if we want to provide CPD for ourselves as librarians and, by virtue of our daily work, to our customers. OPLs in particular have developed as trainers by teaching information literacy (IL) to their patrons, whether they would explicitly call it IL or not. This in turn informs their own understanding of IL, which then guides their search for CPD methods to develop these IL skills. Although the study did not explicitly investigate IL, several OPLs connected CPD with it.

Following an extensive review of research, which included studies on CPD in LIS and in other professions, adult education and learning theories, staff management literature and works on OPLs, the researcher narrowed her focus on two research questions:

- What are Irish OPL librarians' conceptions of CPD?
- How do OPLs in Ireland experience different methods of CPD?

Research approach – Phenomenography

The research questions called for a qualitative approach. Having looked at several qualitative strategies, the researcher decided on Phenomenography, which

> "...takes a *relational* (or *non-dualist*) *qualitative, second-order* perspective, [...] aims to describe the key aspects *of the variation* of the experience of a phenomenon rather than the richness of individual experiences, and [...] yields a *limited number of internally related*, hierarchical categories of description of the variation." (Trigwell, 2006, pp. 368-369; italics in original, E. H.]

One of the founding fathers of Phenomenography, Ference Marton, emphasised that its value to research on learning as it

> "focused on the ways of experiencing different phenomena, ways of seeing them, knowing about them, and having skills related to them" (Marton and Booth, 1997, p. 117)

This means that the researcher is trying to understand the relationships a participant has with a phenomenon and is seeking to describe and interpret these different ways of perceiving. The focus of the analysis, however, is not on an individual's perceptions but on the variety of conceptions as experienced across the sample group. These can be grouped into so-called "categories of descriptions", which are qualitatively distinct from each other. Each category also displays dimensions of variation which are aspects that are common to all categories but are experienced in a different way. The aim is an "outcome space", which shows the relations these categories have to each other and also the dimensions of variations within each category. This is a very short summary and the researcher would invite interested readers to peruse Marton and Booth's (1997) excellent book.

Research design

Having obtained ethical clearance from the University of Sheffield, the researcher conducted a pilot study with three OPLs in Dublin in June and July

2008[1]. Following revisions of the researcher's interviewing techniques and some modifications to the interview schedule, the main study took place between September 2008 and June 2009. This coincided with the biggest economic downturn in the history of the Irish state and its financial implications for the library world became apparent in many of the interviews.

Data was collected through semi-structured interviews with 30 OPLs based in the Republic of Ireland. Phenomenography often uses purposive sampling to maximise variation within the group of study participants. The researcher advertised "calls for participation" in several Irish LIS information sources, both online and in print. She also asked colleagues in other libraries to forward it to non-members of the Library Association of Ireland (LAI) and contacted each volunteer individually by email. The demographic details of participants were as follows:

Gender:	5 men, 25 women
Full-time versus part-time:	22 full-time, 8 part-time
Nationality:	24 Irish, three from the UK, two from other EU countries, one from outside Europe
Age:	2 fell into the 20-30 years category, 14 into the 30-40 bracket, 7 were between 40 and 50 years of age and 7 were aged between 50 and 60.
Level of support:	20 worked completely on their own, ten were supported by one assistant or more
Location:	11 rural, 19 urban
Location by province:	19 Leinster, 9 Munster, 1 Ulster, 1 Connaught
Library settings:	9 Health, 9 Special (in wide range of subject areas), 6 Academic, 3 Corporate, 3 School/Public

Table 1: Demographic information of interviewees

Their LIS experience ranged from 3 months to 32 years. The mean average was 13.4 years. When it came to their actual OPL experience they also showed a lot of variation: from two months to 30 years with a mean average of about seven years. 16 answered that their current position was their first job as an OPL. 14 had held an OPL job in the past, some even several of them. Nearly all interviewees (27) were members of the LAI, with 13 being members of LAI

---

1   The researcher presented some of the results at the 2009 satellite meeting in Bologna, see references.

and at least one other association. Seven librarians were involved in one of LAI subgroups at committee level.

Interviews lasted between just over half an hour and 110 min. Additional data, such as reflective impressions, pre- and post-interview conversations, and a sketch of the physical library environment, was also captured in notebooks and helped the researcher to develop a deeper understanding of the interviewee's life world. All interviews were recorded and transcribed verbatim by the researcher. Phenomenographic interviews result in rich descriptions which can be grouped into categories. As there are no guidelines for the novice phenomenographer to follow, the researcher, in consultation with her supervisor, decided on a "cut-and-paste" technique using the printouts of the transcripts. She kept a record of the emerging categories and documented the filtering and regrouping through a photographic trail of evidence. At several meetings the researcher discussed the analysis with the supervisor, who played "devil's advocate" and challenged some of the decisions taken.

Findings

Five categories of description and four dimensions emanated from the data. OPLs in this study perceived CPD as outlined in Table 2:

Categories of description: CPD is…

Category 1: Upskilling for the sake of the organisation/library service (service orientation)

Category 2: Developing as a professional librarian (LIS profession orientation)

Category 3: Helping you to do all the jobs an OPL does (OPL orientation)

Category 4: When you have learned something and you want to do things in a better way when you come back (personal orientation)

Category 5: Your development as a human being (lifelong learning orientation)

Table 2: Overview of categories of descriptions

The following four dimensions also emerged (see Table 3):

Dimensions

Dimension 'role' – responsibility, motivation and support

Dimension 'time' – current job or career or life in general

Dimension 'style' – formal or informal with examples

Dimension 'networking'– types of networking, reasons for doing it

---

Table 3: Dimensions of variations

Depending on the category the aspects of these dimensions were more to the forefront or in the background (see Appendix for an overview of the outcome space). Of particular interest in the context of this article are dimensions 'style' and 'networking'. Looking at the dimension 'style' the following types of CPD were mentioned in each category:

Category 1	Category 2	Category 3	Category 4	Category 5
Both formal and informal; formal strong	Both formal and informal;	Doesn't need to be formal; much more informal	Both formal and informal	Both formal and informal, very strong on both
Examples: Training courses (both in the org. and outside), seminars, academic degrees; being involved in work committees; Internet (email lists, online tutorials, free resources); on the job	Often informal more important, but accreditation or formal structure strong	Examples of informal: Internet (Web, email, email lists, online tutorials), database providers, phone; reading journal articles; on the job activities	Examples of formal: Short seminars, training courses, refresher courses	Every opportunity to learn!
	Examples of formal: Courses, conferences, seminars; training courses as part of a conference; case studies		Examples of informal: Internet (email lists, newsgroups, restricted groups); hands-on, people show you how to do things (shadowing people); Newsletters from vendors; journals	
	Examples of informal: hands-on, people showing you things; email lists, help forums, web seminars, online learning, correspondence courses, email, phone; reading, especially professional literature; informal networking evening			

Table 4: CPD activities by category

This overview shows a wide variation of CPD activities with distinct preferences for either formal or informal means or both. OPLs were engaged in many different types of CPD in order to meet their own IL needs and by extension those of their organisations and patrons. When probed about formal ways of updating their IL skills, one solo librarian elaborated further:

"... I used to **go to the [mentions library organisation] based in England**, just to see what they were doing over there and I think it was there that I learned most about **information literacy**, because they were on the ball sooner than we were and **about virtual learning environments and all of that sort of stuff**. So at least when they were talking here in [mentions own organisation] then about e-learning, at least I knew what they were talking about [laughs] and I was able to through in my few little bits that I had learned..." Interviewee 5 (counter number 00:17:13)

One interviewee talked about the broadening of skills in the context of CPD and went on to explain that they thought that a degree course outside the LIS world would help them with their knowledge in IL:

"I suppose the broadening would be, I did a **Diploma in Journalism** three years ago, now just a Saturday morning Diploma course, but I think in terms of marketing and communication it was very helpful and **I wouldn't say I did [it], you know, because I wanted to necessarily broaden my library and information side, librarian's work**, but I did know at the same time it would be helpful, that **there was a clear relevance**, because of the **whole raise of interest in information literacy and communication with people** and, **giving our message to people** [...] And I thought a communication skill **broadening my skills there clearly would be relevant**." Interviewee 23 (counter number 00:17:25)

Promotional and career aspects featured strongly in the context of pursuing IL-related CPD:

Researcher: "When you reflect now on your own experience so far as a librarian, how important, do you think, CPD will be for your future?"

"... Just to get me involved in areas that I may not already have been involved in, I suppose, updating me on what's happening out there in terms [of] how technology's affecting libraries, trends in, I suppose user interaction with libraries and so on, particularly now that we're dealing with the digital natives. Yeah, it would be absolutely crucial that I'd continue with CPD. I just don't think an employer would look at me [laughs], if I turned around in a year's time "I haven't done anything!" [...] And I think for promotional prospects as well, you know, if you're just doing the same job day in, day out, then you can expect to stay in the same job forever!" Interviewee 18 (counter number 00:14:33)

So which CPD activities might help other OPLs become more information literate? Training courses and seminars offered by the library associations and library schools were mentioned quite frequently by the solo librarians in this study. They suggested, however, that they should be run either in the evenings or on weekends with perhaps an online option for librarians who were too remote to travel. The researcher would encourage OPLs to subscribe to free Webinars, which can be followed in people's own time. Instantly accessible information resources, such as RSS feeds and online videos, could help solos to quickly update on IL issues. Being an OPL herself, however, the researcher is aware of the fact that a lot of learning happens in the actual workplace. The nature of the information need as well as personal learning preferences dictate the CPD strategy the solo librarian will use. The next section will explore OPLs' ideas on how they could pass on their own increased understanding of IL to their clientele.**OPLs are IL teachers as part of their role as CPD providers**

Most solo librarians improved their customers' CPD opportunities by monitoring relevant websites, email lists and newsletters in their respective professional fields. Interestingly some OPLs mentioned their role as trainer or CPD provider. They talked about educating their patrons to become information literate as being one of their tasks:

> "That's what I *love* about my job, it's the part of my job that I really like is giving training and I kind of think if I'm not giving training I don't know what I would be doing with that time, because it's so important for me. We spent a lot of money on databases and online resources and you're dealing with different generations of staff..."
> Interviewee 21 (counter number 00:26:03)[2]

The interviewees displayed an awareness of being in need of more teaching skills. Some OPLs met this by attending courses including third level degrees, which were usually run by non-LIS institutions, such as teacher training centres. Several OPLs reported having a teaching background and they generally felt that to be of benefit. Those who didn't often felt it would help them enhance their status within the organisation as the role of the library and the librarian expands into IL teaching and training:

> "...Ehm, as I said, I would like to do something on 'the librarian as teacher', again, I suppose, to... it would *help* [...] gain acceptance among my peers here that the library has a role in teaching and in delivering information literacy. That's about the only thing, but whether

---

2   Bold text in the interview quotes highlights important passages, italics denote emphasis by the speaker; "R" is Researcher.

I would commit myself to doing anything formal, I don't know…" Interviewee 5 (counter number 00:23:33)

"…I've gone to a lot of them [training courses] and I always find them interesting. It's things like "**training the trainer**". I would have done those **kind of courses at work as well**. I did presentation skills training and because we have a [mentions organisation] orientation programme, **which would be induction training for new staff, so I do a lot of that with new staff. I've been involved with the Intranet, so now I would, I give the spiel about the library and the library services and now I'm gonna be giving a big spiel about the Intranet, what's up on that, how would you use it, how would you search it**, etcetera, etcetera. But I just find that's all **very good for raising my profile and raising the library's profile in the organisation anyway**, 'cause I have about an hour's slot with all new staff. So they know who I am and they know my name at the very least and know that I'm in the library, etcetera. So that's, I find, **you have to kind of broaden your horizon a bit**…" interviewee 20 (counter number 00:12:03)

OPLs naturally contribute to the CPD of their patrons by training them in IL. Because of the nature of their work and the diverse group of users they serve, however, one-to-one tutoring is often more effective than a formal training course. A good way of establishing a presence in the professional life of a new employee is to give some references at the induction session on how the librarian can help and then to follow it up with more targeted support. Another useful tool might be setting up an IL online tutoring course which patrons can follow in their own time. Examples are available from larger libraries' websites which can be tailored towards the organisation's needs.

OPLs often need to go where their clients are as they might not have the time or are too remotely located to frequent the physical library. Web 2.0 technologies can support IL training for these individuals. OPLs can set up interactive websites, such as blogs that encourage comments, which can include an "ask a librarian" type information service, as well as remote access to the library OPAC and other information resources. This should be fairly inexpensive as most organisations have Internet access for their employees. A lot of online how-to-do support is available to librarians. Sharing sites of interest or establishing Wikis with their patrons might encourage a more interactive learning environment and benefit both sides. Additionally, podcasts and videos could be used as IL training aids. Free software can be accessed online.

Networking and information literacy

All OPLs relied on some form of networking with other human beings in order to find solutions to work-related or personal problems (see Appendix), albeit for different reasons and by choosing different sets of people. One example from Category 2, dimension networking, shows how it informs them about IL:

> **R:** O.k. What do you like most about networking then?

> "[…] It's clearly good for you to **compare with your peers** as to what kind of things are interesting people and exercising their kind of energies at that time [...] And just to kind of test the levels or **what are you doing in terms of your information literacy** or **the range of subjects**, where everybody is, you know. Am I very far behind or am I doing o.k. [laughs] considering all the usual difficulties?..." Interviewee 23 (counter number 00:24:07)

IL was also about the exchange of information, which created new knowledge in the organisation:

> "These are the people who are shelving, these are people who know where everything is! And **they had such knowledge and they had, I mean, I learned so much *from* those people. And they weren't qualified at all**, like they weren't qualified librarians **and they had *such* knowledge to give and you'd learn it from everybody you meet**, d'you know. **So you just *pass* it on, it's exchange**, yeah. And pass the information on. There's no point clogged up here [points at head], you know. [...] **And the more people you can pass it on to, the more the information disseminate out there.**" Interviewee 30 (00:38:27)

Networking facilitated keeping up-to-date with new information resources, a crucial component of being information literate:

> "Ehm, probably, all of those different networking opportunities [like] email lists. Newsletters you get from various database vendors about the new sort of features that they have in their products would give you an idea of the way things are going. Like library journals, like speaking to people at conferences..." Interviewee 12 (00:27:57)

It could be argued that participating in networking is an intrinsic part of being an information literate person. Without a constant exchange of knowledge with other professionals it would be impossible to be able to find, evaluate and use information effectively and efficiently. The researcher found all participants in this study to be enthusiastic and skilful networkers who shared their skills with the people they served.

Discussion

Despite a general lack of financial support, time restrictions and other barriers these OPLs managed to engage in professional development. Information professionals in this study used a wide range of informal and formal types of CPD as outlined in table 4. It became evident that a "one-size-fits-all" approach to CDP and therefore to updating of IL skills does not exist for solo librarians who work in a wide variety of organisations and settings. The same could be said to teaching IL to patrons. Even though the researcher did not explicitly ask the OPLs about their IL needs, she feels that it would be safe to assume that these CPD methods were applied in order to build on people's existing IL knowledge. The researcher believes that their experiences and suggestions are valuable to other librarians as they approach CPD to develop their skills in IL. Informal activities in particular might suit busy individuals who do not have a huge amount of resources at their disposal. In this regard Web 2.0 technologies could offer OPLs inexpensive, effective ways of not becoming more proficient in IL themselves, but also for teaching IL skills to their patrons.

Other LIS professionals emerged as the information source most likely to be contacted by these OPLs, usually in person but also online or by consulting LIS literature (see Table 4 above). This corresponds with findings in Long and Applegate's (2008) study where information professionals participated predominantly in informal CPD means, namely discussions with colleagues, reading the professional literature and email lists, with only conferences and workshops mentioned in any significant numbers in the formal activities category.

Any chance to network with other LIS professionals should provide librarians with CPD opportunities to enhance their own IL skills. By forming communities of practice (CoPs), such as being an member of their library association, they will be able to share their knowledge. Informal CoPs could be created through participation in online forums. Web 2.0 technology has advanced and simplified this process and provides low cost channels for information professionals to reach their target groups. Huvila (2011) noted that information creation should be part of information literacy. This researcher believes that librarians are well placed to actively engage in social media and also help their clients find their way through this new digital world.

Final remarks

IL is a core part of the work librarians do. Library associations, library schools and individuals themselves must ensure that these skills are being developed on an on-going basis. Courses offered as part of a library degree can only be the first step on the path to lifelong learning. Librarians are best positioned to facilitate their customers in their information literacy journey. This can pose a challenge, but can also be a source of immense satisfaction. OPLs in particular can help shape this future by being up-to-date with their own knowledge on this two-way street of learning: CPD does influence their role as IL providers and vice versa. In a modern workplace environment,

"becoming information literate has more to do with complex outcomes such as developing a workplace identity, learning to work collabora- tively, learning about work performance, or understanding how to par- ticipate in a collaborative setting, than it does about learning a set of generic skills." (Lloyd, 2011).

Being an intrinsic part of the organisation is the best defence in times of finan- cial turmoil and funding cuts. The library needs to be the heart of the organisa- tion and its OPL the blood that keeps it going.

References

Andretta, S. (2008). Promoting reflective information literacy practice through Facilitating Information Literacy Education (FILE). *Health Information and Libraries Journal*, *25*(2), 150-153.

Bruce, C. S. (1999). Workplace experiences of information literacy. *International Journal of Information Management*, *19* (1), 33-47.

Clyde, L. A. (2005). Librarians and breaking barriers to information literacy. *Library Re- view*, *54* (7), 425-434.

CONUL Advisory Committee on Information Literacy (2011). *Integrating information lit- eracy into the curriculum*. Retrieved from the DIT website: www.dit.ie/media/documents/library/CONULACIL.pdf

Hornung, E. (2009). The smart ones: one-person librarians in Ireland and continuing profes- sional development. In J. Varlejs and G. Walton (Eds.), *Strategies for regenerating the library and information professions; Eighth World Conference on Continuing Profes- sional Development and Workplace Learning for Library and Information Professions, 18-20 August 2009, Bologna, Italy* (pp. 301-316). (IFLA Publications 139). München: Saur.

Huvila, I. (2011). The complete information literacy? Unforgetting creation and organiza- tion of information. *Journal of Librarianship and Information Science*, *43* (4), 237- 245.

Information Literacy Working Group of the Library Association of Ireland (n.d). Retrieved from the Library Association of Ireland website: www.libraryassociation.ie/working-group-on-information-literacyx/

International Federation of Library Associations and Institutions (2012). *IFLA Media and Information Literacy Recommendations*. Retrieved, from the IFLA website: www.ifla.org/files/information-literacy/publications/media-info-lit-recommend-en.pdf

Long, C. E., & Applegate, R. (2008). Bridging the gap in digital library continuing education: how librarians who were not "born digital" are keeping up. *Library Administration & Management, 22* (4), 172-182.

Lloyd, A. (2011). Trapped between a rock and a hard place: what counts as information literacy in the workplace and how is it conceptualized? *Library Trends, 60* (2), 277-296.

Marton, F., & Booth, S. (1997). *Learning and awareness*. (The Educational Psychology Series). Mahwah, NJ: Lawrence Erlbaum Associates.

Raseroka, K. (2003). Libraries for lifelong literacy: IFLA Presidential Theme 2003-2005. *IFLA Journal, 29* (2), 109-112.

Russell, P., & O'Brien, T. (2009). The Irish Working Group on Information Literacy (WGIL), Part II: Report on cross-sector activity 2006-2008 and recommendations for action. *SCONUL Focus, 46*, 101-104.

Shuter, J. (1984). *The information worker in isolation: problems and achievements*. Bradford: MCB University Press.

Siess, J. (2003). One-person library. In M. A. Drake (Ed.), *Encyclopedia of Library and Information Science* (2nd Ed.) (Vol. 3; Lib-Pub, pp. 2209-2217). New York: Marcel Dekker.

Slater, M. (1988). *Internal Training and External Short Courses: a study of informal continuing education in the special sector of the library/information field*. (British Library Research Paper 52). Boston Spa: British Library Board.

Webber, S., and Johnston, B. (2004). Perspectives on the information literate university. *SCONUL Focus, 33*, 33-35.

Weiner, S. (2011). Information literacy and the workforce: a review. *Education Libraries, 34* (2), 7-14.

Wheeler, A. (2007). Information literacy, technology, and forgotten barcodes: the life of a solo academic librarian. *College and Research Libraries News, 68* (6), 368-369.

Williamson, J. B. (1990). *The further education and training needs of one-man-band library and information workers*. Unpublished Master's dissertation, University of Aberystwyth, Aberystwyth.

Planning for Succession: Building Upon an Information Literacy Instruction Experience

Juanita Jara de Súmar
McGill University, Montreal, Canada
juanita.jaradesumar@mcgill.ca
and
Julie Jones
McGill University, Montreal, Canada
julie.jones@mcgill.ca

Abstract

The authors, a senior academic librarian and a junior colleague propose an un-official but structured succession planning project to ensure that valuable knowledge developed during a decade of conducting information literacy workshops is not lost when the senior librarian retires. The methodology proposed combines techniques of reflective writing with the systematizing of experiences, a procedure with roots in adult education that is used to preserve best practices in various types of communities. Particular attention will be given to the analysis of intergenerational relationships and to the identification of areas where generational differences may affect the project.

Introduction

In recent years, the Humanities and Social Sciences Library (HSSL) at McGill University in Montreal, Canada, has hired a number of recently graduated librarians to take the positions left open by retiring senior librarians. This has resulted in a present staff composition of a small number of senior librarians approaching retirement age, and a new cohort of librarians who are working towards reaching tenure. There is a gap where one might expect to find tenured, mid-career librarians.

At the time of writing, the library has not established an official succession planning program, or a mentoring program. This is partly due to the fact that the library is going through changes in internal structure, which may require a revision of position responsibilities and the redefinition of services offered. Until the end of 2011, the structure of HSSL consisted of four teams, each with a mixture of junior and senior librarians, as well as library technicians and library assistants. With the dismantling of this team structure, it was apparent to the authors – a junior and a senior librarian from one of the teams – that the opportunity to pass on knowledge and expertise that the working relationships the team structure afforded was no longer there. Feeling that simply handing a portfolio to a junior librarian to take over was not an effective way to pass on responsibilities, the authors wondered if there was a way to compensate for the absence of organizational-level succession planning and transfer knowledge and experience in a manner that would be appropriate and beneficial to the continuing professional development of both librarians.

The knowledge and expertise in question relates to the delivery of information literacy sessions for courses on Academic Writing that the senior librarian is heavily involved with. She works with another senior librarian on these offerings and had been considering the need to mentor or train another librarian who could share, and eventually take over, the delivery of these workshops. The junior librarian was looking for opportunities to develop her expertise in library instruction, as this is one of the position responsibilities that factors heavily in the tenure dossier. Because library instruction experience is preferred, but not mandatory at hiring, and the emphasis the MLIS programs place on these skills varies (Sproles, Johnson, and Farison, 2008), junior librarians typically have differing levels of expertise in this area. The junior librarian is also interested in the impact of the generation gap in the workplace, and the ways different generations can learn from each other and enhance each other's careers.

These facts came to light during a casual conversation. The authors decided to develop a plan that would allow them to systematically evaluate and reflect on the content and presentation methodology of the current workshops, then work collaboratively on updating the workshops with the new vision and ideas that the junior librarian could bring to this activity. The idea being that, through a collaborative process, the material would not only be preserved and passed on, but also reviewed, evaluated, enhanced, and transformed. Rather than simply giving junior librarians tasks and material to take over in a rote manner when senior librarians retire, or having junior librarians rewrite material from scratch, the goal here is to facilitate the transfer of experience and knowledge between *both* librarians. This will positively impact the workshop material, the two librarians involved, and the library system as a whole when the knowledge and experience is applied to other projects.

The authors hope that by applying a systematic reflection to how the workshop has evolved over ten years that is recorded for future revisions, we will provide the library with an information literacy activity that can be integrated into the creation of instruction offerings for newly created units that the library serves, such as the Writing Centre and the Arts Research Internship office. This transformative capacity building has potential far reaching benefits for the organization as a whole. We hope that our exploration can lead to the creation of a toolkit of best practice, so that the activity may be replicated by other librarians who are also looking to preserve knowledge and experience in a manner that will enhance current library services. While one of the goals is replication elsewhere, this is a case study at one institution and may not transfer elsewhere. However, many components of this project will be easily adopted by other libraries.

Literature review

We looked at background literature on succession planning, intergenerational issues, and reflective practice. Finding a fair amount of literature regarding succession planning, we only looked at selected papers and reports, prioritizing those from Canada and the United States (8Rs Steering Committee, 2005; Kieserman, 2008; McMahan and Masias, 2009; Singer and Griffith, 2010; Summerfield, 2002; Topper, 2008; Webster and Young, 2009). The concept of succession planning is associated with an overall official planning activity of library administration. We also found that succession plans almost always have the goal of ensuring leadership continuity in directive roles and of identifying among the staff those who could take those roles. Furthermore, the main reason why most of these documents have been produced is because of the impending retirement of the baby-boomer generation of librarians.

Vicki Whitmell (2002) adds to the main themes in succession planning the need to consider: the availability of internal and external training opportunities; formal mentoring programs; and incorporating activities that don't necessarily depend on a succession plan. A few years later, she proposed the need to include the concept of workforce planning, a concept that seems more relevant for the purpose of this paper:

> "While succession planning includes identifying and training people for specific key positions, workforce planning goes beyond this to include strategies for education, recruiting, retaining, training, developing and mentoring staff throughout an organization" (Whitmell, 2005, p. 135).

Jason Bird relates succession planning to the need to support new librarians. He advocates for providing training, experience and opportunities to participate in internal projects and committees (Bird, 2005). Hartman and Delaney (2010, p. 36) acknowledge the importance of senior librarians in this process when they discuss "retaining the institutional knowledge of librarians", stating that we must "identify and retain their departing expertise—the gold in the library's intellectual vault", and that we "need to be proactive in finding ways to hold on to valuable skills and knowledge". Similarly, while examining the impact of the influx of younger librarians entering the library workforce as a result of the high rate of retirements, Wilder points out that "staff take incalculable expertise with them when they retire" (2007, p. 1). Specifically focusing on academic libraries, Wilder goes on to suggest that the "youth movement" the library world is seeing "could afford ARL libraries the opportunity to retool in ways that might otherwise have been impossible" (2007, p.2). Edge and Green reiterate the opportunity that this unique intergenerational context provides. They highlight the fact that the younger generation often introduces senior colleagues to emerging areas (mobile technology and Web 2.0 being common examples). While the senior generation can introduce younger librarians to classic skills they may not find elsewhere. "We can make this type of connection a two-way communication" (2011, p. 104). Rather than just focusing on the knowledge that may be lost when boomers retire, Edge and Green urge us to realize the "huge potential for a revitalizing influx of new professionals whose more recent and relevant training bring new outlooks to librarianship" (2011, p.105). It is precisely this potential for intergenerational "give and take" that we wish to explore.

We were unable to find literature addressing specifically strategies to identify and record for the future valuable practices developed by senior librarians during their career in the organization, what we can call best practices. These practices are not necessarily related to leadership in directive positions of the library and, yet, many of them are a real asset for the day-to-day services offered by the library. Being able to build on successful programs developed by local staff, instead of starting from scratch, as well as having a record of unsuccessful efforts, can result in better and faster projects in the future. As Hartman and Delaney indicate, recording experiences doesn't mean the we would be focused on "keeping the old ways", but rather that we may be "building bridges between traditional knowledge and mastery and newer skills" (2010, p. 36).

We looked at the literature to explore the methodology to use to assess the quality and value of practical work, as it is performed in the workplace, and how these actions can be studied and then translated into a systematized corpus of experiences that can be used in the future. This relates to the skills applied when performing particular actions or services and determining if this was done in a competent manner.

Because of a personal relation[1], the senior author has been aware since 1994 of a methodology called Systematization (or Systematizing) of Experiences. With roots in the field of popular adult education in Latin America, this methodology has extended worldwide to many areas of social intervention,

---

1   One of the main developers and promoters of this methodology is the brother of one of the authors.

such as health, education, development projects and others. Antoni Verger i Planells defines Systematizing experiences as

> "el proceso de reconstrucción y reflexión analítica sobre una experiencia de acción o de intervención que permite interpretarla y comprenderla. Con la sistematización se obtiene un conocimiento consistente que permite transmitir la experiencia y confrontarla con otras experiencias o con el conocimiento teórico existente. Así, se contribuye a la acumulación de conocimientos generados desde y para la práctica, y a su difusión o transmisión" (Verger Planells, 2007). [2]

To achieve this process of reconstruction and analytical reflection and ensure that consistent knowledge about our action or process can be preserved and transferred for later use, a series of forms and techniques have been developed. They have been explained in the various books on this subject, which unfortunately are only available in Spanish and Portuguese at the present time. See for example Sistematizando experiencias, anexo 2 (Jara Holliday, 2005, pp. 87-98). Yet, looking at the forms and explanations that they use, it becomes apparent that they are somewhat related to the reflective method of learning.

One of the early advocates of reflective practice, Donald Schön, argues that good practitioners obtain professional knowledge from what they do. He studied how five professionals in different areas approached their interventions. His findings show that practitioners reflect in action. When facing a new, uncertain case, they reflect on what they know and apply this knowledge to the situation at hand (Schön, 1983).

Librarianship literature offers a certain number of publications that explain the use of reflective practices in the educational process of future librarians, and for evaluating knowledge via the analysis of reflective journals written by the students. McGuinness and Brien explain the use of reflective journals at University College Dublin to evaluate the knowledge acquired about the research process (2007). Mansourian writes about using a learning diary for a similar purpose at Tarbiat Moallem University in Tehran (2008). Stephen Hackett establishes relationships between competency-based training and reflective practice to determine if they can be combined for educational or training purposes. He surveyed the literature and highlights a model developed by Andressen et al. The model includes three stages of reflection: preparation, re-

---

2   [Systematizing experiences is] the process of reconstruction of and analytical reflection on an action of intervention experience, in order to interpret and understand it. Systematization produces consistent knowledge, allowing the transmission of the experience and its comparison with other experiences, or with existing theoretical knowledge. Thus, this process results in the accumulation of knowledge produced from and for practice, and its wide exposure and transmission (Translated by J. Jara).

flection during the activity (noticing and intervening), and reflection after the event (Hackett, 2001, p. 110). Barbara Sen of the University of Sheffield also studied the reflective writing of their Information Studies students (2010). Her research focused on the actual reflective process and on the impact of this method on academic outcomes related to management skills. Although it focused on academic outcomes, she found that "[t]here was some evidence of non-academic learning with reflective writing, but in this case was not significant. The most benefit was apparent when students were most analytical in their reflection and expressed that in deeply analytical reflective writing" (2010, p. 91).

Our current information literacy workshop

The activity for our mentoring and succession plan is the 90 minute hands-on information literacy workshop provided by the senior librarian to groups of students enrolled in the Faculty of Arts' Academic Writing courses for native speakers of English. We will not include in this project the writing courses for non-native speakers of English, which has different learning outcomes and a targeted clientele.

The number of groups taking the course every year – 22 to 25 students in each group – as well as the number of teachers who participate in teaching these courses varies, but in recent years there have been at least 15 groups and some 6 teachers every year. Some groups are homogeneous: all are first year students in the same or similar disciplines; other groups are formed by a mix of upper and lower undergraduate level coming from backgrounds across faculties. Some teachers teach to more than one group and/or participate in each of the three academic terms. Five of the groups receive their library instruction from another senior librarian, who originally developed the workshop. As she works part time, the other groups receive their instruction from the senior librarian involved with this paper; she has been teaching this workshop for the last nine years. The presentations developed by this second librarian are the ones that will be the subject of this project.

More than fifteen years ago the instruction librarian at the time received an invitation to introduce library instruction to the students in the academic writing courses. Since then the library is invited every term to provide this 90 minute workshop. Although there have been administrative changes in the reporting units, and the course has gone through name changes, the objectives of the course remain: to help the students improve the quality of their academic papers, including the use of appropriate bibliographic material and citation styles. The content of the workshops is continuously updated to reflect changes in the library collections, database availability, citation software and, particularly, to adjust to each of the instructors class plans, specific group composition, and to make sure that the learning outcomes of the workshop are in accordance with current course objectives.

As has been mentioned, periodic administrative changes have affected the reporting structure of the Academic Writing course. The latest change occurred last year when the university created a Writing Centre. Their courses are the same as the previously delivered writing courses in the Faculty of Arts, and taught by the same instructors. As their mandate is much larger than previously, our library is considering having a larger involvement via workshops. As such, we think that the current information literacy workshop can serve as important groundwork for expanding our involvement with the Writing Centre. Also, in 2011, the Faculty of Arts decided to give more emphasis to research activities of undergraduate students and partnered with our library to offer a three-module information literacy program, which has been repeated this year. One of these modules was based on the current sessions offered to Academic Writing courses. Here again there is an opportunity for us to see how much of what has been developed in previous years can be used to develop the new workshops.

Intergenerational issues: a hindrance or an opportunity?

A valid question might be, is such a reflective process realistic for the younger workforce, made up of Generation X and Y? There is a tendency in the literature to focus on the fears that older and younger generations in the library workforce have of each other. The generational difference often being characterized as one "with so-called Baby Boomers born after World War Two often at odds with their Generation X and Y colleagues — all born since the early to mid-1960s" (Sayers, 2007, pp. 474-475). The younger generation is, for the most part, made up of "digital natives" and "there is some truth to the generalization that this generation has a leg up on previous generations in terms of computing ability and use of the Web" (Edge & Green, 2011, p. 101). This new generation is a varied group that values diversity, change, continuous learning, and, in many cases, "greater degrees of personal flexibility, professional satisfaction and immediacy" (Sayers, 2007, p. 480). As a result of this quest for satisfaction and immediacy, this generation can be construed as one with a short attention span and little patience to stick with projects when it may feel like they are not immediately succeeding. However, the reality is that this generation values the reflection of mentoring as much as those before them, perhaps even more so, given that it is increasingly less common. In his 2007 examination of the CAVAL's 2006 Training Needs Survey, as well as previous survey data, Sayers urged academic libraries to realize that they must "[p]rovide rich and varied access to mentors and other living career guides," and that, "[d]espite an outward confidence and independence, Generations X and Y do not have all the answers. Like generations before them, they still require guidance from older and hopefully wiser colleagues." (2007, p. 485).

At the same time, generalizations must not be made about senior librarians either. Common stereotypes about this generation are that they stop embracing challenge, become unmotivated, and are resistant to change (van der Walt & du Plessis, 2010). A project such as this one demands that they be open to the point of view and ideas of the younger generation. Inherent in this heavily collaborative approach is a commitment to the potential for give and take between generations and the notion of no employee ceasing to be developing as a professional, no matter how close to retirement they are — a commitment to age diversity in the workplace, in other words.

As a profession we place emphasis on continuous learning, but what about learning from each other? And what if we view each other as drastically different from ourselves? This difference must be embraced rather than fought; differences must be viewed as opportunities. This type of project aids in this goal, as it is precisely because the generations we are looking at have differing knowledge and experience, that this project is possible. Dinwoodie nicely summarizes this approach to diversity, commonly referred to as the *information-processing and decision-making* approach: "In this view, heterogeneity among members of workgroups is generally a positive factor in that it enhances performance, providing the group with a broader range of knowledge, skills, and abilities relevant to the tasks at hand and allowing the group to process information more thoroughly" (2005, p. 2). The reality is that there is complexity and tacit knowledge involved with much of the work that we do as librarians. Many skills we need in this field in the twenty first century are not taught in library school, but acquired via experience, problem solving, and team building (Chute, 2007), and projects such as this one tease them out and preserve them for future use.

Intergenerational knowledge transfer project

As a prerequisite to working on the project it is necessary that we become proficient in both reflective writing and the methodology to systematize experiences; these activities cannot be learned through only studying the theory behind them. Both librarians need to be practitioners, and this is the part of the project that may be the main conditioning factor for success, and for establishing a calendar.

We will approach McGill Writing Centre to see if there is a member of the staff who can provide instruction on reflective writing. Alternatively, we can search for available course offerings, and have at least one of us enroll in it. Or we may need to teach ourselves. In that case it may be necessary to contact a center such as The Learning Centre of The University of New South Wales, which has offered those courses in the past, to gain additional information about the course content for this writing technique. To obtain support for participating in systematization of experiences activities, we can make contact with an expert facilitator and arrange some sessions via Skype. This would be an appropriate technology, as it allows for the face-to-face interaction required by this methodology.

The initial stage of the project will consist of reflecting on past actions. There are records of the evolution of the presentations during the past nine years, but unfortunately the correspondence between the instructors and the librarian has not been kept. It will be necessary to rely on retrospective reflection based on the senior librarian's memory of how the presentations were developed and modified. Both librarians need to participate interactively, to ensure that their understanding of the historical development is identical. Intergenerational knowledge sharing starts from this early stage; each of us will need to learn how the other works and thinks. Though the actions being examined are not hers, the junior librarian will also spend time reflecting on what has been done in the past.

The retrospective reflective process will follow the guidelines developed for systematizing experiences. We hope to obtain facilitator support at the beginning of the process. Some sample questions to be asked are: What elements should be taken into consideration for the historical recovery? What elements are necessary to organize and classify the information? What are the steps and procedures for this exercise (Jara Holliday, 2005, p. 88)? We will look into developing appropriate recording forms and the results of the exercise will be recorded following the principles of reflective writing. The goal here is for the senior librarian to gather knowledge of the experience that is readily available to her and easily described, and also that which is tacit and therefore more difficult to articulate. So much of what we do can quickly becomes "invisible" to us as we grow accustomed to it. A recovery exercise like this can help uncover and extract this tacit knowledge. The two librarians will analyze and assess what has been done and explore things that were done that did not work. Gaps between theory and practice may emerge.

Reflecting-in-action and reflective writing should be applied to all subsequent actions. Some researchers argue that trying to reflect while performing an action is disruptive and interferes with the action, and sometimes paralyzes the performer. Schön deals with these objections and suggests that reflecting-in-action is possible, and that fear of paralysis can be overcome by reflecting on the rationality that causes the paralysis (1983, p. 281). Indeed, making a conscious choice to make the time to reflect on action, instead of just reacting to situations, allows the performer to consider past, current, and future possibilities, which can be understood as the opposite of paralysis.

An important aspect to observe is whether variations in approach emerge that are related to the generational difference. As previously mentioned, the younger generation is often cited as one that is made up of workers who value immediacy and instant success. Will junior librarians from younger generations have the patience to engage in an exercise like this one?

The process from this point will be about continued knowledge sharing and the standard procedures of learning on the job, all recorded in reflective writing done by both librarians. An iterative process will be set up that will allow the junior librarian to slowly take over responsibility for the presentations and that will allow the two librarians to work together to enhance the material. The junior librarian will observe presentations as they are currently delivered, and both librarians will apply reflecting-in-action and reflective writing after each workshop. Subsequently there will be some workshops where the junior librarian will share the presentation. She will conduct various sections, to gain full insight of the current process. The resulting written documents should provide a full picture of past and present development. Once the past actions have been analyzed and reflected upon, we will be ready to determine what has to be kept and what can be improved, both in terms of content and presentation.

At this point, the junior librarian should be ready to try her ideas and materials in some of the sections of the workshop. One or more of the instructors will be approached with the proposal and, if agreed, the material will be taught by both librarians, in tandem, the next time the workshop is offered. Besides the usual reflecting-in-action and reflective writing, we will request commentaries from the instructor who agreed on the presentation. It will be important to find out if the workshop contributed to the students achieving the learning outcomes and the instructors' expectations. These commentaries will be incorporated in the systematization. As we are looking for information transfer and sharing, the senior librarian will be presenting the material prepared by the junior librarian, and most probably using new technologies. Because these workshops are repeated three terms a year and for various groups each term, there should be ample opportunity to test and apply new approaches to the various sections.

In a final phase, we will agree on a new presentation that corresponds with the findings of the whole reflecting and systematizing process. At this point we may be conducting the same workshop for different groups and then comparing experiences. Or we may find it more effective to teach the workshop presentations together, as a pair. We must continue to apply reflecting-in-action and reflective writing each time we conduct a workshop, and register any finding that will help systematize the experience. It may be possible that adjustments to the agreed changes are necessary as new technologies become available and new pedagogical theories are developed.

We propose that the materials obtained by reflective writing be utilized to complete the systematizing of experiences exercise. In this way both techniques – reflective practice and systematizing experiences – will be integrated in one result. These systematized materials will be offered to other junior librarians, particularly new hires, in our branch library, starting a new transfer cycle that will incorporate new reflections to be systematized. The material will also be made available to other librarians in our university who may be interested in using this methodology.

A realistic timeline will be prepared once the factors that condition the beginning of the project can be resolved. We are aiming to undertake the reflective writing course and the systematization of experiences training by mid fall of 2012. The retrospective reflection, observation of current workshops, and systematization of past experience will follow. If this can be achieved and we obtain acceptance from the instructors, sharing of the presentations could happen in February 2013. Depending on the status of the Academic Writing courses, we could aim to do some testing of the new presentation created by the two of us for the 2013 summer term.

Conclusion

The recent changes in the generational makeup of the library workforce are vast. As many senior, experienced librarians retire, and the profession scrambles to replace them, we must remember that it is not just about the quantity of employees, but also about the preservation of what they know and what they have experienced. As Chute writes, "we need to cultivate appropriate means to facilitate the growth and augmentation of the knowledge, skills, and abilities of our future leaders The field as a whole benefits if we find a way to transfer the legacy knowledge from our current experts to their future successors" (2007, p.86).

Our proposal to utilize the systematizing of experiences is a new application of this technique. It is a new tool for librarianship that could be widely applied to preserve and enhance knowledge and experience. It is a method of articulating experience – an extraction of tacit knowledge. And this is something that is tremendously needed as large portions of the field retire, often with decades of learning under their belts. At the same time, the method propels the profession forward as the ideas and experience of the younger generation are applied in meaningful collaborative ways.

This project acknowledges that there is as much value in preserving finished projects and teaching material – what to do, essentially – as there is in preserving what *not* to do. Imagine the potential in that – in having access to the metadata surrounding past projects. With this as one of the goals, a future iteration of the project could be the creation of a database of the material gleaned from the systematizing of experiences process. This database could benefit a single workplace, serving as a searchable best (and worst) practices intranet of sorts, or perhaps even the profession as a whole if access was made available to a larger population.

References

8Rs Steering Committee. (2005). Looking to the future: succession planning, continuing education and the 8Rs Study. *Feliciter, 51*(1), 31-35.

Bird, J. (2005). Ready and waiting for the future: new librarians and succession planning. *Feliciter, 51*(1), 36-37.

Chute, M. L. (2007). Efforts in leadership and succession planning, large and small. In A. Ritchie & C. Walker (Eds.) *Continuing professional development : pathways to leadership in the library and information world.* (pp. 85-99). München: K.G. Saur.

Dinwoodie, D. L. (2005). Solving the dilemma: a leader's guide to managing diversity. *Leadership in Action, 25*(2), 3-6.

Edge, J., & Green, R. (2011). The graying of academic librarians: crisis or revolution? *Journal of Access Services, 8*(3), 97-106.

Hackett, S. (2001). Educating for competency and reflective practice: fostering a conjoint approach in education and training. *Journal of Workplace Learning, 13*(3), 103-112. doi: 10.1108/13665620110388406

Hartman, A., & Delaney, M. (2010). Wait! you can't retire without sharing that with us: retaining the institutional knowledge of librarians who will soon leave the profession. *American Libraries, 41*(11-12), 36-38.

Jara Holliday, O. (2005). *Sistematizando experiencias: apropiarse del futuro: recorridos y búsquedas de la sistematización de experiencias.* Xativa: Dialogos Red L'Ullal Edicions.

Kieserman, R. H. (2008). Issues in library human resources management. *The Bottom Line: Managing Library Finances, 21*(4), 135-137. doi: 10.1108/08880450810929134

Mansourian, Y. (2008). Keeping a learning diary to enhance researchers' understanding of and users' skills in web searching. *Library Review, 57*(9), 690-699. doi: 10.1108/00242530810911806

McGuinness, C., & Brien, M. (2007). Using reflective journals to assess the research process. *Reference Services Review, 35*(1), 21-40.

McMahan, J., & Masias, M. (2009). Developing a succession plan for a library. *Information Outlook, 13*(7), 29-32.

Sayers, R. (2007). The right staff from X to Y: generational change and professional development in future academic libraries. *Library Management, 28* (8/9), 474-487.

Schön, D. A. (1983). *The reflective practitioner: how professionals think in action.* New York: Basic Books.

Sen, B. A. (2010). Reflective writing: a management skill. *Library Management, 31* (1), 79-93. doi: 10.1108/01435121011013421

Singer, P. M., & Griffith, G. (2010). *Succession planning in the library : developing leaders, managing change.* Chicago: American Library Association.

Sproles, C., Johnson, A. M., & Farison, L. (2008). What the teachers are teaching: how MLIS programs are preparing academic librarians for instructional roles. *Journal of Education for Library andIinformation Science, 49* (3), 195-209.

Summerfield, M. (2002). CLA's human resources and succession planning survey: analysis and recommendations. *Feliciter, 48* (4), 188-189.

Topper, E. F. (2008). Succession planning in libraries. *New Library World, 109* (9-10), 480-482. doi: 10.1108/03074800810910504

Van der Walt, S., & du Plessis, T. (2010). Age diversity and the aging librarian in academic libraries in South Africa. *South African Journal of Libraries and Information Science, 76* (1), 1-10.

Verger Planells, A. (2007). Sistematizando experiencias: análisis y recreación de la acción colectiva desde la educación popular. *Revista de Educación,* (343), 623-645.

Webster, D. E., & Young, D. J. (2009). Our collective wisdom: succession planning and the ARL Research Library Leadership Fellows Program. *Journal of Library Administration, 49* (8), 781-793.

Whitmell, V. (2002). Library succession planning: the need and challenge. *Australasian Public Libraries and Information Services, 15* (4), 148-154.

Whitmell, V. (2005). Workforce and succession planning in special libraries. *Feliciter,* (3), 135-137.

Wilder, S. J. (2007). The ARL youth movement: reshaping the ARL workforce. *ARL Bimonthly Report, 254,* 1-4.

Incorporating Information Literacy Competency Standards and Information Literacy Competencies Into Staff Development Programmes: A Case Study of the National Library of Uganda

Sarah Kaddu
World Digital Library (U) Project Coordinator
sarkaddu@yahoo.com

Abstract

The aim of this paper is to examine action taken by National Library of Uganda (NLU) in conceiving and implementing a programme towards Information Literacy Competency Standards (ILCS). The objectives of the paper are to establish the nature of the programme related to standards and competencies NLU has put in place, the impact of the programme, challenges and the future strategies. Methods of data collection included literature analysis, one on one interviews with NLU management, staff and users and personal on job recollections. Beneficiaries include management, staff, users and community at large through services offered. This work is heavily informed by the activities of the Association of College and Research Libraries of the American Library Association which compiled the four information literacy competencies standards used.

Introduction

The aim of this paper is to examine the National Library of Uganda's (NLU) incorporation of staff development in implementing Information Literacy Competency Standards (ILCS) and Information Literacy Competencies (ILC). The paper will establish the NLU activities the programme has adopted to achieve the standards and competencies. It will also establish the impact of the programme, identify challenges encountered and provide strategies to overcome the challenges. Methods of data collection included literature analysis, one on one interviews with NLU management, staff and users, personal on the job experience, and reflection by long service staff. Many of the issues explored in this paper are relevant to management, staff, users and the community at large.

Information literacy is a pre-requisite to providing effective public library services. This is so because library users at whatever level must conceive their information need, have the desire to satisfy that information need, know where and how to get the information, extract the information and utilize it. At the end of the 'assembly line' they have to evaluate whether the information secured solved the information need that set in motion the information seeking process. Teaching information literacy involves applying information literacy competency standards (ILCS) as explained by Eisenberg et al (2004) who listed the five information literacy competencies namely: resources, interpersonal, information, systems and technology. This has to be supported by information literacy competencies and Information Literacy Competency Standards such as those developed by the Association of College and Research Libraries (ACRL) (Eisenberg et al, 2004).

The National Library of Uganda was set up by the National Library Act, 2003. It repealed the Public Libraries Act (1964) that set up a Public Libraries Board to establish, equip, manage and maintain libraries in Uganda. Following the enactment of the Local Governments Act in 1997, management of public libraries was decentralized to local governments rendering the Public Libraries Board redundant. The NLU Inspection, Research and Extension Services Department (IRES) is responsible for promoting a reading culture through libraries and other reading activities; monitoring of library services; developing guidelines and standards for public and community libraries and publishing for the NLU (National Library of Uganda, 2012).

Information literacy competency standards and information literacy competencies

The beginning of the 21st century has been called the 'Information Age' because of the explosion of information output and information sources. It has become increasingly clear that students cannot learn everything they need to know in their field of study in a few years of college. Information literacy equips them with the critical skills necessary to become independent lifelong learners. Information literacy implies becoming "critical consumers of information to avoid overload and to develop new intellectual skills in order to manage information effectively and transform it into usable knowledge" (Martin and Williamson, 2003).

An insight into information literacy can be gathered by exploring the concepts of Information Literacy Competency Standards and Information Literacy Competencies. ILCS can be construed as guides or tellers or pointers in the information literacy competence universe. In other words, what level should we attain to qualify as being information literate competent? The standards include the:

- determination of the nature and extent of the information need
- identification of types and formats of potential sources for information
- construction and implementation of effective search strategies
- retrieval of information online or in person using a variety of methods
- extraction of record, and managing information and its sources plus evaluation of the nature and extent of the information need
- accessing needed information effectively and efficiently and considering the costs and benefits of acquiring the needed information

There is a subtle difference between Information Literacy Competency Standards and Information Literacy Competencies although they supplement each other and lead to the same end result – effective information provision. The Big 6 (strategy) is an information problem-solving approach developed by Eisenberg and Berkowitz (1990). It is one of the most popular models for information literacy skills and includes the following steps: task definition; information seeking strategies; location and access; use of information; synthesis and evaluation. Although The Big 6 includes only six steps, some primary teachers find it overwhelming for their young learners. As a result, teachers have developed modified versions to meet their needs. For instance, Eisenberg and Berkowitz (1999) have developed an approach called the Super 3 for very young children which includes three steps: plan, do and review. NLU staff need ILCs which will enable them to identify their information need/s, identify their sources and be able to get the needed information, document the acquired information and finally evaluate that information. Other relevant literacy competencies include computer, digital, media, visual, and Library Management/Administration literacies as explained below:

- Computer literacy : this includes anatomy of the computer, structure and functioning such as booting, maintenance, hardware and software
- Digital literacy : includes new ICT based skills such as instant messaging, blogging, web browsing, social networking, music videos, podcasting, photo sharing, digital storytelling, online discussion, fan fiction and digital mashups
- Media literacy : includes an awareness of the theory of interpretation and application of information from the media
- Visual literacy : includes the theory, interpretation and application of photographic, pictorial and diagrammatic objects
- Library Management/Administration literacy: relevant areas include principles and application of management/ administrative competencies

Many of the above competences are already present in some NLU staff. These include literacy competencies on producing line charts, photo sharing, music, videos, and social networking which they have used or are using knowingly or unknowingly. Some NLU staff use Facebook to communicate with colleagues within or outside NLU. They also upload and download images or videos from Internet.

NLU and staff development programme

Staff development refers to the processes, programs and activities through which every organization develops, enhances and improves the skills, competencies and overall performance of its employees and workers (Dutta, 2012). At NLU, the Administration and Finance Department which has the Human Resource component is generally vested with the task and responsibilities of staff development. The NLU makes use of trained staff from Library and Information Science (LIS) education institutions at para-professional, undergraduate and graduate levels. It also offers in house staff training through seminars, workshops and retreats organized periodically. Furthermore, NLU supports its staff to go for further training at graduate or other professional avenues.

Staff development is addressed in other ways by the NLU. Regular staff appraisals are held where further areas of individual staff training are pinpointed and addressed. Staff are sponsored to attend a range of courses in areas such as conservation of cultural heritage materials, digital management and archive management, metadata and sensitizing and evaluating seminars. Some other staff, through their own initiatives, identify programmes and sponsors themselves. A few have won private sponsorship to short term courses, seminars and travel grants through personal initiatives and innovation. NLU gives permission to attend and at times facilitates such staff.

It is apparent that the NLU is lacking supplying detailed IL courses. There are a range of strong and valid reasons for NLU to mount IL specific courses. The relevance of all the above staff development ventures is to prepare NLU staff to shoulder the responsibility of teaching and applying information literacy skills to school children and other stakeholders such as students and researchers who customize services under NLU auspices.

Challenges

There are many challenges NLU faces in the context of IL. A few key ones are highlighted below:

Lack of an effective staff development programme: NLU does not have an effective staff development programme and this does not allow a systematic approach to teaching practical assessment. Effective staff development focuses on the knowledge, skills, and attitudes required of staff so that all staff can learn and perform at high levels.

Inadequate computers: inadequate computers do not meet demand, also corresponding prohibitive costs of software and maintenance.

Computer illiteracy: many users are not computer literate which demands prior computer training before information literacy skills. One staff member commented:

> "NLU is small in size, budget and space. We have only six computers. They cannot serve many users at one go. We have electronic resources but they are not accessed by the users. The users do not have the skills to access them. Neither have we taught them how to search for information from the few computers that provide Internet access."

Lack of IL competency skills: some library staff do not have IL competency skills to ably pass on IL skills to the users. During the interviews, the staff working in the Reference Library did not know what IL was, neither had they heard about ILCS.

Unwillingness to mobilize students: there is an unwillingness on the part of schools to mobilize their students to participate in the IL programmes because IL courses are not examinable by the Uganda National Examinations Board examination. Some effort has been made by some NLU staff to pass on IL skills to the little children during the reading tents, but many schools fail to mobilize their students because IL is not an examinable subject.

Lack of continuity in applying IL skills: lack of continuity in applying the acquired IL skills among many Ugandans due to poor reading culture/utilitarian reading among Ugandans.

Mobilization of IL training: mobilizing participants to undertake IL training is a challenge because potential users regard it as a waste of time as it shows no immediate benefits.

Lack of IL skills curriculum: no agreed and well formulated IL skills curriculum in place to follow when teaching IL.

Conclusion and recommendations

ILCS are a necessity in the information age. ILCS equip users with Information Literacy Competencies which empower users to be independent lifelong learners and critical consumers of information. Users learn to manage information overload and to develop new intellectual skills to manage information effectively and transform it into usable knowledge. For NLU to overcome the challenges faced in conceiving and implementing a programme towards ILCS a considered and managed strategy is necessary. Below are a range of recommendations which (if implemented) should empower the staff and users to become independent lifelong learners and critical consumers of information.

Developing IL skills: IL skills can be developed in a variety of ways. It is possible to teach the theory behind the various literacies, the application of the literacies through hands on experiences such as website searching, blogging through seminars and staff professional development workshops

Partnerships: NLU should be a dynamic partner to actively seek opportunities to collaborate with schools, teacher librarians; telecenters, community centers, to introduce, develop and evaluate information literacy within the curriculum and a range of associated programs

Design and delivery of IL programmes: NLU should design effective information literacy programs to be taught and evaluated at various levels by trained staff. Furthermore NLU should continue to develop complementary generic programs – introductory and orientation programs

Monitor and evaluate external programs: NLU should monitor and evaluate external programs for potential use in its information literacy programs

Funding: NLU should seek more funding from central and local government to have a national drive towards information literacy as well as other literacies – computer, visual, digital and media for staff development and training, resources – like teaching spaces, technology, allowances, salaries, transport, and other overheads

Marketing: IL and related literacies are a new phenomenon to the majority of people in developing countries. There is therefore need for well planned marketing for the programmes. It would be advisable when marketing to consider improving the facilities and services offered

More qualified staff: NLU should acquire well educated and trained ICT personnel who can effectively educate and train users as well as information professionals

Government leadership and support: The government should take leadership in promoting ICT in the countries because ICTs are bound to have big impact on the development of any nation. Consequently appropriate policies and legal backing should be put in place

Mandatory teaching and examination: ICT should be a taught and examinable subject at all levels. This will make it more appealing to students as well as the teachers and education administrators.

References

Dutta, P. (2012). *What is the definition of staff development?* Retrieved from the ehow website: www.ehow.com/facts_5059005_definition-staff-development.html

Eisenberg, M.B., & Berkowitz, R.E. (1990). *Information problem-solving: the big six skills approach to library and information skills instruction.* Norwood, NJ: Ablex.

Eisenberg, M.B., & Berkowitz, R.E. (1999). *Teaching information & technology skills: the Big6 in elementary schools.* Worthington, OH: Linworth.

Eisenberg, M.B., Lowe, C.A., & Spitzer, K.L. (2004). *Information literacy: essential skills for the information age* (2nd rev. ed.). Westport CT : Libraries Unlimited

Martin, L. & Williamson, S. (2003). Integrating information literacy into higher education. In A. Martin & H. Rader (Eds.) *Information and IT literacy: enabling learning in the 21st century* (pp144-150). London: Facet.

National Library of Uganda. (2012). *About NLU.* Retrieved from NLU website: www.nlu.go.ug.

Nature or Nurture? Case Study Perspectives on Developing a Team of Passionate Instruction Librarians at the Li Ka Shing Library, Singapore Management University

Rajen Munoo
Head Instructional Services and Research Librarian, Li Ka Shing Library,
Singapore Management University
rajen@smu.edu.sg

Abstract

Developing and sustaining a team of passionate instruction librarians willing to conduct training and go the extra mile is hard to do, especially with limited resource. Successful instructional programmes depend on teamwork and collaboration especially in academic libraries. In this paper the author who is Head of Instructional Services at the Li Ka Shing Library, Singapore Management University, will share how this has been done with a team of thirteen, each with different levels of skills and competencies. The first part of the paper will cover some of the new ways information literacy programmes are being delivered at the library. Woven within this description are some of the skills needed to teach effectively. The author then discusses the different techniques used to develop the team such as co-training and training coordination meetings as a platform for communication and sharing. A selection of survey data is presented showing how the instruction librarians are evaluated for trainer preparedness and content delivery. This is useful in identifying intervention strategies and professional development opportunities to address the 'nature or nurture' question. An overview of the Advanced Certificate in Training and Assessment as part of the Singapore Workforce Skills Qualifications programme is presented in the concluding section of the paper as a possible 'outsourced' training model for the instruction librarians.

Introduction

Today information literacy and instruction has 'matured' in many academic institutions. The number of librarians involved in teaching, training and instruction programmes have also increased. This then warrants the question, where and how are instruction librarians being equipped with the necessary skills to design, develop and deliver programmes? Oberman (2002, p7) noted importantly that "the curriculum for the master's programmes in library science do not cover pedagogy and learning theory if at all, let alone teaching skills." To this LaGuardia, Griego, Hopper & Melendez (1993) writing in the early years, highlighted that most of the learning and experience is obtained by 'trial by fire'. The need for librarians to be equipped with skills and competencies has become evident in the literature and with agencies advocating information literacy and instruction. A case in point being the Association of College and Research Libraries (ACRL) which, in 2008, published the *Standards for Proficiencies for Instruction Librarians and Coordinator*. The ACRL task force identified twelve categories of proficiencies each with their own core skills. Some of which include, communication skills, curriculum knowledge, information literacy integration skills, instructional design skills, leadership, planning and presentation skills, to mention a few (Association of College and Research Libraries, 2008). This is a useful reference document for determining the skills needed to teach and furthermore identify Continuing Professional Development (CPD) interventions to help develop them. One can then adapt and use this document in one's own context.

The author, who assumed the role of Head of Instructional Services at the Li Ka Shing Library, Singapore Management University in 2009, contextualises and describes the teaching skills library staff need and the related CPD interventions using the range information literacy programmes offered by the library. This is significant as most of the instruction librarians had no or limited instruction or information literacy experiences. Today, they are all immersed in instruction related activities. Addressing the question, nature or nurture, the author highlights leadership insights on managing the team of thirteen shared staff. The library offers a range of instructional programmes as part of its information literacy programmes but does not market or brand these explicitly, they are neither credit bearing nor part of the curriculum. For the purpose of this paper the terms training and instruction will be used interchangeably.

Contextualisation: instructional services and programmes

The Singapore Management University (SMU) was established a decade ago as the third university in Singapore. There are six schools adopting a North American pedagogical approach using case studies and group work in seminar-style classroom settings. The academic year commences in August and ends in April. Being a 'new' university, the Li Ka Shing library's collection comprises mostly electronic resources and the vision and mission of the digital library is to "support the University in generating a world class, leading edge research and learning organization through a personalized e-knowledge hub in which knowledge is acquired/generated, organized and shared...to bring together digital and non-digital intellectual assets that benefit the University and its stakeholders by providing value-added e-services to facilitate research, teaching and learning." (Li Ka Shing Library, 2010). In order to realise this the Research Librarians, who also form the Instructional Services Team, support the six schools in teaching, research and learning too. The Instructional Services Team comprises seven Research Librarians with subject-domain expertise and three non-school Research Librarians having functional responsibilities such as Web Librarian, Customer Services Librarian and Research Librarian for Research Centres and Institutes. Two para-professional staff provide the team with support. They all design, develop and deliver training programmes for the SMU community which includes students, faculty and staff. These programmes equip students with lifelong learning skills during their academic journey and beyond SMU. The team constantly looks for learning solutions by embracing elearning and working with strategic vendors such as Bloomberg to train the students. Drawing on the critical skills listed in the ACRL (2008), *Standards for Proficiencies for Instruction Librarians and Coordinators*, staff need to have skills in communication, information literacy integration, instructional design, leadership, planning and presentation.

New ways to deliver information literacy programmes

Embedding instruction throughout the term

The team advocates, in addition to contemporary research and media literacies, the concept of information literacy where users know "when and why they need information, where to find it, and how to evaluate, use and communicate it in an ethical manner." (Chartered Institute of Library and Information Professionals, 2004). Figure 1 shows the range of instructional programmes offered by the library. This is represented as a pyramid highlighting the progression from a broad-based mass training to personalised research consultations.

The just-in-time instruction aligned closely to the term illustrates how the programmes are embedded throughout the 15 week term to cater to student's research needs making them timely and relevant. Each programme or activity is accompanied by related teaching approaches, tools and skills.

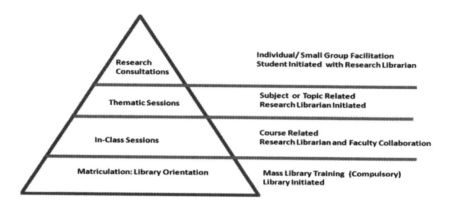

Figure 1: Schematic representation and overview of instructional programmes

Reaching out to the masses via elearning

The matriculation library orientation training is made up of two major learning activities. The first being that upon registration students are sent a link to complete an elearning activity on library etiquette. There is a quiz at the end and they stand a chance to win lucky draw prizes. An elearning working team was set up to design and develop this. Team members used a business model concept where the Customer Service staff were seen as the 'client' and the elearning team was the 'vendor' who used the ADDIE approach (Branch, 2008) to create the course. They learnt new skills such as instructional design, project management and they also evaluated new software. Subsequently the elearning team has been creating reusable learning objects, such as the creation of search strings, which other instruction librarians can use.

The second activity is a face-to-face class where students attend a 1-hour hands-on training on how to use PYXIS, the digital library. Using a sample course reading list, they learn how to look for e-journals, e-resources and books. There has been an increase in the enrolment over the years and this meant that all staff had to be deployed to cater for the increased number of training sessions. The Instructional Services Team teach the classes and staff from other sections are involved as co-trainers. This acts as a refresher for all staff to update their knowledge in searching the digital library and further know what the students will be taught to better assist them once the term starts. The Head, Instructional Services prepares the 'matriculation kit' comprising the roster, PowerPoint slides, trainer script and the activity sheet. The train-the-trainer sessions and briefings in advance help to allay new staff's fears and also create a 'safe environment' for the trainers and co-trainers. This has worked very well over the years and for the more experienced instruction librarian it is an opportunity for informal coaching and mentoring.

Week	Programmes/Activities	Teaching Approaches/Tools/Skills
0	Matriculation: Library Orientation [Duration: 1 hour]	Lecture, Presentations, Hands-On, Video eLearning Instructional Design Skills, Information Searching and Retrieval Skills, Communication Skills, Classroom Management Skills, IT skills including new software; Promotion and Marketing Skills, Social Media Knowledge and Skills
1-7	In-Class Sessions [Duration: Vary depends on faculty collaboration] Academic Writing [Duration: 1.5 hours] Research Consultations [Duration: Typically 1 hour]	Lecture, Facilitation, Presentations, Hands-On, Research Guides Instructional Design Skills, Information Searching and Retrieval Skills, Communication Skills, Classroom Management Skills, IT skills including new software; Promotion and Marketing Skills, Social Media Knowledge and Skills
8-11	Thematic Training [Duration: 1 hour] Research Consultations [Duration: Typically 1 hour]	Lecture, Presentations, Hands-On, Research Guides Instructional Design Skills, Information Searching and Retrieval Skills, Communication Skills, Classroom Management Skills, IT skills including new software; Promotion and Marketing Skills, Social Media Knowledge and Skills
12-14	Research Consultations [Duration: Typically 1 hour]	Small Group Discussions, Facilitation, Hands-On Information Searching and Retrieval Skills, Communication Skills
15	Exams	

Figure 2: Instructional programmes offered during a typical term period

Value-added in-class instruction using research guides

For this type of instruction, the Research Librarians work closely with faculty to customise a session for the course using the curriculum or syllabus. These are one-off sessions and range between 3 –90 minutes depending on the available time given by the faculty. The value-add of this session is that students are introduced to scholarly subject related resources such as journals and databases (so that they do not rely solely on Google and Wikipedia-type resources). Furthermore students get to 'meet and greet' their Research Librarian whom they can follow-up with for a Research Consultation. Most Research Librarians create and use Research Guides to teach their in-class sessions. The Research Guide is a knowledge portal of key resources tied to the course and students make reference to this throughout their term. It also acts as an elearning tool where students can refer to it throughout the course and it can be easily repackaged for the faculty for future requests. Some of the Research Guides created include Business, Government and Society, Legal Research and Writing, Academic Writing and Country Studies or Business Study Missions. Staff learned how to create Research Guides and were able to integrate these into their teaching, evaluating their impact by seeing the usage statistics.

The number of faculty collaborations increased in 2010/2011 as can be seen in Figure 3 below. The library initiated training includes programmes such as the mass matriculation library orientation sessions and other presentations. These decreased significantly in the last year from 261 to 201. Looking at this trend one notes that faculty have become aware, through promotion and marketing, about their Research Librarian's subject-domain knowledge and their ability to teach customised research skills. The Research Librarians migrate from teaching in the familiar library training room to the initially unfamiliar seminar rooms in the respective schools and share the same teaching space with the faculty.

Fiscal Year	No. of Students Receiving Some Form of Instruction		
April to March	Faculty Collaborations	Library Initiated	Total
2010/2011	4,927 (261 sessions)	3,633 (201 sessions)	8,560
2009/2010	3,432	4,235	7,727

Figure 3: Number trained by type

Reflecting on the literature, this is our example and form of being the embedded librarian. Kvenild and Calkins (2011) in their introduction described embedding as a proactive process whereby the librarians collaborates and engage with clear outcomes in events and activities with another person or group. They elaborated this role further noting the importance of being visible and involved in understanding the department pedagogical and learning approaches highlighting their subject or domain expertise. Translating this for implementation requires that instruction librarians need skills in instructional design principles where they must know how to write clear and measurable learning objectives and develop and deliver effective instruction. Additional skills such as promotion and marketing what they do to both faculty and students have become necessary. Many of the instruction librarians at the Li Ka Shing library did not possess these skills initially and this will be discussed later in the section on CPD interventions.

Amongst the instructional services team, there are some who are more 'embedded' in their courses than others as they use different techniques to achieve this. They are in congruence with Oberman's (2002) observation in that "they consult on integrating information literacy assignments, they team-teach, and they even grade work together." However, she cautions that informal ad hoc collaborations with known faculty are unsustainable in the long term, "rather, sustainable information literacy programs must have an institutional mandate, commitment and structure. This allows the players to change, but the program to remain." (Oberman, 2002)

Thematic sessions: subject or topical related instruction

These sessions are offered during recess week and closer to assignment and term paper deadlines. Research Librarians conduct courses on different topics, popular ones include Finding Company Information, Statistical Resources, Legal Resources for non-Law Students, Industry and Market Research, Research Clinic for Business Government, EndNote and Prezi. These sessions are open to all students some whom might not have had an in-class session, those wanting a refresher generally benefit from these classes also. Research Librarians volunteer to conduct these sessions as they are related to their subject areas and again co-trainers help out. These classes benefit the Research Librarian as they keep up-to-date with the latest database and web content as they package the course. Again skills such as promotion and marketing and scheduling determine the hallmark of success for these sessions.

Research consultations: individual/small group facilitation

Research Consultations are targeted specifically to individuals or groups of students to help them find resources based on research topics/problems in a more private setting. Research Consultations are promoted during in-class and matriculation library orientation sessions. It is an opportunity for the Research Librarian to offer the most individual form of instruction and at this point both build rapport in getting to know each other. Students taking the Academic Writing classes have been proactive in setting up Research Consultations as they need help with narrowing their broad topic into a problem statement or research question and finding resources for their papers. Research Librarians need to know how to facilitate small group discussions in addition to using the reference interview as a tool for understanding the respective student's topics.

Using CPD interventions to develop skills

Coaching and mentoring using feedback

The Instruction Service team members posses a range of skill sets ranging from developing to proficient, in addition to their different personalities. This can be ascertained especially when the instruction librarians have to all teach the same courses or conduct the same training. Thus, for mass training that requires the involvement of different instruction librarians, two standardised questions are asked relating to trainer preparedness and trainer delivery of content. An online survey feedback form using SurveyMonkey is administered to measure learner reaction at Level 1 in the Kirkpatrick's evaluation model (2011). The summary data is shared at communication platforms such as meetings and confidential individual feedback is given to the respective instruction librarian as this forms part of their performance appraisal.

Data from the last four years indicate a steady increase in the number of respondents strongly agreeing that the trainer was well prepared. A significant increase can be seen in Figure 4 where in 2010 where there was a 7% increase in the number of respondents strongly agreeing (63%) that the trainer was well prepared. The percentage of respondents being neutral, disagreeing or strongly disagreeing had declined from 8% in 2008 to a constant 4% in 2010 and 2011.

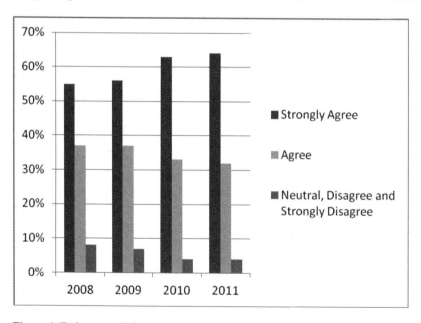

Figure 4: Trainer preparedness responses

Similarly, more students strongly agreed that the trainer delivered the content effectively. The trends can be been in Figure 5. In 2008 and 2009, a higher percentage of respondents agreed (average of 60%) rather than strongly agreed that the trainer delivered the content effectively. In the last two years this has shifted where on average now 50% strongly agreed that the trainer delivered the content effectively. The feedback responses for neutral, disagree and strongly disagree decreased too from 15% in 2008 to 5% in 2011.

The improvement in feedback ratings for trainer preparedness and delivery of content responses could be a result of the appointment of the Head for Instructional Services who co-ordinates and also reviews the programme regularly in addition to providing feedback and developing intervention strategies. This is one of the administrative skills listed in the *Standards for Proficiencies for Instruction Librarians and Coordinators* where it is noted that he or she, "documents the activities, effectiveness, and needs of the instruction program through statistical analysis, formal reports, presentations, and data analysis." (Association of College and Research Libraries, 2008, 6).

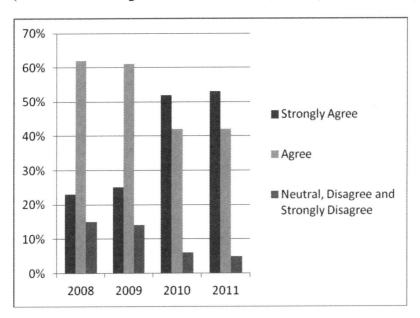

Figure 5: Delivery of content

Mining qualitative feedback to identify training courses

Open-ended feedback though difficult to process is a useful intervention strategy to also identify training courses for staff development. Below is a sample of some of the open-ended feedback received and the 'coding' or categorisation of the responses to identify themes or topics for intervention.

Comment/Feedback	Identifying Themes/Topics for Intervention
It packed slightly too much information	Content
Maybe can provide a printed step by step instruction	Learning Materials
It was a little dry	Delivery Techniques
There is not enough time to brainstorm or think of ideas. It would be more useful if we can do it before lesson and bring our mindmap to class	Time Management
It's not necessary to attend the session, since all information is covered in the research guides	Managing Expectations
The class was distracted and unfocused	Classroom Management
The boolean method is overly emphasized	Content
There were videos to enhance though provoking ideas about the topic of research the trainer was engaging and helpful	Use of Media
It would have been better if the instructors provided handouts on what to type in the fields when searching for an article in the database	Learning Materials
Interesting and fun delivery	Positive Delivery Techniques

Figure 6: Identifying themes or topics for intervention using qualitative feedback

When reviewing staff's individual feedback, learning and development pro-grammes can be identified and this can then be included in the staff's training plan for the year. These areas can be monitored or tracked on a regular basis and if necessary, the staff may be advised to co-train with another instruction librarian possessing strength in a certain skill or competency. The collated and analysed feedback is shared with the instruction team at the Training Coordi-nation Meeting (TCM).

Voices during the training coordination meeting (TCM)

The TCM is a 90 minute session that is held monthly where the team members discuss and share issues and experiences. Typically, the meeting reviews the minutes of the last month, and follows up on actions needing closure. The training statistics are reviewed too. Data and documents are stored using SharePoint. The team reflects on the training achievements for the previous month. Resulting from this is a round-table open discussion where each in-struction librarian shares about the classes they conducted. They highlight both the positive and negative issues experienced, the latter being mainly IT related. This is a similar practice used by LaGuardia, Griego, Hopper & Melendez (1993, p60-61) where "team members do informal "debriefings" after each presentation, discussing how the class went, what worked, what bombed." Interestingly, even though LaGuardia, Griego, Hopper & Melendez wrote this article in 1993, it is a common but effective communication technique used today and the author believes many other instruction teams worldwide still do this. There is a lot of laughter during the 'debrief' and this becomes a cathartic session as it provides again, that 'safe environment' for the team members to seek help, solutions and support. Everyone is given a voice and everyone's voice is heard at the TCM.

Opportunities to 'showcase' something new or another team member's achievement such as a published paper helps to build morale, innovation and creativity. The Head, Instructional Services also use the meeting to introduce new concepts, approaches and strategies, interesting articles and invite guest speakers to talk on the latest trends and developments. Issues and action items from the senior management meetings are also shared at this meeting. Guest speakers or presenters are also invited, a case in point being a recent demonstration of WebEx.

Conference attendance sharing platform: the learning circle

The library's monthly Learning Circle is another avenue for the Instructional Services team to keep up to date with trends and developments. Staff who have attended conferences both locally and internationally share key learning points and best practices at these sessions. Finding and creating opportunities for the instruction librarians to present and share is a way of nurturing them so that they are rewarded and recognised for their efforts. The Learning Circle has also been used for sharing of professional readings, trends and best practices from site visits, or teaching other staff a new social media application.

Internal collaboration: faculty and other key departments

The Head, Instructional Services is also the Research Librarian for the School of Business and supports the Corporate Communication discipline in addition to two other subjects. Having built a close working relationship from the numerous in-class sessions and other research help provided, some faculty extend an invitation to team members to attend relevant topical lectures and talks by industry speakers in the area of presentation and communication. Again, this highlights one of the many benefits from being an embedded librarian and also helps to build the required skills staff need to teach effectively.

Over the years the library has developed strong ties with many departments on campus, a case in point being the Centre for Teaching Excellence

(CTE). The role of the CTE is to promote teaching excellence and build best practice in pedagogy. They also help facilitate the use of new technologies for faculty. The Head, Instructional Services invited CTE staff to share with team members, during the TC, themes and topics such writing learning objectives using Bloom's Taxonomy and an overview of instructional design using the ADDIE model. For the latter the team contextualised their own training where reflected on the different phases such as Analysis, Design, Development,Implementation and Evaluation. The team appreciated the theoretical foundations to instruction and pedagogy. The more experienced instruction librarians applied what they learnt and reviewed their own instructional programmes to align it to sound pedagogical principles.

Another example of collaboration was when the library was invited to participate in the inaugural Teaching Innovation Week held in September 2011. A small task force was set up and the instruction team involved in the Academic Writing programme showcased the blended learning approach used to teach this course. This was a refreshing experience for the team as it highlighted the need to 'tell and share their stories' and in this case they shared the same platform with faculty using innovative teaching methods.

Recently the university implemented a new elearning management system, Desire2Learn. Again the CTE were invited to the TCM to share how the instruction librarians can use the elearn system to embed themselves. Currently the Research Librarian for the School of Information Systems is prototyping a curriculum for the new students in the new academic year. An elearning project team also work closely with the CTE team where necessary to co-create learning objects.

External training and 'outsourcing' professional development

Partello (2005: 115) passionately remarked and highlighted:

> "Whether librarians teach outside the library or not, we need to learn to teach. We should know about learning theories, including multiple intelligences, and how to construct a class so that we reach learners of all abilities. Too many of us focus on what we think is important and not what the students need. We cram too much information into 50- or 80-minute sessions and don't allow time for students to reflect and retain the information".

This again warrants the need for continuing professional development opportunities for instruction librarians who are passionate about teaching. Instruction and training librarians receive on-the-job training or in-house arranged training typically on topics such as communication and presentation skills. The latter are often offered by commercial training providers and whilst generic enough, often lack customisation and contextualisation.

Workforce Development Agency (WDA) programmes

Recently in Singapore, the Workforce Development Agency (WDA) launched the Workforce Skills Qualification (WSQ) framework for Training and Adult Education. The Institute of Adult Learning (IAL), one of the various training providers, offers the Advanced Certificate in Training and Assessment (ACTA). It is targeted at individuals in training and adult education to become certified trainers. The university arranged for an in-house run of the course and the Head, Instructional Services together with two other staff, one of whom is involved in instruction, successfully completed it and found it to be useful. The course is made up of six competency units such as: Applying adult learning principles and codes of ethics relating to training; Designing and developing a WSQ training programme; Preparing and facilitating a classroom training programme and Developing and conducting a competency-based assessment. The entire duration of the course is 15 days and learners can pick and choose the modules and dates making it a flexible learning programme. This certificate programme provides an opportunity for experienced instruction librarians wanting a specialised qualification and also an opportunity for those needing to develop their skills and competencies in training in general. Currently a para-professional staff member is completing the programme with two other staff having expressed interest to do the course. This 'outsourced' programme can help raise the skills and competencies of instruction librarians. The Head, Instructional Services will encourage other team members to pursue this certification programme and include it in their training plan.

Library Association of Singapore's Professional Development Scheme (PDS)

Recently the Library Association of Singapore (LAS) Professional Development Scheme (PDS) was established as a means to motivate librarians to keep up-to-date with their professional training and development. Using a points system members can participate in a range of development areas such as:

- Expertise development : activities that will help to upgrade and improve the skills and knowledge of practitioners
- Industry knowledge development : activities that keep the practitioner informed of current developments in the information industry
- Personal development: activities that help the practitioner improve on his/her work productivity, personal management skills and general knowledge.

Upon attainment of the required points they will be awarded the title of "Practicing Professional" by the PDS Board. Their names are listed in the gazette and on the official LAS website (Library Association of Singapore, Professional Development Scheme Guidelines, n.d.). Librarians, including the Instructional Service Team at the Li Ka Shing Library, are not formally required to participate in this scheme but benefit from the courses, programmes and activities arranged by the LAS.

CPD: The bottom line for instruction

Developing a team of passionate instruction librarians

So how do librarians teach, ask LaGuardia, Griego, Hopper & Melendez (1993)? They describe the situation practically as being, 'usually a trial by fire'. Elaborating this further they describe the process as being fast paced where the instruction librarian is required to package a class and 'pack and go' to deliver the instruction. Most times using 'instinct', and seizing the opportunity by setting aside the frills and the luxury of time to develop 'perfect' instructional designed programmes. But how long does it take? In the typical solo-act "trial by fire school", probably years, but in today's context it has become on-the-job (LaGuardia, Griego, Hopper and Melendez, 1993).

This scenario is characteristic of the Li Ka Shing Library and it begins upfront during the interview where anyone applying for a professional position has to do a 30-45 minute presentation on any topic to the interview panel, in our unique case the entire library staff. This is very significant and critical as it helps to determine whether the prospective staff member has the necessary communication and presentation skills. It helps to ascertain whether they 'fit'. It also helps the Heads of Departments to determine the learning curve required for the staff to transition from understudy to going 'solo'. Over the last few years, all the Research Librarian positions have been filled and this has helped the team members to bond and work as a team creating a nurturing and caring environment celebrating our diversity.

Unity in diversity

Our unity in our diversity comes from the complementary strengths amongst us and we leverage on the subject-domain knowledge that each one brings. Many of the Research Librarians have industry and practical experiences and this immediately inculcates a sense of respect for the individual. As Head of Instructional Services, the author realised the importance of building a 'safe environment' of trust and care, as not everyone enjoys teaching, thus echoing

LaGuardia, Griego, Hopper & Melendez's (1993; p.58) approach of team cohesiveness and teamwork. The culture and work ethic in the library is one of helping and this has transcended to training and co-training activities. This has been one of the hallmarks of success amongst the instructional team members who exude a sense of passion and make training and teaching less burdensome as they are willing to share and transfer knowledge. The benefits of co-training are well documented in the literature, the salient one being a holistic beneficial learning experience for not only the trainer but also the students and faculty.

Conclusion

Revisiting the *"Standards for Proficiencies for Instruction Librarians and Coordinators"* (2008) instruction or teaching embraces communication skills, curriculum knowledge, information literacy integration skills, instructional design skills, leadership, planning and presentation skills. Similarly, reflecting on the question of nature or nurture, the author's personal answer and response to this is that it is both, especially if one has a diverse team and has seen the team grow and develop over the years. If you are in a leadership role such as co-coordinator or head, then it is important to have a holistic perspective and profile for each of the instruction librarians where a mental map is formed for each team member noting their related areas of strengths and development. For instruction librarians displaying characteristics of 'nature' it important to give them the freedom to be innovative and creative where through advice and guidance they transfer their skills and passion by helping to coach and mentor other team members. Nurturing relates to creating a 'safe environment' and making everyone feel inclusive by providing leadership, direction, mentoring and a 'safe environment'. These have been some of the qualities that has made the information literacy and the instructional services team passionate as they strive for excellence in training and teaching. As Head, Instructional Services, the author advocates and celebrates the nature-nurture process as part of the continuing professional development of the instructional services team.

References

American Library Association. (2008). *Standards for proficiencies for instruction librarians and coordinators: a practical guide*. Chicago: Association of College and Research Libraries. Retrieved from:
www.ala.org/acrl/sites/ala.org.acrl/files/content/standards/profstandards.pdf
Branch, R. M. (2008). *Instructional design: the ADDIE approach*. New York ; London : Springer. DOI: 10.1007/978-0-387-09506-6. Retrieved from:
www.springerlink.com.libproxy.smu.edu.sg/content/w5640r/#section=263149&page=1

Chartered Institute of Library and Information Professionals (CILIP). (2004). *Information literacy: definition*. Retrieved from:
www.cilip.org.uk/get-involved/advocacy/information-literacy/pages/definition.aspx

Kirkpatrick Partners. (2011). *The Kirkpatrick Model*. Retrieved from:
www.kirkpatrickpartners.com/OurPhilosophy/tabid/66/Default.aspx

Kvenild, C., & Calkins, K. (Eds.). (2011). *Embedded librarians: moving beyond one-shot instruction*. Chicago: Association of College and Research Libraries, American Library Association.

LaGuardia, C., Griego, A., Hopper, M., & Melendez, L. (1993). Learning to instruct on the job: team-teaching library skills [Electronic version]. *The Reference Librarian, 18(40)*, 53-62.

Library Association of Singapore. [n.d]. *Professional Development Scheme: PDS Guidelines*. Retrieved from: sites.google.com/site/laspds09/Home

Li Ka Shing Library. (2010). *Strategic Plan, 2011-2012. Revised 2010*. Singapore: Singapore Management University. Retrieved from:
http://library.smu.edu.sg/aboutus/LKSLStratPlan2011_12.pdf

Oberman, C. (2002). What the ACRL Institute for Information Literacy Best Practice Initiative tells us about the librarian as teacher. In *Libraries for life: democracy, diversity, delivery*. The Hague: IFLA Council and General Conference: Conference Programme and Proceedings (68th, Glasgow, Scotland, August 18-24, 2002).

Partello, P. (2005). Librarians in the classroom. *The Reference Librarian, 89/90*, 107-120.

Singapore Workforce Development Agency. *Training and Adult Education*. Singapore: Singapore Workforce Development Agency. Retrieved from:
http://app2.wda.gov.sg/wsq/Contents/contents.aspx?contid=987

Develop @ Your Library – Meaningful Partnerships Through Information Literacy in Liasa Gauteng South Branch, Johannesburg

Julia Paris
Campus Librarian, University of Johannesburg Library and Information Centre, South Africa
juliap@uj.ac.za

Abstract

Develop @ your library was the celebration theme of the 2012 South African Library Week. The aim of the chosen theme was to join forces with governmental skill development initiatives aimed at job creation. In South Africa there are masses of unemployed people who use the public library resources to find information about employment opportunities. There is a great need in South Africa for literacy development and more specifically information literacy skill development to assist library users in their search for information. There is also a need for information literacy to be recognized as a critically scarce skill among librarians in the public library sector. Academic librarians are deemed to be much better skilled in the area of information literacy training as a result of the academic environment they function in. To augment the information literacy training skill development gap, a partnership has taken shape in the spirit of 'Develop @ your library. The aim is to develop and implement an information literacy blueprint in the City of Johannesburg, under the auspices of LIASA Gauteng South Branch. The call to "Develop @ your library" created the space for focused conversation about how to approach and close the information literacy training skills gap, future collaboration, design, implementation and evaluation of information literacy training programs. The paper reflects the first steps taken towards such an initiative. The project is a work in progress.

Introduction

This paper describes the pioneering work started in the City of Johannesburg between academic and public librarians who joined forces against illiteracy and the overwhelming rate of unemployment in South Africa (SA). The aim of the collaborative partnership was a focus on an information literacy training blueprint for the public library in this precinct. The conversation started on an informal basis after the 2011 Library and Information Association of SA conference. Early in 2012 the conversation was followed by an invitation to make a presentation to the Head Librarian and her eight regional library managers. The presentation was followed by a meeting where the possible terms of reference were mooted and a follow-up workshop where the work to be done was outlined. The discussions were held in the spirit of the theme of 'Develop @ your library'.

The state of literacy in South Africa

Literacy is a basic human right in South Africa. As in most countries, literacy is enshrined in the right of an individual to be educated and to acquire literacy to be able to function in society at large. The demands of the 21st century workplace are impacting South Africa in a serious way and increasing rapidly as a result of the information explosion brought about by the growth and popularity of the Internet and advances in technology. The knowledge held by a minority of people is becoming a valuable divisive commodity in economic terms seen against the big majority of people who are unemployed. Evidence exists that the demands made on the South African economy is for a new kind of worker, one who is equipped with adequate levels of computer and information literacy skills in order to find or create a job. The knowledge worker is expected to have a very high, almost sophisticated information literacy skill set which would include critical reading and critical thinking, as well as knowing how to search, find, evaluate and use the information for his or her well- being. The experience in the South African environment is evidence that the role of librarians had become even more important within this highly demanding knowledge intensive context. The dire unemployment rates are creating an urgency for librarians across all spectra to join forces to train the South African public in information literacy skills.

High levels of unemployment and low levels of literacy within South Africa were addressed by the theme of the South African Library Week which called on all librarians nationwide to answer the call to action and create the opportunity in their libraries for people development through information literacy skill training. The South African Library Association took a deliberate decision to encourage development of basic skills to assist library users in all library sectors to address the issue of capacity building to assist job hunting whilst trying to address the high rate of unemployment.

The main goal of the Develop @ your library campaign was to step up and become part of the national initiatives to create information literacy skill development opportunities to those citizens who daily frequent our libraries. Each contributing partner answered the call to contribute to the national agenda of the South African government. All the contributions were made in the spirit of voluntary participation in the library association and general need for skill development to alleviate poverty in the country. The participation of individual librarians was pledged as a gift to the profession. This generosity of spirit is well known in the library and information science profession in South Africa.

Definitions of concepts used

Library Literacy, Computer Literacy, and Information Literacy

The concepts of library literacy, computer literacy and information literacy all depict a level of literacy which requires a specific set of skills in order for a person to be rated as literate in today's society. Library literacy is the required skills to be able to adequately use a library. This kind of skill is usually imparted during a library orientation session. Library literacy is the skill and confidence with which an individual uses the library. Computer literacy is the skill of knowing how to use the computer as a tool to find the information that is sought, at a basic level this means keyboard skills. Computer literacy is the skill and confidence with which an individual uses the computer or any form of technology to access information.

Information literacy, in a nutshell, is the skill to know when information is needed, where to go to find it, how to search for it, find it, evaluate it and use it to make a decision which fulfils the need for the information. Due to the fact that this is such an important skill for survival in the information intensive environment we are in, information literacy is deemed:

> "... as the ability to effectively access and evaluate information for problem-solving and decision making... in short, information –literate people know how to be life-long learners in an information society. They know how to learn because they know how knowledge is organized; how to find information; how to use information in such a way that others can learn from them" (Erasmus, 2000; p.2).

The skills gap experience of some public libraries in the skill development domain

Public libraries are well used facilities in South Africa. Most of them have relevant programmes geared towards addressing children and adult literacy needs, however, very few of these facilities have focused, well developed training sessions and enough skilled librarians to facilitate information literacy programmes. This discovery was made in the knowledge sharing meetings between public and academic librarians. Alliances were formed between the two sectors' librarians, which led to a decision to uncover the shortfall of information literacy training skills in the public sector and capitalize on the strengths found in both public and academic sector environments to address the issue. The alliances formed and needs discussed endorsed the formulation of active work to assist in promoting a culture of reading, as well as partnering on the design and introduction of formal literacy and information literacy training programs in public libraries. The librarians were aware that the promotion of and advocacy for reading were important imperatives. However, something more fundamental was required. The 'something more' was manifest in the formation of a collaborative initiative which is currently in its infancy.

The collaboration initiative defined

The initiative formed was in the spirit of collaboration, an agreement to co-operate to advance mutual interests, as well as the interests of the profession and the citizens of the country. This partnership was formed in a spirit of mutual contribution and exchange of knowledge and information beneficial to the bigger vision, mission and strategy of the library profession in South Africa. The reality is that "Johannesburg public libraries are well developed hubs of education, giving residents access to books, magazines, and audio-visual material. Besides lending out material, the city's libraries offer a wide range of other services including literacy classes, story-telling sessions for youngsters, classroom support, gatherings for older residents and literary competitions." (Libraries, 2012) which makes it very easy to address this skill development need in an organized way and in a short time frame.

The partnership between academic and public librarians is geared towards well researched quality programmes, impactful interventions, and life-long skills development. In Johannesburg alone there are four major universities: one international and three local universities. The legacies and strategic capabilities of these universities are well established and developed. The competencies and skills of the librarians at these educational institutions are highly recognised and in great demand. Academic librarians know how to advocate with new faculty for the inclusion of IL into departmental curricula, how to respond to accreditation bodies and how to make use of grant opportunities for library programs. These are skills which could be shared with public librarians. Academic librarians are comfortable in the use of the innovation provided by social media tools to service their clients. This is a skill which is not well developed in public libraries in South Africa currently.

Public librarians on the other hand have the benefit of knowing the political, economic, social, environmental, legal and societal needs of the broader public. They are also closer to the educational sectors, and in touch with the educational needs of primary school learners, unemployed youth, and unemployed adults. Community librarians have insight into what is happening in their communities and what the main needs of these communities are, and where focused information literacy programmes could make a difference. Public librarians also use very creative ways to encourage a culture of reading with all their users, have very interesting participative programmes pitched to various levels of readers, and have a wide range of information sources and resources to provide to their varied user base. A marriage between the two sets of strengths is a powerful recipe for collaboration and success. The common goal of empowering people to build their capacity to improve their skills and well-being is also an empowering one. Working together in a focused formalized partnership could serve to strengthen the region, offer a blueprint for the other regions, and strengthen the library profession in the country in a holistic way. Collaborations, cooperation, partnerships and alliances are not foreign concepts to librarians. In South Africa, funding is not easily available, so librarians collaborating in this way through the library association could ensure optimal use of training budgets too. In the past collaborative efforts through the Gauteng and Environs Library Consortium (GAELIC) had served very adequately to cement librarians and develop very pertinent skills, as well as minimize the impact of dwindling budgets. The consortium was declared redundant as a result of changes in the South African higher education landscape.

Within the skill development domain tacit and explicit knowledge is seen as the new capital of the 21st century. Librarians, who are at the core of the knowledge workspace have invaluable knowledge as citizens of the country. They are well placed to serve the information literacy skill development and training agenda to help alleviate illiteracy. The workforce required in the South African knowledge environment is different as a result of a vast transformational metamorphosis brought about by the democratic environment, technological advancements and the social, political, and economic needs of the country. Librarians use their minds, knowledge, intuition, and skills collectively to process information and apply it to their daily work. This is the context in which South African citizens too are required to seek employment, and librarians can make a huge contribution in this regard. What is even more powerful about this new economy is that customers of our library services, whether public or academic have vastly different demands, and have been transformed by this new way of thinking, doing and being. In the past companies used to rely on the tools or instruments to execute the job. In this new knowledge intensive corporate and civic environment, companies and governments now rely on people to know how to access, process, and change knowledge into meaningful use and value for living and innovation for personal and economic profit. This new set of circumstances places great pressure on public and academic libraries to develop strategies to service the demands of the day. Again, librarians are the best placed to play this role.

Libraries and intellectual capital

The concept of intellectual capital emerged in the 1990s. Loosely defined, intellectual capital refers to various sources of intangible knowledge of great value to the individual and the organisation the individual works for. Librarians are included in this conceptual understanding. It is clear from the literature that intellectual capital is a valuable asset that is very important for libraries competent to survive in the knowledge- based economy. There is a business case for sharpening and honing this understanding and development of intellectual capital in public libraries as well. South Africa is seen as the most developed country in Africa, and this fact provides even more emphasis to this need. Librarians are vital for the development of the South African workforce. Librarians are even more crucial to assist the masses of illiterate, and semiliterate job seekers in the country. The intellectual capital of librarians is the country's social intelligence. The recognition of this fact of librarian tacit and explicit knowledge is highly overdue. This joint initiative if pursued nationwide could prove to have far-reaching social impact for the citizens and economic progress of the country.

In the public sector libraries there is a very complex mix of staff. Some of the librarians do not hold a degree in Library and Information Science. In some instances where the public librarians have a degree some do not have the infrastructural capacity to develop the innovative skills required to competently serve the new economic needs. The meaning of intellectual capital and the subsequent interpretation of the intellectual capital in the library sector is a very complex situation and will require good planning and deep thinking. Execution of practical innovative methods is important. Ryan (2012, p.43) is of the opinion that "execution is what matters, and execution relies on human talent". The success of the four university libraries in Johannesburg is evidence that the academic librarians found in these libraries do possess this talent. It is also true that most of this untapped tacit and explicit knowledge is well developed as a result of how they approach challenges and ride the wave to change as their information environment changes. It is imperative that this joining of human talent be the springboard for the proposed collaborative effort to address the literacy, information literacy and unemployment crisis in South Africa.

Possible tools mooted for further development:

Needs assessment tools

An open online literacy forum where conversations and opinions could be logged, ideas could be exchanged, and feedback could be given on the collaboration on an ongoing basis.

A formal mentoring program.

A skills-development program for information literacy training of the trainers program.

A blueprint for skill development for library users of various ages and societal levels.

A measurement instrument for measuring the effectiveness of training programs and skills developed.

User feedback instrument for impact measurement.

The Balanced Scorecard as a tool for the measurement of intellectual capital across both sectors.

Examples of areas identified for collaboration

Art faculty librarians with the art programmes of the public library

Business faculty librarians with the entrepreneurship programmes of the public libraries

Education faculty librarians with children's services in public libraries and school libraries

Humanities faculty librarians with the general reading and writing programmes in public libraries, and assignment and project research in school libraries

General reference librarians could be matched with the need for computer, digital and media literacy of public and school library users.

Partnership through a formal agreement – the next step

A formal contractual agreement is the next logical step in the collaborative partnership. In the formal agreement, the goals and objectives, as well as the terms of reference of the collaborative project will be thoroughly discussed and unpacked to give structure to the partnership. The agreement will be followed by a series of workshops organised around the training processes to be used, training objectives, skill development methodologies to be considered, trainers and trainees, venues for training, monitoring and evaluation of outcomes, and finally review of the whole partnership and its impact. All of this information and knowledge will be packaged in an information literacy skill-development toolkit. Additional points of clarification identified for follow-up discussion were:

Any restrictive organisational policies

Rules of engagement

Target populations and their needs

Communication plans

Training plans

A training curriculum

Funding of such projects

Timelines for projects

Monitoring and evaluation and risk register

Review of partnership for challenges and benefits of collaboration

Reporting on partnership to strategic stakeholders

All these points will be dealt with and impact investigated. The whole idea is mutual benefit, ensuring collegiality and personal growth for all participants and organisations who decide to participate.

Conclusion

The initiative taken to form the collaborative partnership between academic and public librarians through the library association is a unique one. In the past consortiums encouraged interaction and skills development. The library association interest groups transferred skills in silos in the various interest group structures. The dire need for skill development of a vast majority of semi-literate and non-literate people in South Africa had made it necessary for librarians to work across their workplace boundaries and unite in one mission – to educate and skill the citizens of their country. "Develop@ your library", the 2012 South African Library Week, created the conversation and action to do it.

References

Erasmus, S. (2000). *Information literacy level 1: library literacy.* Johannesburg: Technikon Southern Africa

Libraries (2012). Retrieved from the official website of the city of Johannesburg: www.joburg.org.za/index.php?option=com_content&task=view&id=68&Itemid

Working Together Beyond Borders – Capacity Building in Information Literacy Education at Three University Libraries in Namibia, Tampere and Helsinki

Menete Ndapandula Shatona
University of Namibia
mshatona@unam.na

Janika Asplund
Tampere University Library
janika.asplund@uta.fi

Tiina Heino
Helsinki University Library
tiina.m.heino@helsinki.fi

Päivi Helminen
Helsinki University Library
paivi.helminen@helsinki.fi

Abstract

The main function of university libraries is to support higher education's core missions of research and education. However, lack of experience coupled with inadequate technological know-how impedes libraries, especially in Africa, to execute their mandates. It is against this background that the University of Namibia (UNAM), University of Helsinki (UH) and University of Tampere (UTa) formed a collaborative partnership to share experiences and skills to improve competency of the library staff. All three participating university libraries have an opportunity to learn from each other and to evaluate and modify existing practices. The project covers several capacity building areas and among them, as central components, are content development for Information Literacy (IL) instruction and pedagogical skills to plan and teach IL skills to students and academic staff. This paper will review the collaborative activities between the three university libraries. In addition, the paper further seeks to explore what was learnt and how working together has benefited and reshaped the experiences of the participants coming from three different libraries.

Lastly, it concludes by identifying the best practices and key elements of teamwork which are critical to ensuring success.

Aim and background

Helsinki, Tampere, and Namibia University Library have started a co-operation, funded by the Finnish Foreign Affairs Ministry's HEI-ICI project, for the years 2011-12. The aim of the project is to improve human resources capacity at the University of Namibia Library. The main areas of capacity building are information literacy (IL) teaching for students and staff, peda-gogical skills of the librarians, modern practices for providing access to elec-tronic resources of information, methods of marketing, joint quality improve-ment and benchmarking, strategic planning skills, collection development and management, research and academic writing and publishing articles in peer-reviewed journals. The enhancement of the skills of library staff will benefit the University of Namibia students and staff by improving library services and access to scientific information.

Both Tampere University Library and Helsinki University Library have a long history of teaching information literacy, starting from user education and moving on to information literacy education. IL has been embedded in the cur-riculum for a good number of students for many years and is considered a cru-cial skill for students to succeed both in their academic studies and for lifelong learning. Therefore, the work we do now is based on solid ground and exper-tise gathered during the years.

The University of Helsinki faces the challenges of a multidisciplinary and multi campus university. We try to offer IL services equally in each faculty and yet take into account differences between disciplines and pedagogical ap-proaches. The previous curriculum change (Bologna Process in 2005) involved every faculty launching the Information and Communication Technology (ICT) Driving Licence as a compulsory course for all students of the Univer-sity of Helsinki. Information literacy has an important role in the ICT Driving Licence (Helminen, 2007).

The Teaching Council of the University of Tampere has confirmed the status of IL education in the guidelines for the new curricula. Therefore good-will exists at a high level towards IL education; not only in negotiations be-tween faculties and library. In the new curriculum, IL education is planned to be offered equally and the education is evenly structured in different study programs. Students in various disciplines have equal access to IL education in different phases of their study. Information literacy is considered a crucial skill for students to succeed both in their academic studies and for lifelong learning. The more extensive amount of IL education means that in the library an in-creasing number of library staff will be teaching as part of their daily work –

more pedagogical training for library staff is required as well. In Tampere University library, a good number of library staff have attended university pedagogy training for university teachers or have had some tailored pedagogical training for library staff (for different training options of library staff; (see Iivonen, Tevaniemi and Toivonen, 2007). There is also a need for a critical look at the existing job descriptions of each library staff member to make sure they meet the new requirements. Most notably, there are various factors which need serious consideration, such as how librarians' pedagogical training is organized and how active co-operation on course content and curriculum issues between library management, university management, library information specialists and university staff is organized. It is also important to describe core issues which are defining the learning objectives of each IL course at each study level to reach a generally accepted model.

In Finland, both the Tampere and Helsinki Universities, we have had good results in cooperating with various stakeholders within the university. Furthermore, the universities have seen the good learning outcomes our students gain from IL education, and we have also seen the library status getting stronger within the university. As all the participating universities are multidisciplinary, it is useful to share our experiences and good practices. In this project, the participating universities could explore how IL practices could be implemented at UNAM keeping in mind the local academic conditions.

Collaboration between academic libraries

Lluís M. Anglada (2007) points out that libraries have, throughout history, created different forms of cooperation, and the development of organizations such as libraries depends on their ability to work together. He uses the concept of social intelligence to define the kind of collaboration that is needed in academic organizations in order to survive: the accumulated social capital – social intelligence – means either success or failure. In our cooperation, we believe that together we can accumulate social capital and learn things from each other. Academic libraries are knowledge-intensive organizations where the best results are achieved when expertise and knowledge are shared and best practices benchmarked.

Information literacy skills as well as teaching skills are important for librarians. At the libraries in-house training sessions play an important role, they provide a possibility to share expertise and help us to achieve the common goal – the best services to our customers (Jankowska and Marshall, 2003). Kuhn et al. (2011) point out that librarians should have regular meetings to share their expertise, since a growing number of librarians are teaching, and often lack formal teacher education: "Learning from colleagues and sharing experiences is a valuable way of improving practice". Study circles where IL trainers teach each other and share experiences proved to be useful for staff development (Heino, 2010). The seminars in our cooperation project work as "training the trainers" sessions for both parties. Internet and social media collaboration tools lower the threshold of finding time to create collaboration and partnerships (see also Ahola and Asplund, 2010). The internet has increased cross-border relations, and nowadays it is fairly easy to establish new companionships with other libraries including internationally (Anglada, 2007). Neyer and Yelinek (2011) conducted a survey to assess mentoring experiences and attitudes towards work, and they listed important criteria for a successful mentorship: the mentor's professional experience and expertise, mutual respect between the mentee and mentor, and the issue of time. Mentoring is one of the key issues in our project.

The library's crucial role within the university

Anglada (2007) mentions the library's changing role and says it should be considered as an integral part of the academic community. Libraries are not separate islands. The importance of the library for the academic community is seen clearly in the following quotation by Huotari and Iivonen (2005; p324):

> "One way to integrate high quality library services with the long-term planning of the university is to understand the library as an internal strategic partner".

The companionship should be based on competence and trust:

> "The cooperation in information literacy education and planning IL education has meant for Tampere University Library the possibility to build partnership within the university. There is no doubt that this partnership brings added value for the whole university, but also for the library whose status and impact in the academic community will be cemented in this way " (Iivonen, Tevaniemi and Toivonen, 2007;p.163; translation: Asplund).

It is important that cooperation is active between library upper management and university upper management as well as between information specialists in the library and the schools or faculties within the university.

Appleton, Stevenson & Boden (2011) say that libraries should form strategic partnerships with the university faculties, take initiative, and influence change, not just respond to change. They would like to see the "library as a central hub of teaching, learning and research in the university" (p.357). Throughout our project, we have kept in mind the library's role within the university, whether it is sharing ideas on how to integrate IL into the curriculum or reflecting on faculty's needs in order to enhance collection development. All three universities agree upon the important role of libraries in the university, and how IL education is vital for academic success. In this project the libraries could share ideas on how to communicate with the university and its faculties, as well as to how to integrate IL into the curriculum.

The national and international collaboration aspect: libraries are fast learners

Anglada (2007) mentions the long history of cooperation in libraries: networks and associations had organized collaboration a couple of decades earlier, but it was at the end of the 1990's that various consortia were developed throughout the world, and soon the idea was spread to many countries to organize joint issues via consortia. Prior to that, many issues had been handled by associations. In Finland, national cooperation provides us with tools and experience and helps us to collaborate in international forums. We are already used to working together, and we are used to diversity, because libraries in Finland have various working environments and organizational cultures. Often within the organization there is only one person who is doing a specific task, but there might be several people working with similar tasks in another organization, whether it is nationally or internationally. That is the reason why we have several networks in Finland to gather people working with similar issues, like the national IL network. The FinELib consortium and the networks launched by the Council for Finnish University Libraries have given us strength to join forces with people with certain expertise to act more powerfully, and to save time and effort. Thus it is natural that we would like to act globally as well. The HEI ICI project is a proof of that strength.

Finnish libraries have several people acting in international associations: the survey made by the Council for the Finnish University Libraries in 2011 clearly reveals that approximately half of the university libraries in Finland have representatives in international associations (Asplund, 2011). The Information Literacy network created by the Council for Finnish University Libraries has done systematic work with IL education at the national level, for example creating national recommendations for universities to include IL in educational programmes in 2004 (Finnish recommendations …,2004; Juntunen et al 2008). The IL national recommendation for universities has been a useful tool for university libraries. Libraries have used it actively in IL teaching and planning. This shared guideline has provided a backbone when curricula have been planned together with the academic community. Some parts of the recommendation are still valid but new needs have emerged. Therefore, it is time to renew the recommendation and this work is going on in the IL community between people in different higher education institutions (the universities and universities of applied sciences). This renewal process has opened up the dialogue between the different library sectors, and the library community will evaluate whether there is a need for separate recommendations for universities and universities of applied sciences or whether one recommendation could cover all different levels of higher education. The updated recommendation is due at the end 2012.

Information literacy at UNAM

Bundy (2003) states that university students should be equipped with IL skill as this would encourage them to do research to provide evidence-based research to problems affecting their countries. Also, the findings could be used for policy formulation and decision making. Like any other university in the developing world, UNAM is faced with a general lack of IL programmes at the university, further compounded by a lack of an IL policy at a national level. However, the absence of an IL programme does not mean that IL is not offered at UNAM. Some subject librarians teach IL to both undergraduate and postgraduate students in the disciplines for which they are responsible. This teaching is offered on an individual or group basis. Notably, IL teaching is usually done at lecturers' request. The teaching of IL is not examined and nor it is evaluated. On the other hand, students also sometimes request one-on-one training on how to search the library e-resources, and the library catalogue (OPAC).

What are the activities planned for the project, and what has been done so far

At a seminar held in April of this year, we have planned several presentations on IL in Finland and group work for gathering ideas on different aspects of IL education and staff capacity building. In and between the seminars the Namibian library staff have development sessions to keep working on their own. Although the current funding period of the project is short, less than two years, it makes it possible to start the capacity building program. The main highlight of the project includes two seminars to be held in Namibia. In addition, several UNAM Library staff members will come to Finland for four week study visits. Two weeks are to be spent at the UTA and the other two weeks at the UH. A few staff members from UNAM Library will come to Finland during the IFLA Conference in August 2012. Collaborative activities are also carried out over the internet and these activities will continue after the funding period. UNAM Library has adopted a Trainees-Become-Trainers approach to expand the knowledge base amongst its staff: UNAM librarians who learn new skills in this cooperation will become trainers of the others.

UNAM librarians' work visit to Finland

In November 2011, two librarians from Namibia came for a study visit to Finland, one of whom was more oriented to library management and marketing and the other visitor was a subject librarian with keen interest in IL and information services. During her stay the subject librarian visited the libraries and benchmarked their services. Her main interest was health information and emphasis was on the following topics: the content of information literacy, planning IL education in cooperation with the unit and the information specialists. The subject librarian learnt that the concept of IL is ultimately centered on the user at the two universities. In addition, she found it interesting to see how the teaching of IL was conducted in training labs. This was because the training was practically oriented and then followed with a one on one individual training session.

Further to that, it was important to learn that gathering user feedback in terms of the teaching of IL was pivotal to the improvement of the course. The feedback forms which users had to complete before the end of the lecture were worth considering for implementation at the UNAM Libraries. She also visited several libraries in both cities and became acquainted with all the main functions of the library. More specifically she studied the modern services of the health sciences library. In the words of the visiting subject librarian:

> "I was overwhelmed to see a mini collection (Lux Humana) of fiction books in a health sciences library. This just shows that healing and therapy comes in different shapes, bounds and is not limited to health/ medical books only. Reading a good novel is another form of therapy and it is a good idea that we could adopt at our libraries to blend our collections".

The conversations with colleagues in Finland played a key role during the whole visit.

The information literacy recommendations have provided a solid backbone for all the university libraries in Finland although each library has its own way of working in IL. In our opinion, for the Namibian visitors, it is a good thing to see how IL is implemented in two different academic organizations in Finland. The learning outcome is accumulated when the visitor can share and evolve the ideas in her/his organization.

Working seminars

There was a launch seminar in Windhoek, Namibia in October 2011; eight experts from Tampere University Library and Helsinki University Libraries went to Namibia. The seminar was attended by staff from the University of Namibia, Polytechnic of Namibia and other library institutions, all together there were over 40 Namibian participants. The topics covered were evidence-based librarianship, collection development, strategic planning, quality of services and scientific writing and publishing. The feedback from the launching seminar was encouraging. While some indicated that the seminar deepened their understanding of academic library services, others mentioned that it amplified their opportunities for international networking and collaboration. The respondents further agreed that the seminar was beneficial and useful to them in many different ways.

There will be another cooperation seminar in Namibia in April 2012, where there are several topics planned. This seminar will have more presentations and group work around IL issues. There will be eight people going to Namibia from Finland, four of them specialists in IL and information service issues. The UNAM Librarians will present a series of lectures about the information behaviour of students, staff and researchers and the UNAM IL education programme initiative, and we will work together on this issue. One session will give an outlook of the Finnish IL education landscape, where the speakers will present the national framework for IL in Finland and an overview of IL education in Tampere University Library and Helsinki University Library. One session will be on pedagogical skills, with examples of best practices from real life IL work, the aligned model of information literacy education (planning, execution, evaluation), a case-study of a Bachelor level information seeking course module, problem based learning in IL education for medical students and IL study circles for library staff. We will have team work in the second seminar as that was found fruitful in the launching seminar. We will also be practicing pedagogical methods with some preliminary reading tasks being given to all participants before the seminar.

Both of the seminar programs have been designed and planned together with the Finnish and Namibian partners in order to make the seminar relevant and achieve the kind of learning experience both of us find useful

How the impact of the project will be evaluated

The outcomes of the programme will be reported to the Ministry of Foreign Affairs by the end of 2012. The project period is so short that it is not possible to provide quantitative indicators. We will use qualitative evidence on the impact of the programme, such as the feedback surveys from the seminars, the reports of the study visits, and possible interviews with the UNAM academic staff and students. A peer-reviewed publication will be published at the end of the project and it will partly provide evidence on the impact of the project.

Benefits of the project to the librarians of the three universities

It was discovered that the three universities shared similar benefits as identified by Scherlen, Shao and Cramer (2009) in China and the United States, that international collaboration opens up new perspectives and gives ideas on alternative solutions. Staff members of the participating universities learnt about their different and unique cultures. The project has deepened our understanding about cultural differences. These experiences can be utilized when library staff work with international students and staff in each participating university.

Scherlen, Shao and Cramer (2009) specify that it is important to choose the development areas and after that, focus on these areas. Their idea on dividing the benefits of cooperation into long-term benefits and short-term benefits makes sense (see also Kidd and Roughton, 1994). During the funding application process we defined our objectives, activities, expected results, and indicators of achievement carefully, but the plans need to be readjusted as our understanding about our partner libraries and staff members increases. If we focus on the change issue, we should define more precisely what benefits concerning IL we would like to achieve. We have had a wide variety of topics in our seminars. As we move on with our project, it would be a good idea to focus our attention on some development areas and continue to work with these. It takes time to achieve long term benefits, and which will be lasting benefits can only be assessed after the project. After we have shared ideas on IL education in the April 2012 seminar the experts in Namibia could focus on those areas in IL education they find useful and train the trainers.

The project has increased the awareness of the different library services in various sections of the participating universities. This has provided an opportunity to network with academic staff who work with similar development projects. We can also expect that the staff members participating in these visits, exchange programs and cooperation seminars will have improved motivation and inspiration to develop their work. Kidd and Roughton (1994, p.297), who made an extensive study of international exchange programs in academic libraries, drew the conclusion on the benefits that: "Most staff members experienced improved motivation as a result of their exchange."

In the participating Finnish universities, the project provides an opportunity to view our own practices through the eyes of the outsiders. As we prepare the programme for the collaborative seminars, exchange ideas on the web, or present our activities for the visiting UNAM staff members, we are compelled to evaluate our own practices and expose ourselves to the sharp questions of the outsiders. Self-evidently, those staff members who are the most involved benefit most. In the events and through written communication, all staff members have a chance to reflect on their own work and become acquainted with the Namibian visitors and library services.

Suggestions on the way forward

The following experiences could be tapped by UNAM library to ensure that IL is adopted, implemented and becomes part of the curriculum:

- In the words of Amunga (2011), there is a need for all information professionals to meet and collectively develop a national IL policy.
- The UNAM library can learn from their Finnish counterparts and appoint an IL coordinator for all IL activities such as training and support for IL teachers, and planning of joint practices such as feedback collection, the use of statistics, marketing and sharing best practice between campuses
- The UNAM library could carry out a study on the perceived challenges of implementing an IL course at UNAM (if there are any)
- The current crop of students trained in IL could be used to advocate for the implementation of an IL course at UNAM Library.

Conclusions

The success factors of this project have been that commitment from both partners has been forthcoming. In addition, networking and collaboration between staff members from all partners continues to bear fruitful results and we are determined to continue to network. The project not only involves the exchange of knowledge and expertise, but it also promotes well-being at work by entailing mutual sharing and enthusiasm into daily activities. Seeing innovation from other libraries and putting this to good use in one's own library is a positive outcome of any collaboration. It is obvious that each library could have carried on their development work on their own and reached similar results eventually. The gem of this project is the collegial support and pressure which make the participating staff members work harder. Organizing events and preparing presentations and papers also put pressure on each participant. Creativity stems from right kind of pressure.

References

Ahola, M., & Asplund, J. (2010). The possibilities and challenges of social media in the work practices of university libraries: Tampere University Library Case Study. In *Discover new ways of working in the linked and social web*, pp. 141-150. Online Information 2010 Conference Proceedings. London: Incisive Media.

Amunga, H.A. (2001). *Information literacy in 21st century universities: the Kenyan experience.* Retrieved from: http://ir.inflibnet.ac.in/dxml/bitstream/handle/1944/1636/44.pdf?sequence=1

Anglada, L. M. (2007). Collaborations and alliances: social intelligence applied to academic libraries. *Library Management*, 28(6/7), 406 – 415.

Appleton, L., Stevenson V., & Boden, D. (2011). Developing learning landscapes: academic libraries driving organisational change. *Reference Services Review, 39*(3), 343-361

Asplund, J. (2011). *Yliopistokirjastot ovat kansainvälisesti aktiivisia.* Retrieved from: http://synblogi.wordpress.com/2011/10/31/yliopistokirjastot-ovat-kansainvalisesti-aktiivisia/

Bundy, A. (2003). A window of opportunity: libraries in higher education. *Library Management, 24*(8/9), 393-400.

Finnish recommendation for universities for including information literacy in the new degree structures. (2004). Retrieved from: www.helsinki.fi/infolukutaito/ILopetus/recommendation.pdf

Heino, T. (2010). *Continuing education/professional development for information literacy teachers at the Helsinki University Library.* Retrieved from: www.apdis.pt/eahil2010/en/images/stories/docs/fulltexts/e2_05_heino_full.pdf

Helminen, P. (2007). Ensimmäisen vuoden opiskelijan informaatiolukutaidon perusvalmiudet: Helsingin yliopiston tvt-ajokortti. In A. Nevgi (Ed.), *Informaatiolukutaito yliopisto-opetuksessa.* (pp. 183-196). Helsinki: Palmenia, Helsinki University Press.

Huotari, M-L., & Iivonen, M. (2005). Knowledge processes: a strategic foundation for the partnership between the university and its library. *Library Management, 26*(6/7), 324-335.

Iivonen, M., Tevaniemi, J., & Toivonen, L. (2007). Informaatiolukutaidon opetus – kumppanuutta käytännössä. In A. Nevgi (Ed.), *Informaatiolukutaito yliopisto-opetuksessa.* (pp. 147-165). Helsinki: Palmenia, Helsinki University Press.

Jankowska, M. A., & Marshall, L. (2003). Why social interaction and good communication in academic libraries matters. *Reference Librarian, 40*(83/84), 131-144.

Juntunen, A., Lehto, A., Tevaniemi, J., & Saarti, J. (2008). Supporting information literacy in Finnish University Libraries – standards, projects and online education. In J. Lau (Ed.) *Information literacy: international perspectives.* Munchen : K. G. Saur. IFLA publications; 131.

Kidd, T., & Roughton, K. (1994). International staff exchanges for academic libraries. *Journal of Academic Librarianship, 20*(5/6), 295-299

Kuhn, I., Barker, C., Birkwood, K., Carty, C., & Tumelty, N. (2011). *TeachMeet – librarians learning from each other. University of Cambridge Medical Library.* Retrieved from: www.dspace.cam.ac.uk/bitstream/1810/237027/3/eahil2011_teachmeetkuhn.pdf

Neyer, L., & Yelinek, K. (2011). Beyond Boomer meets NextGen: examining mentoring practices among Pennsylvania academic librarians. *The Journal of Academic Librarianship, 37*(3), 215–221.

Scherlen, A., Shao, X., & Cramer, E. (2009). Bridges to China: developing partnerships between serials librarians in the United States and China. *Serials Review, 35*(2), 75–79.

Information Literacy Education in Higher Education Institutions in South Africa

Leoné Tiemensma
Midrand Graduate Institute, South Africa
leonet@mgi.ac.za

Abstract

Many students in South Africa come from a disadvantaged background and lack information literacy skills needed in academic studies. There is an under-provision of computer and internet facilities as well as library resources. Only 7% of schools in South Africa have a functional library. Challenges are enormous. Information literacy skills are very important to information/library science students. As librarians they will be the ones that will help their user communities to become information literate and to act as facilitators of learning. Information skills tuition is not just about learning about specific tools, but a process that involves identifying an information need, finding and critically using resources to meet that need, managing the information found as well as understanding the information environment. Developing information skills for lifelong learning is the ultimate goal, as Pinto, Cordon & Diaz (2010) states: "to create people who learn throughout their entire lives, and who are capable of resolving their information needs by finding, evaluating and using information to resolve problems or take decisions." An overabundance of information and rapid developments in information technology information necessitate approaches and tools to satisfy information needs. In this paper the standards and benchmarks with which to measure information literacy competencies will be highlighted briefly. Approaches and tools taught to information science students at a leading South Africa university will be discussed. The focus is on the following learning outcomes: the student should be able to plan an information task, to retrieve information for an information task, to organize the information, to use various reading and thinking skills and to complete an information task. These approaches and tools can also be applied in information literacy training and staff development programs in the workplace.

Introduction

The concept of Information Literacy emerged in the 1970s with the development of new technologies. Online technology development and sophisticated electronic retrieval systems have a huge impact on the information environment and particularly on the library environment in terms of information literacy. The means of accessing information as well as the format in which information is stored has changed. Books and electronic resources organise information in different ways. In order to access and locate electronic databases, specific information literacy skills are expected from the user. During the Colloquium on Information Literacy and Lifelong Learning held 2005 at the Bibliotheca Alexandrina it was proclaimed that Information Literacy and lifelong learning are the beacons of the Information Society (IFLA, 2006).

Developing information skills for lifelong learning is the ultimate goal, as Pinto, Cordon and Diaz (2010) states: "to create people who learn throughout their entire lives, and who are capable of resolving their information needs by finding, evaluating and using information to resolve problems or take decisions." Information literacy would include information skills, library skills, information technology skills, academic literacy and media literacy. The need for information depends on particular circumstances and needs. Each individual has his own background and experience in terms of information literacy. To be information literate, one should be aware of possible sources of information as well as the routes to get to that information to fulfil an information need.

The importance of information literacy is recognised beyond formal educational environments to communities, the workplace and other institutions. Developing an information literate person is a continuing process, as the information world is constantly developing and changing. Information literacy development should thus be seen in a wider context than an individual's personal Information Literacy landscape to include the broader information landscape.

The need for Information Literacy (IL) skills by learners at all levels in the education system and especially at higher education level has been widely documented by international bodies such as the International Federation of Library Associations (IFLA, 2006), the United Nations Economic, Social and Cultural Organisation (UNESCO) (Ito, 2008), national bodies such as the Society of College, National and University Libraries (SCONUL) in the United Kingdom (SCONUL, 2011), the American Library Association (ALA) and the Association of College and Research Libraries (ACRL) (Saunders, 2009).

An overabundance of information and the continuous development of new information technologies necessitate approaches and tools to satisfy information needs. Developing information literacy is not just about learning about specific tools, but a process that involves identifying an information need, finding and critically using resources to meet that need, managing the information found as well as understanding the information environment. In this paper these approaches and tools at higher education level in South Africa will be discussed.

Information literacy: theoretical framework

In the 21st century IL is a key attribute for each individual. At the World Summit on the Information Society (WSIS 2003) the *Geneva declaration* no. 29 stated that "each person should have the opportunity to acquire the necessary skills and knowledge in order to understand, participate actively in, and benefit fully from, the Information Society". IL stretches further than an educational context, and impacts on the broader context of society, work, economic activities and well being. Sayed defines IL as the lifelong ability to access sources of information, locate information and critically evaluate information, not only in the academic environment, but also on the work and home fronts (1998).

In UNESCO's concept of IL and knowledge societies (Ito, 2008), IL is shown as the foundation on which knowledge societies should be built. In this model, IL enables access to information and develops the ability to supply and use information. Social participation, learning, cultural expression is the result thereof and that can lead to development, prosperity and freedom in building knowledge societies.

According to Britz and Lor (2010) limited IL skills have negative abilities:

- It affects the ability to access relevant and accurate information;
- The inability to make meaningful use of retrieved information not only limits our choices, but also limits our ability to participate in the different information-based socio-economic and other activities.

The American Library Association (ALA) and the Association of College and Research Libraries (ACRL) have actively promoted IL as necessary for an informed society in general and especially for students in higher education institutions (Saunders, 2009). The focus in this article is on IL in higher education. IL in an academic setting is different from what could be considered information literacy in an everyday or in the workplace setting. Students do not only need to access information, but ought to have the necessary skills and knowledge to find, use and manage information effectively.

There are various IL models to teach IL competencies in the higher education environment. The Association of College and Research Libraries "Information literacy competency standards for higher education" (2000) identify five standards that an information literate student should meet:

- Determines the nature and extent of the information needed;
- Accesses needed information effectively and efficiently;
- Evaluates information and its sources critically and incorporates selected information into his/her knowledge base;
- Uses information effectively to accomplish a specific purpose;
- Understands the economic, legal and social issues surrounding the use of information and accesses and uses information ethically and legally.

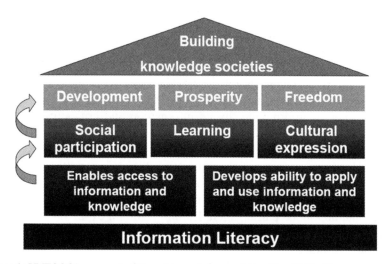

Figure 1: UNESCO's concept of IL and knowledge societies (Ito, 2008 p7).

Searching for information is often seen as a *process*. Kuhlthau (2004) developed the Information Search Model – that describes information seeking as a sense-making learning process of different phases each with its own strategies. Kuhlthau further suggests that the purpose of a library's IL education program is to develop student's insight into the process of information handling and into how each if its phases connect.

The Eisenberg and Berkowitz (1990) model known as the Big6 is an information problem-solving model that integrates information searching and use skills in a systematic process. The six stages of the Big6 model are:

Stage 1: Task definition
- Define the information problem;
- Identify information needed to solve the information problem;
Stage 2: Information seeking strategies
- Determine possible sources;
- Select the best sources;

Stage 3: Locate and access information
- Locate sources (intellectually and physically);
- Find information within sources;

Stage 4: Use of information
- Engage (e.g. read, view);
- Extract relevant information from a source;

Stage 5: Synthesis
- Organize information from multiple sources;
- Present the information;

Stage 6: Evaluation
- Judge the product (effectiveness);
- Judge the information problem-solving process (efficiency).

The Big6 is a widely used approach to teaching IL. Information seekers go through these Big6 stages when they seek information to solve a problem or to make a decision. This model is a very helpful framework to develop an IL course.

The SCONUL (Society of College, National and University Libraries) Working Group on Information Literacy in the UK developed a model "Seven Pillars of Information Skills". This model has been adopted by librarians and teachers around the world (SCONUL, 2011). This model defines the core skills and competencies (ability) and attitudes and behaviours (understanding) at the heart of IL development in higher education and encompasses the following (SCONUL 2011):

- Identify: Able to identify a personal need for information;
- Scope: Can access current knowledge and identify gaps;
- Plan: Can construct strategies for locating information and data;
- Gather: Can locate and access the information and data they need;
- Evaluate: Can review the research process and compare and evaluate information and data;
- Manage: Can organise information professionally and ethically ;
- Present: Can apply the knowledge gained: presenting the results of their research, synthesising new and old information and data to create new knowledge and disseminating it in a variety of ways.

These models share a number of elements, for example the ability to access information, evaluation of information, presentation of information and the understanding of ethical practices involved with information. These or other models could be used as basis to develop IL education programs.

 **SCONUL**   **Seven Pillars of Information Literacy**

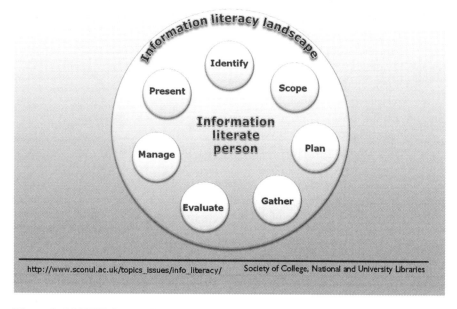

Figure 2: SCONUL Seven Pillars of Information Literacy (SCONUL, 2011)

Librarians as facilitators of learning and their role in information literacy education

Librarians as facilitators of learning are "the interface between the work required of students and researchers and their information needs" (Esterhuizen and Kuhn, 2010; p.88). Information Literacy education has become a core function of academic libraries across the globe. Academic libraries subscribe to expensive electronic information resources and librarians should ensure that their users are effectively trained to use these databases.

Librarians can use their expertise to assist students. Librarians have expertise in analysing a topic, identifying information needs, finding information in web pages, databases, journals and books, evaluating the quality of information sources and citing and managing references (Toteng, Hoskins and Bell, 2010). Academic librarians can act as facilitators to teach a wider range of IL skills and competencies. Students need to be made aware of the role of librarians in assisting students in the IL process.

Information literacy skills are important to information science students. As librarians they will be the ones that can act as facilitators of learning and help their user communities to become information literate. Ongoing training for librarians is an issue that needs constant attention. Practicing librarians should keep track with trends and developments.

Library / faculty collaboration

One of the findings of research on IL education at tertiary level highlighted the need for collaboration and partnerships between librarians and faculties as a key issue (Hart and Davids, 2010; Lawal, Underwood, Lwehabura and Stilwell, 2010). Many academics assume that students have already acquired IL skills. They do not recognise the need for IL education and argue that students should not spend time on activities that do not contribute to their official assignments and study. This poses a great challenge to IL educators who wish to implement IL programmes. The major recommendations of the Hart and Davids study (2010) are that more periods in the timetable should be allocated to IL and that lecturers should recognise the educational role of librarians.

IL as part of a university's educational strategy cannot be achieved by librarians alone. Collaborative partnerships between librarians and academic staff as well as support from management will be needed to accept librarians as facilitators of IL education. IL training should be part of the institution's policy. The responsibility of IL programmes as part of the educational strategy of the institution thus goes further than the library.

Information literacy education in South Africa

A National Benchmark Tests Project by the association HESA (Higher Education South Africa) showed that in terms of academic literacy 47% of the students were proficient in English, the dominant language of higher education and 7% had only "basic" academic literacy skills (MacGregor, 2009). From this Benchmark Project it was also clear that South Africa's school system is continuing to fail its learners and that universities will need to do a lot more to tackle what appear to be growing proficiency gaps.

Various research studies on IL at higher education level have been undertaken in Southern Africa, for example Sayed (1998), De Jager and Nassimbeni (2003), Toteng, Hoskins and Bell (2010) and Hart and Davids (2010). Findings of research on IL education at tertiary level highlighted key issues for IL education (Hart and Davids 2010: 28):

- The under-preparedness of students for university education;
- The need for collaboration between librarians and faculties;
- Challenges in assessing information literacy programmes;

 – The challenges and opportunities of information and communication technologies.

The general finding is that a huge number of students are not equipped for the demands of university education. There is a lack of skills in the use of electronic resources, information evaluation, including internet information and computer use.

Many students in South Africa come from a disadvantaged background and do not have information literacy skills needed in academic studies. There is an under-provision of computer and internet facilities as well as library resources. Only 7 % of schools in South Africa have a functional library. IL at school and community level is under-developed. There are significant differences between students from historically advantaged and historically disadvantaged environments. Because of these differences IL programs should take previous experiences into account. Other reasons documented why students are not prepared for university studies include:

 – Varied socio-economic and cultural backgrounds;
 – In a country with 11 official languages, for most students English is a second, or even third or fourth language. English is the lingua franca in South Africa, although only 8% South Africans use English as their home language;
 – A rote learning experience;
 – The particular and diverse nature and language of academic discourse. (Jansen, 2004; Van Rensburg and Lamberti, 2004).

Computer literacy is an important component of IL. Prior computer literacy might contribute student IL. Computer literacy instruction is not the norm in South African schools and the computer skills of incoming students range from highly proficient to non-existent (Hart and Davids, 2010). In the digital world of the 21st century, students need to be able to use online resources successfully. Most students seeking information use the Internet as first choice, but are unable to evaluate the credibility of the sources.

The concern that students lack the ability to find and use information, resulted in a *LIS Transformation Charter* of the National Council for Library and Information Services. This Charter identifies IL education as a priority for academic libraries (*LIS transformation charter,* 2009). The South African Qualifications Authority (SAQA) lists IL as a cross-field critical outcome for students. From the late 1990s higher education institutions have been engaged in curriculum reform to bring their academic programs in line with the National Qualifications Framework of SAQA (Esterhuizen and Kuhn, 2010). Draft national IL training guidelines for university libraries were compiled under the auspices of the Committee for Higher Education Libraries of South Africa (CHELSA). Data about existing IL programmes was gathered via surveys, webinars, and written submissions from participants (Esterhuizen and Kuhn, 2010). Consensus was reached on the guidelines and core competencies to be included in IL training. The value of these guidelines is the promotion of a common core curriculum for IL at university level in South Africa. Although this is an ongoing process, these guidelines provide a basis to work from.

According to De Jager and Nassimbeni (2005) a large number of institutions and libraries in South Africa are including IL training in their strategic mission statements and acknowledge the need for IL skills for graduates. It is, however, not always clear what, when and how IL should be taught. CHELSA advised that each higher education institution should deal in their own preferred way with matters such as:

- Accreditation of the training program;
- Decision on whether the offerings should be compulsory or not;
- Selection and usage of available training materials according to need;
- Adoption of training methods;
- Participation of academics in the compilation and offering of the IL training program (Esterhuizen and Kuhn, 2010).

Institutions which offer Library and Information Science in South Africa have declined the last few years, mainly due to the merger of many higher education institutions. Another trend is that Library and Information Science schools are merging with other disciples and the focus is on areas such as information and knowledge management, information technology, multimedia, information systems technology, and not librarianship.

Information literacy programs: different options

Few universities make any structured provision for developing IL skills. An investigation into the status quo of IL programmes at universities in South Africa showed that programmes are either compulsory or voluntary, range from basic to advanced IL teaching, and teaching methods vary from online to contact or mixed teaching methods. A wide variety of IL practices exists. It is often a problem to attract students to attend IL instruction sessions when the programme is not mandatory. Librarians play an important role in presenting IL programmes.

Library instruction

At some universities, for example the University of Pretoria (UP) and the University of South Africa (UNISA), a distinction between IL and library instruction is made. Library instruction is considered a subset of IL. Library instruction is compulsory for first year students at UP, and at UNISA the onus is on the student to book for library skills training. At UNISA the training in library skills consists of two separate training units, which, in the end, form one unit. These two units are: Basic Library Skills and Advanced Library Skills. The basic library skills training focuses on how to find your way around the UNISA library. This two hour training session is aimed at new undergraduate and postgraduate students and equips students with the knowledge and skills of how to use the Library and its resources effectively. This training includes orientation in the library (Library Tour), understanding information literacy, finding library material and using library services/facilities, procedures for borrowing, returning and renewing books and library etiquette. The Advanced Library Skills training is aimed at the various sources of information, including both online and printed reference sources. The ethical use of information (plagiarism and copyright) is also covered, as well as distinguishing between printed and online sources, defining reference sources, characteristics of reference sources. Training in the use of the UNISA Library Catalogue with details of nearly two million items is also given and that includes basic search skills (author, title, journal, etc.) and advanced searching skills (how to refine a search to retrieve more relevant information and how to download) (UNISA 2012). Two workshops for students run by the Cape Peninsula University of Technology in Cape Town cover the library's online public access catalogue (OPAC), the library's electronic databases (for example EbscoHost), and referencing techniques, and included hand-on practice. At Midrand Graduate Institute first year students across faculties get instructed on library use and basic information literacy skills. This is part of an induction/orientation program, but is not compulsory.

Full course

There have been arguments that an IL course should be integrated into the academic curriculum across subject fields (Lawal, Underwood, Lwehabura and Stilwell, 2010). At the University of Pretoria a full course on IL is a compulsory course to all first year students and they get credit for this course. It is offered by the Department of Information Science (Bothma, Underwood, and Ngulube, 2007). At UNISA a course *Developing information skills for lifelong learning* is compulsory for Information Science students. Students from other departments can also enrol for this course, but it is not compulsory.

Online

In the 21st century universities and their libraries focus more and more on distance education services. There is a need to develop online programmes and resources and there is a shift to the application of e-strategies. The Cape Peninsula University of Technology (CPUT) has developed an online information literacy course. This Information Literacy course was implemented by institutions of the Cape Higher Education Consortium. It takes the users through the information literacy process in five steps (Lockhart, 2011)[1]. This online course is compulsory for all first year students and they write an online test after completing the course. At the University of North West, an online Computer and IL module is also compulsory for first year students.

CHELSA information literacy survey 2011

CHELSA did an Information Literacy Survey in 2011 among 22 universities. A summary of the responses revealed the following (Pearce et al, 2011):

- All of them (100%) offer an information literacy training programme in their library;
- Components covered in this programme: Library orientation/basic library skills (95.2%), using the library online catalogue (100%), using electronic databases (95.2%), using the Internet (e.g. Google Scholar) (90.5%), referencing and plagiarism (95.2%), and other components (47.6%) such as evaluating information, search strategies, identify keywords, and information sources;
- The IL program of more than two thirds (71.4%) is subject/discipline/faculty specific;
- The majority of respondents (85.7%) do not have the IL program integrated in all curricula;
- Most of the IL training programs (86.4%) are not SAQA (South African Qualifications Authority) accredited;
- The responsibility for offering the IL training program at the institution lies with dedicated full time trainer librarian(s) (45.5%), Library and Information Science Department (18.2%), Faculty/Academic staff (18.2) and other such as subject librarians, reference library staff, faculty librarians, and trained lecturers (77.3%);
- Student assessment on IL skills is done via a generic assignment with multiple choice questions (84.2%), a formal test (21.1%), a formal discipline specific assignment (26.3%) or a self-marking quiz with results sent to the lecturer//librarians (36.8%);

---

1   This course is available at: http: ixion.cput.ac.za/library_2/infoLit/index.html or at www.lib. uct.ac.za/infolit/index.html

- The majority of respondents (90.5%) have the support of the university management and/or faculty for the IL training program;
- All the institutions have an IL training coordinator.

From this survey it is clear that IL training is a priority on the agenda of most higher education institutions in South Africa, although a number of issues need to be addressed. Assessment guidelines and quality assurance measurement need to be refined.

Conclusion

The challenges of new technologies demand that students have essential information literacy skills that enable them to resolve their information needs. A lack of IL skills indicates a need for IL education. Higher education institutions offer information literacy education to help students understand the importance of information and to have the competency to manage information. Challenges are still enormous to reach a wider audience and to address IL education in South Africa. Information Literacy training is an ongoing process. There exists a wide variety of IL practices and guidelines and core competencies that need to be included in IL training have been identified. The changes that information technology brought have not only changed the needs of users, but also the role of librarians. The library can be a key role-player in an empowering environment. IL education is accepted as part of academic librarians' mission. The main conclusion is that IL education needs a strong place in academic programmes and that the best facilitator of this learning is the librarian. Librarians as IL specialists are educational partners. Librarians are learners as well as teachers.

References

Association of College and Research Libraries (2000). *Information literacy competency standards for higher education.* Retrieved from the ALA website: www.ala.org.ala.mgrps/divs/acrl/standards/standards.pdf

Bothma, T.D.J., Underwood, P., & Ngulube, P. (Eds.). (nd). *Libraries for the future: progress and development of South African libraries.* Pretoria: LIASA. Retrieved from: www.dissanet.com.jsp/ifla/book.jsp

Britz, J., & Lor, P. (2010). The right to be information literate: the core foundation of the knowledge society. *Innovation,* 41, 8-24.

De Jager, K., & Nassimbeni, M. (2003). An exploration of the current status of information literacy tuition in South Africa tertiary institutions and proposals for curriculum design. *South African Journal of Libraries and Information Science,* 69(2), 108-114.

Eisenberg, M., & Berkowitz, R. (1990). *Information problem solving: the Big 6 approach to library and information skills instruction.* Norwood: Ablex.

Esterhuizen, E.,& Kuhn, R. (2010). CHELSA draft guidelines on Information Literacy: paving the way to a South African national framework? *Innovation,* 41, 83-106.

Hart, G., & Davids, M. (2010). Challenges for information literacy education at a university of technology. *Innovation,* 41, 25-41.

International Federation of Library Associations and Institutions. (2006). *Beacons of the information society: the Alexandria Proclamation on information literacy and lifelong learning.* Retrieved from the IFLA website: archive.ifla.org/111/wsis/BeaconInSoc.html.

Ito, M. (2008). *UNESCO and information literacy.* Paris: UNESCO. Retrieved from: humanit.org/PID/Unesco_april08/Ito_InformationLiteracy.pdf

Jansen, J.D. (2004). Changes and continuities in South Africa's higher education system, 1994-2004. In L. Chisholm (Ed.), *Changing class: education and social change in post-apartheid South Africa* (pp.293-314). Cape Town: Human Sciences Research Council

Jiyane, G.V., & Onyancha, O.B. (2010). Information literacy education and instruction in academic libraries and LIS schools in institutions of higher education in South Africa. *South African Journal of Libraries and Information Science,* 73(2), 11-23.

Kulhthau, C.C. (2004). *Seeking meaning: a process approach to library and information services.* Westport: Libraries Unlimited.

Lawal, V., Underwood, P., Lwehabura, M. & Stilwell, C. (2010). Information literacy for higher education institutions in Nigeria and Tanzania: efforts and prospects for educational reform in teaching and learning. *Innovation,* 41, 42-61.

LIS transformation charter (2009). Pretoria: Department of Arts and Culture and National Council for Library and Information Services. Retrieved from: www.nlsa.ac.za

Peninsula University of Technology (CPUT). *Library Papers and Reports.* Paper 20. Retrieved from: http://dk.cput.ac.za/lib_papers/20

MacGregor, K. (2009). *South Africa: shocking results from university tests.* Retrieved from: www.universityworldnews.com/article.php?story=20090816082

Pearce, Robert J. et al. (2011). *CHELSA information literacy survey.* Port Elizabeth: Nelson Mandela Metropolitan University.

Pinto, M., Cordon, J.,& Diaz, R.G. (2010). Thirty years of information literacy (1977-2007): a terminological, conceptual and statistical analysis. *Journal of Librarianship and Information Science,* 42(1), 3-19.

Saunders, L. (2009). The future of information literacy in academic libraries: a Delphi study. *Portal: Libraries and the Academy,* 9(1), 99-114.

Sayed, Y. (1998). *The segregated information highway: information literacy in higher education.* Cape Town: University of Cape Town Press.

Society of College, National and University Libraries Working Group on Information Literacy (2011). *The SCONUL Seven Pillars of Information Literacy. Core model for higher education.* Retrieved from the SCONUL website: www.sconul.ac.uk/groups/information_literacy/seven_pillars.html

Toteng, B., Hoskins, R., & Bell, F. (2010). Information literacy and law students at the University of Botswana. *Innovation,* 41, 62-82.

University of South Africa (2012). *Library: library training.* Retrieved from the UNISA website: www.unisa.ac.za/library

Van Rensburg, W., & Lamberti, P. (2004). Language of learning and teaching in higher education. In: S. Gravett & H.Geyser (Eds.), *Teaching and learning in higher education* (pp. 67-89). Pretoria: Van Schaik

World Summit on the Information Society (2003). *The Geneva declaration:building the information society: a global challenge in the new millennium.* Geneva: WSIS Executive Secretariat. Retrieved from: www.itu.int/wsis/docs/geneva/official/dop.html.

Raising Librarians' Disciplinary Information Literacy: Can Libguides Help?

Jana Varlejs

Associate Professor Emerita, Rutgers – The State University of New Jersey
varlejs@rutgers.edu

Abstract

There are many continuing education opportunities for academic librarians responsible for information literacy instruction, ranging from immersion institutes to webinars, listservs, and voluminous literature. Usually focus is on
pedagogy or technology, with emphasis on generic information finding skills.
Rarely covered through professional development is how librarians learn
enough about unfamiliar curricular areas in order to guide students toward information literacy in the context of disciplines. If one assumes that librarians
must know enough to lead students not only to sources but also to an understanding of scholarly communication in a particular subject field, then how can
that knowledge be acquired? Using chemistry and physics as examples of
fields less likely than humanities and social sciences to have expert subject librarians, LibGuides for those disciplines were examined to see if they appeared to be authored by experts and could serve novice science librarians as a
means of professional development. The study confirmed the value of learning
from others' LibGuides. When asked about the worth of a librarianship qualification versus a science degree, most had a preference for the library qualification, but agreed the latter would help. Librarians who had a science degree
said it enabled them to understand how science worked and made them more
effective.

Introduction

Writing about the challenges of being a new academic subject librarian in an
unfamiliar technical field (mathematics), John Meier (2010a) emphasizes the
importance of forging relationships with faculty, consulting relevant professional guidelines, and seeking informal advice from colleagues. He cites a
study showing that in addition to reference and collection development, the
subject librarian is frequently expected to provide instruction in information

resources (White, 1999), which is borne out by current position announcements. Another study by Meier (2010b) of science librarian responsibilities, including instruction, found those to be more numerous than what they were in the past. Thinking about the array of disciplines that typically appear in North American college and university curricula, it is difficult to imagine how a library staff in all but the largest and wealthiest schools could be equally competent across the entire range of subjects. Since the library/information science (LIS) profession continues to attract primarily humanities and social sciences degree holders (Kim, Chiu, Sin and Robbins, 2007; p. 538), it is easy to understand why it is hard to fill science librarian positions with degree holders in both LIS and science. To add to the dilemma, only 30 percent of LIS education programs offer a course in science and technology information, and about half of those do not do so with "reasonable frequency" (Murphy, 2008). The challenge of recruiting science librarians has been affirmed repeatedly, although the question of hiring specialists versus generalists remains unsettled (Kreitz and DeVries, 2006).

Information literacy (IL) instruction courses are increasing in MLIS programs but are still far from ubiquitous (Westbrock and Fabian, 2010, p. 573). There are, however, many opportunities outside of LIS schools to learn basic IL principles and techniques (Varlejs, 2008). There are immersion programs, workshops, and numerous conferences (American Library Association (ALA), (2011a); the literature is huge (Johnson, Sproles and Detmering, 2011); there is a highly active listserv with a searchable archive[1]; and modular tutorials and animated videos are available for sharing and adapting. The overwhelming focus of all these resources is on fundamentals of instruction, generic concepts of IL, and on implementation issues, rather than on content and scholarly communication in different subject fields. Familiarity with their field, however, makes a difference in subject librarians' effectiveness (Schmidt and Reznik-Zellen, 2011).

There are of course ways to learn and keep up with disciplines. One is to attend subject-specific conferences (Tomaszewski and MacDonald, 2009). It is possible to find literature on IL in various disciplines and professions, but it is sparse, and it is more likely to be published in journals on education for specific fields than in LIS literature (Johnson et al., 2011, p. 551). While LIS research does encompass information behaviour of scientists, knowledge useful for developing IL programs for science students and serving as liaison to faculty, it may not suffice for the librarian unfamiliar with how science works or what comprises its essential knowledge base. To echo Meier, the would-be science librarian who lacks relevant academic preparation must learn on the job as best he or she can.

---

1   ili-l@ala.org

Information literacy and subject expertise

According to Ann Grafstein, the scant attention paid to information in the disciplines is a byproduct of an academic librarianship that sees itself as information rather than subject-centric:

> "The literature conveys a widely held belief that because the content of disciplines is constantly changing, subject content cannot be taught effectively; therefore, teaching should focus on process. As succinctly stated by Maureen Pastine and Linda Wilson, for example, "[t]he process of research is more important than the product" (Grafstein, 2002, p. 200).

Grafstein contends that "An understanding of the discipline, and not simply critical thinking skills, is what provides students with the tools to evaluate research critically in that discipline" (p. 202). Her answer to the process versus content question is to assert that librarians and faculty should share responsibility, course by course, where librarians teach "enabling skills" and faculty teach skills needed for "subject-specific inquiry and research" (p. 202). But faculty often ignore this role, leaving responsibility to librarians (Badke, 2010). If we agree with the standard definition of IL as promulgated in the Association for College & Research Libraries' (ACRL) *Information Literacy Competency Standards for Higher Education* (ALA, 2000), process skills are not enough. In fact, the rationale preceding the six parts of the definition states that IL "enables learners to master content and extend their investigations, become more self-directed, and assume greater control over their own learning." This suggests that IL and content are closely related.

There are signs that the reign of process teaching may be lessening its hold; see, for example, ACRL's wiki on IL and disciplines (ALA, 2011b). One link leads to an article by Leah Solla (2003), the Cornell chemistry librarian, on the importance of the librarian's knowledge of the discipline as a foundation for helping students become "literate in chemical information," which has unique literature and retrieval characteristics. Pali Kuruppu (2006), in a review of the literature on recruiting science subject specialists versus generalists, states that "For science and technology (sci-tech) librarians to be effective, thorough knowledge of the relevant information resources of the discipline they serve is essential and expected" (p. 11). A survey of sci-tech librarians, however, found that while 95 percent of respondents had an MLS degree, only 50 percent had a science background (Eells, 2006), suggesting professional development for science librarians has special urgency. Discussion of and resources for education and continuing professional development for science librarianship can be found in the aforementioned ACRL wiki, as well as in a special issue of *Science & Technology Libraries* on recruitment (2006, v.27, no.1-2). An interesting approach to professional development focused on science rather than on librarianship is the series of "boot camps" arranged by Massachusetts librarians, featuring science faculty who present their research and explain their disciplines in language lay persons can follow (Schmidt and Reznik-Zellen, 2011). This initiative is similar to Meier's (2010a) description of attending faculty seminars and finding other ways to learn about a discipline from experts.

Learning from colleagues

Meier mentions that one way to learn to become a subject librarian in an unfamiliar, technical discipline is to draw on colleagues' expertise. He does not discuss how librarians informally learn from each other, but professional meetings, listservs, and professional literature seem obvious means. He mentions the professional association guidelines. An excellent example of one that includes resources as well as IL principles has been developed by the Special Libraries Association (SLA) Chemistry Division, together with the American Chemical Society's Division of Chemical Information (SLA, 2011). Getting help from colleagues is easy through specialized listservs.[2]

If the novice science librarian needs to go beyond these sources and identify colleagues with specific expertise, one can scan the LIS literature for indications of authors' command of their discipline's content, and then look for their research guides on their library's websites. Or, find those academic institutions that are known for excellence in the sciences and see what research guidance their librarians provide. One can check the Carnegie Classifications (Carnegie, 2010) list of institutions with Doc/STEM programs (offering PhDs in science, technology, engineering, and mathematics) and search their library websites for subject guides. Using the Carnegie Classifications it is possible to identify institutions similar to one's own and thus have a realistic base for comparison. Many library websites will have a list of librarians with their subject/liaison responsibilities and contact information.

Once academic libraries of interest have been identified, an efficient way to find and compare subject guides is to use the list of subscribers to Springshare's LibGuides. The Springshare company offers content management software designed to ease the production of subject and course guides and provide a degree of consistency within and across academic libraries. As of January 2012, Springshare claimed that over 2,000 libraries had mounted some 125,000 guides, all open on the Internet for anyone to consult. In most cases, the authors of a subject

---

2   For example, ALA's science and technology list, sts-l@listserv.utk.edu; the chemical information sources list cheminf-l@listserv.indiana.edu; SLA's physics-astronomy-mathematics list, PAMnet@listserv.nd.edu.

LibGuide are identified, although too often it is hard to find information about their qualifications. True to its name, Springshare encourages sharing content. A librarian who is responsible for IL instruction in chemistry, for example, but has no training in that subject, could adapt a guide published by another library with a similar profile and an expert chemistry librarian.

Methodology

To test how useful it might be to browse Springshare to help a novice prepare guides in chemistry and physics, sample libraries were selected using a list of 272 academic institutions classified by the Carnegie Foundation as "Undergraduate Profile="FT4/MS/LTI," which means that students attend mostly full time for four years, and that admission is "more" selective and "less" accepting of transfer students. This category was chosen in an effort to focus on colleges and universities likely to have traditional liberal arts curricula, high calibre students and faculty, and good libraries. The list does indeed include Ivy League, Oberlin group, and other highly regarded academic institutions.

This list was matched against the Springshare LibGuides community list, and then further reduced by eliminating those institutions with fewer than 50 guides. Exceptions were made for the four that had below 50 guides but were identified as "Doc/STEM" dominant, on the theory that they most likely had librarians with science qualifications. The resulting list of institutions was searched for chemistry and physics subject guides and their authors. In six cases an institution was eliminated because it had neither chemistry nor physics in its curriculum, or no librarian currently holding a position associated with either discipline.

Except for sharing the same Carnegie Classification, the institutions in the final list vary widely; e.g., student body size ranges from 825 to 50,691. It seemed useful to determine a median size so that results could take that difference into account. The median number of students, again based on Carnegie data, is 7037.5.

A basic examination of each chemistry and physics guide first sought to identify the author. The decision to make the librarian rather than the institution the unit of analysis is congruent with the focus of this study on the opportunities librarians new to a discipline might have to learn from those with experience in the subject. The following initial questions were posed:

1. What is the title of the librarian, generic or specific to the subject?
2. What academic or other qualifications does the librarian have?

In addition to the examination of LibGuides in chemistry and physics, inquiries were sent to members of the Springshares Lounge and to science librarian subscribers to the ALA's IL instruction listserv (ILI-L). The message sent to the Lounge and ILI list stated:

> "I am interested in learning about science librarians' experience with developing and maintaining chemistry and physics LibGuides. Do you have an academic background in science, e.g., BA in chemistry, etc.? If not, how do you learn what you need to know in order to prepare a LibGuide? Also, how do you see the relative value of having an MLS or science degree-which is more important?"

Findings from Springshare LibGuides exploration

It quickly became apparent that it would not be easy to answer the question about educational backgrounds of LibGuide authors, nor to ascertain the correct job title. This is true, despite the fact that the LibGuides template has a standard space for adding the position title as well as contact information and more in a sidebar to the body of a guide, and allows for links to be made to directories and biographical information. For example, job titles given in a LibGuide often differ from those in a staff directory, and links to "profile" often don't lead to information about educational background. In many cases, Google was more helpful than a library's website. In those cases where a librarian had created a profile on LinkedIn, it was especially easy to find the relevant data.

For the purpose of this study, "science background" was interpreted broadly, including teaching high school science and experience in a technical or health sciences setting. The most frequent fields of study that could be identified were the biological sciences and chemistry. Table 1 summarizes the educational background of librarian authors of chemistry and physics LibGuides.

Education	Number of Librarians
MLS/MLIS	92
No MLS/MLIS	4
No MLS/MLIS data	42
Science background	53
No science background	31
No science education data	54

*One librarian who is shared by two colleges is counted twice

Table 1. Librarians and their Educational Background (n=138*)

It has to be acknowledged that the 84 cases where the presence or absence of a science background could be determined are not readily compared, despite sharing the same Carnegie Classification. The most obvious difference is that of size, as indicated by the number of students. Even using the median (7,037.5) to divide the institutions into smaller and larger is not especially helpful, as the ranges are very wide: 825 to 6,996 and 7,079 to 50,691.

Of the 31 librarians who do not have a bachelor's or master's degree in a science, nor relevant technical experience, there are 9 with degrees in literature or languages, 5 with history, and 4 with education degrees. The rest have backgrounds scattered across a wide range of humanities and social science fields.

Education/Background	Librarians at Smaller Institutions	Librarians at Larger Institutions	Totals
With Science	20	33	53
Without Science	20	11	31
Undetermined	30	24	54

Table 2. Librarians' Backgrounds Related to Institutional Size (n=84)

It was expected that large universities would be more likely to have subject librarians with educational credentials appropriate for their responsibilities. This expectation is confirmed by the data in Table 2, although it should be noted that in about one third of the cases associated with larger libraries, the chemistry and physics LibGuide authors lack a science degree. Overall, however, 53 of the 84 (63 percent) of the librarians whose complete educational background could be determined have some science in their background.

For the 54 undetermined cases, position titles might serve as an indicator. Institutions with smaller student bodies were excluded from this part of the exploration, since library staff size is also smaller and librarians carry multiple responsibilities, and are therefore not as likely to have a title such as "science librarian." Checking the LibGuides and staff directories for the 24 librarians in the larger half of institutions for position titles and/or discipline affiliation resulted in the following: 11 titles reflecting specific disciplines in the sciences, such as "chemistry librarian;" 5 "science librarian;" 5 generic "research/instruction librarian;" 2 heads of science libraries; and 1 "associate librarian."

One additional breakout was thought to be of interest: data on the 20 librarians at schools identified in the Carnegie Classification as STEM dominant. Only two of these schools have a student body larger than the median, with one just barely so. Of the 20 individuals preparing chemistry and physics guides, only 4 have degrees in science. Seven have general or specific science titles, with most of the rest holding research/instruction positions.

Summary of comments from Springshare Lounge and ILI-l members

Nine of the 15 science librarians who responded to the query sent to the ALA IL list and to Springshare Lounge members stated that they have no science background. All 9 said that the MLIS is more important than a degree in a science, although most feel that the latter would be helpful. Of the 6 librarians who do have a science background, 4 agreed that the MLIS is more important. The other 2 said that both are important, especially in establishing credibility with faculty and understanding how scientists work. As one of them put it,

> "It was very helpful to have that background for several reasons. It did help me with the subject matter and being able to "talk the talk" with the professors. It also gave me more credibility with them. I was more accepted as a colleague than other librarians at the institution".

Another librarian with a great deal of science education agrees:

> "I think both a MLS and some sort of science degree are important because science is a highly specialized language that would be difficult to pick up without taking some classes in it….In regards to libguides I'm always learning new things from my faculty, students, and fellow science geeks many of whom are science librarians. I think one thing you learn as a student of science is that you can never know it all, …so you get used to the idea of constant learning and growth".

The following response makes a case for the MLS as more important than a science degree:

> "I work at a four-year institution. The student population has average information literacy skills. … In this situation, I think the MLS is more important than a science degree, because the students need basic information skills more than advanced skills with science literature. If I were working with graduate students, a science background would be more valuable".

A similar response came from a librarian with an MBA, but no science:

> "I would say having the business background and education was just as, if not more important, than having a science background to do this job, especially in an undergraduate college where I support all the sciences taught here as well as run the library. ... Based on my interaction with area science librarians, I can share with you that many of them do not have science backgrounds, or have a science background different from the one(s) for which they provide library support".

One librarian provided a detailed account of how she copes with myriad subjects in her

> "...community college that teaches college transfer courses in the sciences as well as technology / workforce disciplines such as land surveying technology, computer science... I have been library liaison to physics, astronomy, engineering, computer science, land surveying technology/ geomatics, mathematics and various other disciplines for which I had little coursework as an undergraduate. ... I had to (quickly) learn everything I could about the discipline, beginning with the college catalog and course descriptions. When I could, I met with faculty to discuss their library assignments ... and their "take" on their discipline. I examined the textbook order list to see what the faculty was requiring ... Until recently... we subscribed to at least one periodical title for each discipline... I read the most recent issues...to see what people in the field thought was important. ... It's much easier today, I think, to "learn" a discipline. There are tons of library guides (search *libguide physics* to see what other libraries are offering). ... Usually, if I find something I think is unique on another libguide, I ask the author if I can adapt it. I have never had anyone say "no.""

Other answers to the question of how those who did not have an academic background in the science/s for which they were responsible learned what they needed to know were not as detailed, but overall supported Meier's point that major sources of information are teaching faculty and experienced librarian colleagues. Other strategies mentioned included:

- Examination of one's own library holdings
- Scrutiny of science course descriptions, textbook orders, syllabi, and assignments
- Experimentation with databases and interfaces
- Use of other libraries' LibGuides
- Perusal of journals of education for specific sciences

   - Membership of associations, listservs, and blogs focused on sciences
   - Participation in conferences and workshops for science librarians
   - Examination of vendors'/publishers' catalogs
   - Looking at holdings of similar libraries

In the spirit of not having to reinvent the wheel, one responder stated that "I try to steal from other institutions as much as I can." Acknowledgements, however, are rarely visible on the LibGuides of the stealers.

Discussion and conclusion

The basic question that this study sought to address was how librarians could learn to provide IL in a subject they knew little about. Of particular interest was the notion that newcomers to a discipline would turn to colleagues experienced in the field. Springshares' LibGuides seemed to offer a way for a novice to borrow expertise from subject specialists. Chemistry and physics, subjects not often found in librarians' educational histories, are especially difficult to learn on one's own. Could chemistry and physics LibGuides indeed serve as professional development resources? The answer appears to be yes, although the debt is not always acknowledged.

Using the Springshares "community" database has a number of advantages for the librarian looking to learn from and adapt others' work. Many academic libraries are subscribers, so it is possible to find contributors whose institutions are similar to one's own. The links in the database make it easy to get to the guides of interest. Preparers of guides are almost always identified, and can therefore be consulted for advice and for permission to borrow or adapt. One disadvantage is that the guides are inconsistent in providing biographical information about guide preparers. Even when the "profile" link actually leads to information about the librarian, education credentials are often omitted. Another disadvantage is that it can be difficult to find e-mail addresses, and the links do not work with every kind of e-mail software.

Where it was possible to determine the background of chemistry and physics LibGuide authors, the results suggest that a substantial number of them seem to have at least some education in science. In larger libraries where no biographical information could be located, the position titles generally imply science expertise. Therefore, it should be possible for a librarian with no chemistry or physics education to identify LibGuides authored by better prepared colleagues and to use those as models. The most comprehensive guides will not necessarily be suitable for smaller libraries, as the ultimate determinant of what a library can offer is the budget. Nevertheless, there is value in knowing what constitutes an excellent or good collection of print and electronic resources in order to advise faculty and ambitious students who might want to go elsewhere to use some of the more expensive resources.

It is interesting that the data about science and LIS degrees found via Lib-Guides reflects the distribution of LIS and science degrees that Eells describes in her 2006 paper, where roughly half of the sci-tech librarians in her sample claimed science education. In her literature review, she states that science as a component of sci-tech librarians' education has risen over time. The current results appear to confirm this trend, at least for the larger institutions. It has to be remembered however, that the nature of the Carnegie Classifications/ Springshare sample and the frequent omission of educational information about Lib-Guide authors impose limitations on what can be said with any certitude.

Turning to the responses from science librarians to the question about LibGuides and the importance of MLS versus science degrees, it is gratifying to note that they all see themselves as capable self-directed learners who are able to develop adequate knowledge of fields in which they have no formal training. Even those with the science background strive to continue to master their specialty. The list of modes of learning that are employed is impressive. Overall, they find others' LibGuides helpful, but think first of the needs, resources, and realities of their local situation. If there is a criticism to be made, it is that science librarianship is too inner directed, which is the impression one gets from the relatively rare mentions of involvement with the sciences professional associations and their communications. In a "Viewpoint" article for *Issues in Science and Technology Librarianship,* an engineering librarian lays the inadequacy of IL for engineering students at the feet of the Accreditation Board for Engineering and Technology (ABET) (Clarke, 2011). The ACRL Science and Technology Section does have IL standards (ALA, 2006). In preparing that document, the Section reviewed ABET standards, along with those of other relevant bodies. But "reviewed" is not the same as cooperatively developed, a much more effective way to encourage change. Scanning the science entries of the previously mentioned ACRL wiki on IL in the disciplines, it seems that science librarians are publishing primarily in LIS journals, and much less so in science journals. It no doubt would be beneficial if there were more of a conversation among LIS professionals and science academics. Learning across as well as within each other's fields would benefit their students as well as themselves. An example of such a fruitful exchange between a chemistry librarian and chemistry faculty in developing a seminar incorporating IL is described by Tucci (2011).

Future research directions

Before beginning this study, it was thought that it would be interesting to explore whether LibGuide authors with a science background produced better guides than those without. It soon became apparent that time constraints would not permit that line of inquiry. First, there is the issue of how to define high quality in chemistry and physics LibGuides. Second, it is clear that what would be appropriate for a small liberal arts college differs from what is required by a large research university. Finally, the current project has revealed that there is a great range of qualifications as well as responsibilities among science librarians, and that it would be very difficult to control for all the variables. Nevertheless, it would be worthwhile to attempt such a study, as the results could improve the quality of subject guides and thus support IL instruction for students and continuing education for science librarians, and possibly foster greater collaboration among librarians and faculty.

References

American Library Association, Association of College & Research Libraries. (2000). *Information Literacy Competency Standards for Higher Education.* Retrieved from the American Library Association website:
www.ala.org/acrl/standards/informationliteracycompetency

American Library Association, Association of College & Research Libraries, Instruction Section. (2011a). *Sponsors of Continuing Education Programs for Library Instruction.* Retrieved from the American Library Association website:
www.ala.org/acrl/standards/infolitscitech

American Library Association, Association of College & Research Libraries, Instruction Section. (2011b). Information Literacy in the Disciplines. Retrieved from the American Library Association website:
http://wikis.ala.org/acrl/index.php/Information_literacy_in_the_disciplines

American Library Association, Association of College & Research Libraries, Science & Technology Section. (2006) *Information Literacy Standards for Science and Engineering/Technology.* Retrieved from the American Library Association website:
www.ala.org/acrl/standards/infolitscitech

Badke, W. (2010). Why information literacy is invisible. *Communications in Information Literacy, 4*(2), 129-141.

The Carnegie Classification of Institutions of Higher Education. (2010). Retrieved from the Carnegie Foundation website: classifications.carnegiefoundation.org/

The Carnegie Classification of Institutions of Higher Education, Classification description, doc/STEM. (2010). Retrieved from the Carnegie Foundation web site:
http://classifications.carnegiefoundation.org/descriptions/grad_program.php

Clarke, J.B. (2011). Viewpoints: seeking a paradigm shift for engineering librarian instruction. *Issues in Science and Technology Librarianship,* issue 66. Retrieved from:
www.istl.org/11-summer/viewpoint.html

Eells, L. (2006). Making the science-library connection: A survey of sci-tech librarians. *Science & Technology Libraries, 27*(1-2), 135-158.

Grafstein, A. (2002). A discipline-based approach to information literacy. *Journal of Academic Librarianship, 28*(4), 197-204.

Johnson, A. M., Sproles, C., & Detmering, R. (2011). Library instruction and information literacy 2010. *Reference Services Review, 39(*4), 551-627.

Kim, K.-S., Chiu, M.-H., Sin, S.-C. J., & Robbins, L. (2007). Recruiting a diverse workforce for academic/research librarianship: Career decisions of subject specialists and librarians of color. *College & Research Libraries, 68*(6), 533-552.

Kreitz, P. A., & DeVries, J. (2006). Introduction. *Science & Technology Libraries, 27*(1/2), 1-4.

Kurruppu, P. U. (2006). Recruitment of science and technology librarians: a review. *Science & Technology Libraries, 27*(1-2), 11-39

Meier, J.J. (2010a). Solutions for the new subject specialist librarian. *Endnotes, 1*(1), F1-F10.

Meier, J.J. (2010b). Are today's science and technology librarians being overtasked? An analysis of job responsibilities in recent advertisements on the ALA JobLIST Web site. *Science & Technology Libraries, (29)*1-2, 165-175.

Murphy, J. H. (2008). Schrödinger's course: the availability of courses on resources in science and technology among LIS programs. *Science & Technology Libraries, 28*(4), 307-324.

Schmidt, M., & Reznik-Zellen, R. (2011, August 18). *Science boot camp for librarians: CPD on a shoestring.* Paper presented at the 77th IFLA conference, San Juan, Puerto Rico. Retrieved from the IFLA website:
conference.ifla.org/conference/past/ifla77/2011-08-18.htm

Solla, L. (2003). Low stress opportunity for research students to explore information resources: information literacy for the physical scientist. *Issues in Science and Technology Librarianship, Spring 2003,* issue 37. Retrieved from:
www.istl.org/03-spring/article6.html

Special Libraries Association, Chemistry Division, & American Chemical Society, Division of Chemical Information. (2011). *Information competencies for chemistry undergraduates: the elements of information literacy.* Retrieved from the Special Libraries Association website: http://chemistry.sla.org/il/

Springshare. (2011). http://springshare.com/libguides/

Tomaszewski, R. & MacDonald, K.I. (2009). Identifying subject-specific conferences as professional development opportunities for the academic librarian. *Journal of Academic Librarianship, 35*(6), 583-590.

Tucci, V. K. (2011). Faculty/librarian collaboration: catalyst for student learning and librarian growth. *Science & Technology Libraries, 30*, 292-305.

Varlejs, J. (2008). *Staying au courant*: resources for instruction librarians. In T. Valko & B. Sietz (Eds.), *Moving targets: understanding our changing landscape* (pp. 145-148). Proceedings of the 34th National LOEX Conference, 2006, College Park, MD. Ypsilanti, MI: LOEX Press.

Westbrock. T. & Fabian, S. (2010). Proficiencies for instruction librarians: is there still a disconnect between professional education and professional responsibilities? *College & Research Libraries, 71*(6), 569-590.

White, G. (1999). Academic subject specialist positions in the United States: a content analysis of announcements from 1990 through 1998. *Journal of Academic Librarianship*, 25(5), 372-382.

Learning on the Job, Teaching on the Job: CPDWL and a New Qualification for the Research Information-Literate Librarian

Clare M. Walker

Honorary Research Fellow, Wartenweiler Library, University of the Witwatersrand, Johannesburg

clare.walker@wits.ac.za

Abstract

This was a small informal study to identify requirements for "research information-literate" librarians, particularly in South Africa; to identify a unique focus for research librarian practice; and to propose content for a specialist research librarian qualification with a hybrid modular curriculum. An online exploration of the literature was carried out and a personal email communication was sent to senior colleagues within the Carnegie Research Libraries Consortium project, for information on the local status quo and for input into curriculum coverage for a new qualification. Responses to the email confirmed alignment of thinking with that in other countries, but revealed challenges in South Africa. Strong support was confirmed for a specialist qualification. The discovery of two recent major reports on research librarians (OCLC and Lewis) was central to the direction developed in the paper. These studies have shown that great value is placed on the bibliometric and related expertise of academic/research librarians in the research assessment process and on relationships formed with researchers and research entities, and these elements of practice could be said to define research librarians. A hybrid CPDWL/academic specialist qualification programme would enhance both the skills and these relationships. Research librarianship is therefore not necessarily defined by subject knowledge alone.

Introduction

Academic and research librarians: a global view

In 2007 the report *Researchers' use of academic libraries and their services* listed seven most highly ranked roles of research librarians (Brown & Swan, 2007). In 2009 a study commissioned by OCLC, *A comparative review of research assessment regimes in five countries* (Key Perspectives, 2009), specifically reviewed the role of research libraries in internal and national research assessment processes. The "key premise" of the study was that "librarians have the skills and experience that enable them to make valuable contributions to their institutions, helping to facilitate institutional responses to the requirements of national and internal research assessment systems." (2009; p. 12). The purpose of the study was "to identify good or best practice for libraries in support of national or internal research assessment" (2009; p. 14) and detail of this is reflected in each country report. A strong relationship is also postulated between the establishment and management of Institutional Repositories (IRs) by research librarians and the centrality of the role of the research library to the research institution (2009).

What emerges from the study is a sense that engagement with institutional and national research assessment processes should be the driving force for librarians to acquire and apply those higher level skills and knowledge that define the core nature of the research librarian.

"The library is also perceived to be unique in that it is involved with all parts of the information life cycle, from helping researchers to source the information they need to providing advice on bibliometrics … expertise in data management planning and, ultimately, digital data curation" (Key Perspectives, 2009; p. 47).

Additional research librarian skills that contribute to the research assessment process include:

- Managing IRs;
- Bibliometric expertise;
- Ability to find or acquire information necessary for assessment submissions;
- Understanding of metadata;
- Expertise in cataloguing and curation, especially digital curation.

As every research librarian knows, "these skills are valuable in their own right"; the OCLC study points out that they also contribute to assembling and managing the information required for research assessment (Key Perspectives, 2009). Such new skills must mostly be acquired on the job, by continuing professional development (CPD) in many forms, rather than by advanced academic study.

A major project recently undertaken by Lewis and others to determine the future skills requirements of Australian health librarians (Lewis et al, 2011) reflects the research findings of the much smaller scale project and conclusions outlined in this paper.

Information literacy has traditionally focused on the application of ever more sophisticated library ICT tools in the academic endeavour and the effective use of library resources to develop "critical thinking" skills. Harrington (2009) has explored with positive conclusions the role of the librarian in graduate students' research experience: "... change in the physical and virtual presence of a research librarian will prove to enhance the level of information literacy knowledge of research-intensive graduate students" (2009, p. 188).

The 2011 SCONUL *Seven pillars of information literacy: research lens* provides the research librarian with a holistic model of core generic skills and understanding for "researcher information literacy" ranging from the emerging to the mature experienced researcher. For delivering information literacy rooted in such framework structures with models such as the Seven Pillars and the Vitae *Researcher Development Framework* (2010) the critical nature of re-search librarian advanced skills and understanding is self-evident.

The research librarian cannot deliver information literacy at this advanced level without a deep understanding of the experienced researcher in the re-search environment and the constituent elements of the research publishing and assessment processes (Lewis et al, 2011). It becomes a relationship of in-dividual referral and consultation – a triangular process in a developmental learning/teaching relationship between the research librarian and individual re-searchers and institutional research managers.

Through skills and relationships, research librarians acquire "credibility in the view of senior institutional managers and the researcher communities they serve" (Key Perspectives, 2009; p. 15). Where, how and to what extent aca-demic librarians in South Africa acquire, develop and hone this knowledge, these skills and these institutional relationships, particularly through CPD and high level Workplace Learning (CPDWL), is a key concern of this paper.

The South African academic research environment

Only a few South African "research universities" realistically compete for ranking in the top five or six South African places in the annual global univer-sity "league tables", where research performance is a determining factor (Times Higher Education World University Rankings, 2011-2012; QS World University Rankings®, 2011/2012). Individual and institutional research output is managed within an accredited and assessed national research and publishing environment created by the National Research Foundation (NRF) (National Research Foundation [NRF], n.d.), the Department of Higher Education and Training (DHET) (South Africa. Department of Higher Education and Train-ing [DHET], n.d.), and the Academy of Science of South Africa (ASSAf) (Academy of Science of South Africa [ASSAf], n.d.). Viewed together, these web sites show the holistic national developmental vision for, and products to support, research productivity, quality and capacity development in South Af-rica.

A researcher ratings programme is managed by the NRF (NRF. Knowledge Management and Evaluation, n.d.) and a policy for accredited research publishing and subsidy is administered through the DHET (South Africa. DHET. Policy and development support, 2010; South Africa. Education, 2003.). ASSAf has produced a report on research publishing (ASSAf, 2006), has a *Scholarly publishing programme* (ASSAf. Programmes, 2006,) and supports Open Access through the Brazilian-linked SciELO programme (ASSAf, 2011). University research offices or similar units manage these programmes institutionally. Many academic libraries have taken the initiative to develop and promote IRs for open access to research outputs from the academic research community.

Research librarians in South African universities

South African research librarians need to be familiar with all dimensions of the research environment described above. Kaniki, an executive director at the NRF, and an advocate for research librarian development, identified in 2007 the "new" activities with which librarians should proactively engage themselves (Walker, 2009b). They are explicit or implicit in the role of research librarians referred to above and below.

Currently the most common research support role of South African academic librarians is that of assisting young "emerging researchers" (graduate research students) in recently established Research Commons facilities, and in delivering advanced levels of "research skills/information-literacy" through workshops and individual assistance. Established academic researchers are more usually assisted by senior librarians in individual consultation, for preparation of evaluation submissions through the application of bibliometric tools for citation searches, profiles and related factors. In a few institutions research librarians take on activities associated with "embedded" librarians and deliver high level presentations and services within schools and faculties as well as office consultations.

For most South African professional librarians with basic graduate qualifications in humanities and social sciences, the fields and the terminology of specialist and advanced sciences, technology and social sciences are challenging in delivery of information services. The transition to high level research librarianship is difficult and librarians may not know what they need to know to bridge the gap. The Carnegie Research Libraries Consortium (RLC) project was put in place in 2006 to address this and has been described elsewhere (Darch & De Jager, 2011a, 2011b; Shepherd, 2010; Walker, 2009a).

In brief, the aim of the project was to improve research skills and subject domain knowledge of librarians and build a platform for high level library support of academic research, both for emerging researchers and for experienced academics. Initially three university libraries were selected for the project and, in phase 2, an additional three. All six libraries were from top ranked South African research universities.

Research methodology

Email to library directors: an informal survey

Having retired in 2010 from library management and managerial involvement with the RLC project, the present author communicated in January 2012 by email with five directors/senior colleagues from the six RLC university libraries. One director had very recently moved as director from one RLC Library to another and was therefore asked to comment on both libraries. The former was not mentioned in responses as extensively as the latter.

The email, sent individually to five colleagues all personally well known to the author, was explicitly described as a "personal conversation, NOT a survey" and the responses, received from all five, were similarly conversational and narrative in style. As a result, tabulation and summarising of the responses has required some editing. The six libraries are referred to as UL1, UL2, UL3, UL4, UL5, and UL6 in no significant order, to give identity but retain anonymity in a very small community.

Serendipitously, as part of the response, one director included a paper by Darch and De Jager, to date unpublished (Darch and De Jager 2011b), and a related online PowerPoint presentation was identified (Darch and De Jager, 2011a). In this way the present author learnt that a quantitative evaluation of the RLC Academy participants had recently been conducted by Darch and De Jager (2011a), and that the library directors had reported positive changes in three areas targeted by the Academy (personal development, research proficiency and professional development) (2011a).

The evaluation pre-empted some of the focus of the present author's email to directors; to avoid overlap, only those questions and responses most directly relevant to the idea of a new type of qualification for research librarians (the intended outcome of this paper) are presented below.

Results

Questions and responses

Q.1: How do professional subject librarians in your library build and expand their subject knowledge as well as their technical skills? Are they expected to do so, as part of their performance management goals, particularly as South African librarians come equipped with relatively "thin" subject knowledge at the postgraduate/faculty level?

Directors expect/ encourage/ support:

- Relevant subject knowledge/subject qualification/experience (UL1);
- Basic academic subject knowledge gained from attendance at "101" classes, lectures, non-degree purpose courses (UL1, UL2);
- Attendance at: brown bag lunches, protocol defences, presentations, departmental seminars (UL1, UL2, UL3);
- Involvement in academic research support and research projects, liaison with academics: provides greater understanding of researcher specialization; researcher productivity provides understanding of publication habits and preferences and subject interests (UL3);
- Reading relevant journals, listservs, blogs, e-newsletters, websites (UL1, UL2);
- Development of information literacy course packages increases subject discipline knowledge (UL2);
- Special attention to subject knowledge in training new information specialists (UL1);
- Registering for higher degrees improves subject knowledge; exposure to research process adds value (UL2, UL5); one Library encourages librarians to engage in higher degrees more for experience than broadening knowledge base (UL5).

Performance management:

- Subject knowledge indirectly as a Core Performance Area linked with other CPAs in performance contract; performance management objectives expand subject knowledge (UL1);
- Encourage librarians as part of performance agreement to attend minimum number of seminars / lectures on various research topics on campus (UL3)
- Staff required to discuss plans to expand subject knowledge, as part of performance management objective setting (UL4); initiative should be recognised (UL4)
- University policy for every member of staff to have a development plan (UL5);
- Subject knowledge depends on attitude and effort of information specialists. (UL1,UL2, UL3,UL5)
- Staff may be more concerned with expanding their technical skills, e.g. database searching, than subject specialisation (UL4).

No response for UL6.

Q.2: Do librarians in your library have a structured relationship with the university research office, or research administration in faculties and schools, or graduate research support programmes through which they (librarians) provide support in training and preparation for publication, NRF ratings, personal promotion etc.? How do they gain the confidence of academic researchers and higher degree supervisors?

- Two libraries work closely with Research Office and IP office (UL1, UL3):
    - Experienced dedicated information specialist for University Management offices and decision makers; Library expertise in bibliometrics and patents (UL1);
- Dedicated point of contact for research office; assistance and support in research and research-evaluation-related areas; referrals from various university entities (UL3);
- Library developing expertise in manipulation of new research management tools (UL5);
- Working on closer relationship with new Director of Postgraduate Research (UL2);
- No systematic relationship with Research Office (UL4);
- Subject librarians attend Research Committee meetings; often included on Boards of Colleges, Schools etc; liaise with faculty officers (UL1, UL2, UL3);
- Some but not all subject librarians maintain portfolios on academic staff; provide research needs support and training (UL2); long term relationship between researcher and librarians develops bond and trust in guidance provided by librarian (UL5);
- Higher degrees research supervisors require relationship management with Library (UL4, UL6).

Q.3a: Are there any systematic concentrated specialist library/information staff development programmes planned or already in place in place at your library, by means of which this kind of professional and specialist self-development – in-house staff development programmes of various kinds – could be made available?

- Restructured executive team portfolio taking staff development to a strategic level; in-house training increasingly important (UL1);
- Library restructuring proposed mandatory in-service training programme for all professional staff (one morning every two weeks), basics to sophisticated and advanced elements (UL6);
- Strong library staff development programme encompasses continuing development, skills training and engaging in formal studies (UL5);

- No systematic staff development; considering ways of coordinating internal training initiatives (UL4);
- Individual responsibility for taking advantage of available programmes (UL2,UL3, UL4);
- Vendor (product) training, staff training and development, ICT training, use of specialised new resources, updates on new developments (UL2, UL3, UL4); author workshops presented by Elsevier, training sessions on new research management tools (UL5); journal club (UL3) and workshops that are related to job functions cover various professional aspects and developments (UL3, UL5).

Q.3b: If so, how does the library accommodate higher level staff development within working hours … Does self-development carry a performance reward? And are there alternative kinds of development for different levels of staff? Are any or many such programmes currently in place, recognising that they take up workplace time and possibly personal time, even if this seems slight (e.g. lunch hour lectures, after hours online seminars in USA time zones, etc.) and is any system of in-house credits in place to serve as incentive.

- Performance appraisal system allows for every staff member to have a Professional Development Plan (UL1, UL5); staff evaluated on engagement in development activities (UL5);
- All information specialists sent on courses; other regular one-hour in-house training sessions not in lunch time. Staff attend workshops, seminars, conferences if work-related, well-motivated, with official leave (UL1); Webinars, seminars within work hours are supported; for attending conferences, required to present a paper and submit for publication (UL4);
- Time, money on staff development seen as investment; ROI (Return on Investment) not determined formally, but expected as presentations, articles, new products, new initiatives, innovation (UL1);
- Higher level staff development only through registration for higher degrees programmes: not required or compulsory; no time allowed off work to undertake such programmes (but study leave in conditions of service) (UL2);
- Voluntary; librarians must realise importance of self-development; librarians free to take on campus opportunities to attend seminars, workshops, lectures within own daily scheduled activities (UL3);
- Difficult, unpopular accommodating higher level staff development within working hours; may compromise library operations unless negotiated (UL4).

Performance rewards

- Self-development does carry performance reward (UL1).
- Reward is engagement with researchers, being recognised as part of the team, able to do a better job (UL3);
- No Library incentives or performance rewards (UL2, UL3);
- No reward system; discretionary bonus system could be applied (UL4).

No response for UL6.

Q.4a: Should we be looking at a completely new kind of higher level staff development, an advanced specialist, possibly modular, qualification certificated through portfolio work in the workplace as well as being underpinned by theoretical knowledge, on the lines of the pre-graduate National Certificate (Level 5) unit Standards and Qualifications registered for LIS that were created within the SAQA NQF framework (South African Qualifications Authority, n.d., National Certificate

[Since that time a Higher Education Qualifications Framework has as you know been put in place and a specific postgraduate diploma qualification level 8 between Honours and Masters is part of the structure (South Africa. DHET. 2007, p. 26)]

- Yes (UL1);
- Yes, yes, requiring work within a faculty, with a researcher who is willing to share their research methodologies. We need to know more (UL3);
- Support proposal for new kind of higher level staff development and possibly modular qualification (UL4);
- In many ways, Library is looking at that through own staff development process ; five years ahead ensure Library is providing innovating services using technology: the virtual librarian, the social librarian, the metadata experts and such UL5).

UL2 implies positive response (in Q.4b); no response for UL6; responses tend to overlap with Q.4b.

Q.4b: If the academic library sector could contribute to the purely hypothetical development of such a practice-based qualification, what would you like to see incorporated in it? I see our research librarians now having to know a great deal about new style bibliometrics, research management tools, datasets and similar concepts and tools that have only emerged in relatively recent years.

- Subject knowledge (UL2); research methodology; engaging in research in field of personal expertise; write and publish (UL2);
- Specialised advanced areas of professional expertise, e.g. bibliometrics, research management tools (UL1,UL3,UL5);
- Research practices; work within faculty with researcher willing to share research methodologies (UL3);
- Research management; research performance evaluation, peer review process (UL3);
- Datasets and data management plans (UL3);
- Innovative services using technology (UL5);
- Relationships management in research sector (UL4);
- Higher education and research environment in South Africa and other countries; national imperatives; research-led university (UL3, UL4).

No response for UL6.

New ways of self development for South Africa research librarians

Librarians increasingly engage in higher degree (Masters and Doctoral level) studies, but these tend to be knowledge management and related applications not subject disciplines. On the job, research librarians face the challenge of addressing their own continuing professional development, identifying and acquiring "research information-literacy" both for information literacy programmes to graduate research students and for the demanding support needs of senior researchers, particularly for research assessment purposes. In 2009 the present author proposed ways in which the competencies of research librarians might be expanded (Walker, 2009a; pp. 410-412). Most feature in the responses above.

An advanced specialist qualification for research librarians in South Africa

Given the range and depth of the new roles required of research librarians, a specialist post-basic qualification incorporating CPD is proposed. Question Four in the survey asked for input on such a qualification and, as indicated, received positive responses, suggesting there would be support in developing a new hybrid further qualification incorporating the following:

- On-the-job learning in association with academic researchers and research programmes. Isolated examples of these include "Boot camp:

science immersion for research librarians" (2010; pp. 3-5); "Professional development days" (2011;p.3); a strong focus on the research environment, research assessment processes; and on subject specific
conferences (Tomaszewski and MacDonald, 2009);
- Practical CDPWL elements, that include advanced specialist events;
- Advanced technological skills and tools including bibliometrics, dataset
  management, digital curation;
- Academic study incorporating specialist professional elective contents
  with subject discipline-based elements in mentored professional research writing and publishing.

Such a qualification could be located within the South African Higher Education Qualifications Framework (HEQF) (South African Qualifications Authority, n.d.) with a modular and flexible structure that would be strongly linked to
CPDWL deliverables at an advanced level. Agreement on development, positioning, content and delivery would be negotiated nationally. The HEQF has
incorporated a Level 8 Postgraduate Diploma, a qualification which could accommodate professional specialisation rather than purely academic study.
(South Africa. DHET. 2007). The Diploma is positioned between two post-
basic degree qualifications (Honours and Masters degrees), and would need to
be tested with LIS schools, academic and research institutional libraries and
the South African Library and Information Association. The paper by Lewis
(2011), proposing a modular qualification for Australian health information
professionals, provides a stimulating model for a similar South African development.

Curriculum structure

A specialist advanced qualification is one way to affirm a professional identity
for research librarian practice. Workshops, seminars, short courses and specialist conferences all have their place, but ultimately depend upon internalization
and willingness to change in order to succeed. As the responses from library
directors have shown, this is not always the case in practice. If such CPD contents were however to be embedded in a broad modular framework together
with formal theoretical study, this qualification could deliver the body of
knowledge and skill reflected in a generic research librarian profile.

Research management relationships

The OCLC study and the Australian health librarians project (Key Perspectives, 2009; Lewis et al, 2011) both strongly affirm that the expertise of an ex-

perienced academic librarian is essential for creating relationships in the assessment process, which is informed by sophisticated research bibliometric and analytical tools. Martin, in a very short article, also makes this point (2010), as do some of the South African library directors.

Any advanced programme for research librarians should therefore include an element on relationship-building and management with research managers and research units as well as academic researchers themselves, because librarians, however senior and expert, are not routinely recognised as professional peers. In-depth knowledge and understanding of the research environment and the world of research publishing, including IR management, may alleviate this disjunction.

The IR, providing online Open Access retrieval of institutional research output, is part of the research publishing environment. Research librarians manage IRs; the entire range of knowledge and skills required, including an understanding of the research publication process and IR promotion among sometimes reluctant researchers, should therefore be included in a specialist qualification.

Subject knowledge and technical skills

The premise for the original idea from which this paper grew was that advanced subject knowledge was crucial to the research librarian's relationship with academic researchers, in order to gain their trust and confidence. The one-to-one support relationship referred to above in Question One can be highly successful and productive, but even within a particular school or broad discipline one research librarian cannot be all things to all researchers.

To borrow Jane Austen's opening words in *Pride and Prejudice,* "it is a truth universally acknowledged" by the profession that a competent librarian can become a knowledgeable and skilful subject librarian in almost any discipline -- but may not necessarily become a research librarian. Similarly, the technical skills to exploit databases and complex information resources can be applied at many levels, but in themselves do not define a research librarian. The holistic understanding, relationship-building and expertise that a research librarian can bring to the environment of research assessment have been suggested as the most likely to evoke well-founded confidence and trust.

The products applied to assessment and research management are constantly under development by vendors. Keeping updated through intensive training presentations and short courses or workshops needs to be cascaded down as part of the advanced "research information-literacy" delivered by the research librarian. In the proposed modular framework for specialist qualification such changing technology can be accommodated flexibly by CPD input rather than as a fixed curriculum element.

Writing for presentation and publication

The ability to engage in personal research, write and publish in appropriate forms is increasingly acknowledged as one of the necessary skills of academic and reference librarians -- again, for example, confirmed by Lewis (2011). Darch and De Jager showed that the research article which all Academy participants were required to prepare and write for peer-reviewed possible publication was a daunting task. In their unpublished paper they quote the evaluator of the programme: "having carried out the Research Report writing exercise participants were far more sympathetic towards the researchers in what they experience, the support they need and the continued guidance necessary" (Veldsman, 2009, cited by Darch and De Jager, 2011b; p. 6). This is particularly valid for South African professionals who come from very varied educational and personal backgrounds and who are less likely to have English, particularly academic English, as a first level skill.

The Canadian Association of Research Librarian (CARL) has announced a workshop to be held in June 2012:

"There have been very few opportunities for researching CARL librarians to come together and work on their research in an intensive workshop setting. The inaugural Librarians' Research Institute will fill this gap by providing an intensive workshop experience for academic librarians to hone and further their research skills. The Canadian Association of Research Libraries is developing a unique Librarian Research Institute (LRI), which is designed provide an exciting learning opportunity for librarians who already have some foundational research experience." (CARL, 2012).

The objectives of this CARL workshop suggest that an in-depth CPD opportunity of this kind would provide an appropriate credit-bearing module for a specialist qualification. Professional mentored research writing and publishing should also be a practical requirement for the modular qualification, underpinned if necessary by more basic practical reading and writing development.

Conclusion

Accepting a profile of the research librarian that extends beyond the technically skilled subject librarian, this paper has proposed incorporating practical high level CPDWL with academic study, to attain greater effectiveness and recognition for academic research librarians. It is gratifying to the author to find this idea has been developed for a far larger cohort of librarians on the other side of the world:

"The ALIA/HLA Workforce and Education Research Project has adopted an evidence based approach to determining the future skills requirements for the health library workforce in Australia. Now that the research phase of the project is complete, the next step is to develop a structured, modular education framework to meet these requirements." (Lewis et al, 2011, p. 70).

Acknowledgements

Many thanks are due to my senior colleagues who are directors in the RLC libraries, and the role model Research Librarian at the University of the Witwatersrand, Johannesburg, who all generously responded to my email at short notice and delivered much more than "quick and dirty" input to my ideas and questions in my preparation of this paper. What I have done with their input is my responsibility alone; I hope it will prove a fruitful seedbed of ideas for the future.

References

Academy of Science of South Africa. (n.d.) Retrieved from: www.assaf.co.za
Academy of Science of South Africa. (2011). Open Access: SciELO SA. Retrieved from: www.assaf.org.za/programmes/open-access-scielo-sa/
Academy of Science of South Africa. (2006). *Report on a strategic approach to research publishing in South Africa.* The Academy. (June). Retrieved from: www.assaf.co.za/wpcontent/uploads/reports/evidence_based/assaf_strategic_research_publishing.pdf
Academy of Science of South Africa. Programmes. (2006). Scholarly Publishing Programme. Retrieved from: www.assaf.org.za/programmes/
Boot camp: science immersion for research librarians. (2010.) *Soutte Review, 34*(3), 5. Retrieved from *Soutte Review* website: http://library.umassmed.edu/issue34.pdf
Brown, S., & Swan, A. (2007). *Researchers' use of academic libraries and their services: a report commissioned by the Research Information Network and the Consortium of Research Libraries.* Technical Report. April 2007. Retrieved from: www.rin.ac.uk/researchers-use-libraries
Canadian Association of Research Libraries. (2012). CARL Librarians Research Institute June 2012. Retrieved from: http://carl-abrc.ca/en/research-libraries/librarians-research-institute.html
Darch, C., & de Jager, Karin. (2011a). Reconfiguring the researcher-librarian relationship: evaluating South Africa's 'Library Academy' experience. Presented at the *9th Northumbria International Conference on Performance Measurement in Libraries and Information Services, University of York, 22-25 July 2011.* [PowerPoint presentation]. Available from: www.york.ac.uk/about/departments/support-andadmin/information-directorate/events/performance-conference-2011/presentations/

Darch, Colin & de Jager, Karin. (2011b). Reconfiguring the researcher-librarian relationship: evaluating South Africa's 'Library Academy' experience. Presented at the *9th Northumbria International Conference on Performance Measurement in Libraries and Information Services, University of York, 22-25 July 2011*. Unpublished paper.

Harrington, M. R. (2009). Information literacy and research-intensive graduate students: enhancing the role of research librarians. *Behavioral and Social Sciences Librarian 28* (4), 179-201 (Western Libraries Librarian and Archivist publications. Paper 13.) Retrieved from: http:// ir.lib.uwo.ca/wlpub/15

Key Perspectives Ltd. (2009). *A comparative review of research assignment regimes in five countries and the role of libraries in the research assessment process.* Report commissioned by OCLC Research. Retrieved from: www.oclc.org/research/publications/library/2009/2009-09.pdf

Lewis, S., Hallam, G., Ritchie, A., Clark, C., Hamill, C., Foti, M., et al. (2011). Employers' perspectives on future roles and skills requirements for Australian health librarians. *Evidence Based Library and Information Practice,6*(4),58-71.Retrieved from: http://ejournals.library.ualberta.ca/index.php/EBLIP/article/view/10340/9400

Martin, E. (2010). Director's corner. Untangling the data: new roles for medical librarians in e-science. *Soutte Review 34*. Retrieved from: http://library.umassmed.edu/issue34.pdf

National Research Foundation (n.d.). Retrieved from: www.nrf.ac.za

National Research Foundation. Knowledge Management and Evaluation. (n.d.). Retrieved from: www.nrf.ac.za/risa.php?fdid=2&tab=projects&sub=Projects

Professional development days. (2010). *Soutte Review, 34.* Retrieved from Soutte Review website: http://library.umassmed.edu/issue34.pdf

QS World University Rankings® 2011/2012. Retrieved from: www.topuniversities.com/university-rankings/world-university-rankings

SCONUL (2011). Working group on information literacy. *The SCONUL Seven pillars of information literacy: a research lens for higher education* (2011). Retrieved from: www.sconul.ac.uk/groups/information_literacy/publications/researchlens.pdf

Shepherd, E. (2010) In-service training for academic librarians: a pilot programme for staff. *The Electronic Library, 28* (4), 507-524. Retrieved from: http://eprints.ru.ac.za/1756/

South Africa. Department of Education. 2003. *Policy and procedures for measurement of research output of public higher education institutions.* (June). Retrieved from: www.dhet.gov.za/linkclick.aspx?fileticket=xzuihexfbzq%3d&tabid=416&mid=1225

South Africa. Department of Higher Education and Training. (n.d.). Retrieved from: www.dhet.gov.za

South Africa. Department of Higher Education and Training. Policy and Development Support. (2010). Retrieved from: www.dhet.gov.za/Structure/Universities/PolicyandDevelopmentSupport/tabid/416/Item Id/2546/Default.aspx

South Africa. Department of Higher Education and Training. (2007). *The Higher Education Qualifications Framework.* Retrieved from: www.dhet.gov.za/portals/0/Documents/Higher_Education_Qualifications_Framework_ Oct2007.pdf

South African Qualifications Authority. (n.d.). Retrieved from: www.SAQA.org.za

South African Qualifications Authority. (n.d.). *National Certificate: Library and Information Studies* retrieved from : allqs.saqa.org.za/showQualification.php?id=1341

The Times Higher Education World University Rankings 2011-2012. Retrieved from:
www.timeshighereducation.co.uk/world-university-rankings

Tomaszewski, R., & MacDonald, K. I. (2009). Identifying subject-specific conferences as professional development opportunities for the academic librarian. (University Library Faculty publications paper 40, Georgia State University). Retrieved from:
http://digitalarchive.gsu.edu/uni_lib_facpub/40

Vitae (2010) Researcher Development Framework). Retrieved from:
www.vitae.ac.uk/researchers/429351/Introducing-the-Researcher-Development-Framework.html

Walker, Clare M. (2009a). Pathways to new academic library practices: a South African exploration towards 21st century academic research support. In J. Varlejs & G. Walton (Eds.), *Strategies for regenerating the library and information professions: Eighth World Conference on Continuing Professional Development and Workplace Learning for the Library and Information Professions 18-20 August 2009, Bologna, Ital (pp. 402-415).* Saur: Munich.

Walker, Clare M. (2009b). Pathways to new academic library practices: a South African exploration towards 21st century academic research support. Presentation at *Strategies for regenerating the library and information professions: Eighth World Conference on Continuing Professional Development and Workplace Learning for the Library and Information Professions 18-20 August 2009, Bologna, Italy* [PowerPoint presentation] Retrieved from: www.ifla.org/files/cpdwl/conferencedocuments/presentations/2009/walker.ppt

EFFECTIVE INFORMATION LITERACY
INTERVENTIONS

Information Literacy in a Web-Scale Discovery World – A Case Study of User Experience vs Content at Sheffield Hallam University, UK

Matthew Borg
Information Adviser, Sheffield Hallam University, UK
m.borg@shu.ac.uk
and
Angie Donoghue
Senior Information Adviser, Sheffield Hallam University, UK
a.donoghue@shu.ac.uk

Abstract

When introducing a web-scale discovery system to students and staff at Sheffield Hallam University (SHU), we needed to rethink our approach to how we taught information literacy in this millennial, Net Generation age. Library staff needed to re-evaluate how to introduce information literacy to students and allay faculty staff fears of "dumbing down" the library experience. Although much literature exists on teaching information literacy, not much exists on the way that information literacy can be taught in a web-discovery world. The librarian's traditional role of content gatekeeper is perhaps contentious, but well acknowledged. This paper argues that this focus is no longer relevant, and that a shift in focus toward a first class user experience of accessing content must be made. We provide an historical overview of information literacy teaching at SHU, and describe how the introduction of a web-scale discovery system made us challenge our existing methods of supporting students with information literacy teaching and online help resources. The paper demonstrates how we moved away from the traditional information literacy teaching approach of focusing on content towards providing a first class user experience of content access, and how we used Shoshin, a Zen Buddhist concept, to help us along the way.

Introduction

This paper describes how we redesigned our approach to information literacy when moving into the world of web discovery tools – the hurdles we encountered, the issues we addressed and solutions we were able to implement.

With over 35,000 students and more than 4,000 staff Sheffield Hallam University (SHU) is one of the largest universities in the UK. Until 1992 it was a polytechnic and has a strong tradition of work-based learning across a broad range of subjects. Employability is a key priority for the university. Its widening participation agenda means that many students come from non-traditional backgrounds as well as more traditional ones and also from overseas. It is one of the largest providers of healthcare training and teacher education in the country. It specialises in real-world research including a strong focus on materials science, health, sports, engineering and arts and design. SHU is a large campus based university operating across two sites with a learning centre on each, and offers many courses by distance learning.

With 50% of our undergraduates being under 21 we have a large number of students who fall into the Net Generation category (CIBER, 2008; Oblinger and Oblinger, 2005) in terms of their use of information and technology. These students are generally confident with technology and the internet; indeed they are heavily reliant on the internet to discover information. However, their skills in finding, then evaluating and using that information are less developed. They often do not know much about the different types of information sources they should be using or how to identify resources of an appropriate quality for their university work. Having found material many then struggle with critical analysis.

History of library technology at SHU

SHU has historically been a keen early adopter of technology. In the early 1990s we implemented a web-based library management system. By the mid 1990s we had moved into a new learning centre and also acquired a significant number of information databases on CD which very quickly became web-based. The learning centre model offers students choices about how they engage with learning. Physically such spaces provide secure, supported learning environments over extended hours, where students can learn, interact with others, access learning materials and receive help in meeting their learning needs (Milne, 2006). We wanted to extend some of the principles of this model to the design, provision and accessibility of resources, particularly those online.

In 2004 we moved to a federated search engine (Metalib) and link resolver (SFX) in the hope of simplifying the information search interface for students. However, we still had a separate library catalogue and subject guides. With the introduction of each new technology we solved some problems and encountered others. Although all the technologies worked together technically we were conscious they did not really join up from the user's point of view. Students would need to know what they wanted and where to look before they could start their searching. The disjointed way information resources were presented was a barrier to successful information discovery and it did not reflect their experiences with the well-designed search engines they were already familiar with. "Why can't you be more like Google?" was a frequently received comment.

In the wider university environment a blended approach to e-learning was developing and being promoted with the introduction of a student portal and the virtual learning environment (VLE), provided by Blackboard. This had led to some integration of resources but also to some difficulties as librarians lost ownership and editing rights to subject pages. With the introduction of each new system came the need to rethink and re-design our induction sessions, self-help and subject guides, information literacy teaching for students and also training and advocacy work for learning centre and academic staff.

Historical approaches to information literacy teaching

Information literacy teaching at SHU in the late 1990s to mid 2000s was a mix of face-to-face induction sessions for large groups, information skills workshops, printed self-help material, and one-to-one sessions on request. Sessions varied in content depending on the library support team offering them and the academic discipline of the students. While there was an overview of what was being delivered, we lacked a strategic vision of what was required. Teaching tended to be reactive and partially driven by the requirements of academic staff. There was an expectation that in these sessions library staff would list the information resources that students were expected to use and perhaps demonstrate some of the more complicated ones. Subject librarians were seen as professionals who understood the information landscape in their particular area. They were expected to provide straightforward guidance in how to get to places without contextualising why the journey should be undertaken or developing the skills needed to get there. There was also little focus on how to select or critically analyse the information. We would receive requests for "one shot, single-class sessions" (Finley, 2005) into which we were expected to cram the entire information literacy syllabus. Such sessions were becoming increasingly problematic given the proliferation of sources and the complexity of information literacy skills required.

A partial solution was to develop an online, interactive, information literacy tutorial for students called InfoQuest. It was tailored for each subject and developed primarily for first year undergraduates. We combined simple information literacy teaching, such as how to recognise good quality journal articles, and very practical things such as how books are shelved in the Learning Centre. InfoQuest used interactive Flash elements alongside text and was embedded into students' VLE modules; a generic version was available via the student portal. It was also integrated into the face-to-face workshops for new and returning students. InfoQuest could demonstrate the mechanics of finding and using a database but did not contextualise why a specific information resource should be chosen nor did it empower library staff to teach any critical analysis of resources identified. It was seen as an 'add on' that library staff could use if time was available. The content, not the process, was the crucial focus.

A sample session for business students would comprise of a PowerPoint presentation explaining the rules of using the library (for example fines and loan policies) along with a list of what databases they should be using, and then an online exercise using InfoQuest. At this stage there was limited consideration of interface design or of how to introduce students to searching for information at academic level. Even if the librarian had considered the various learning styles identified by Honey and Mumford (1992) there was limited scope to integrate such theory into the sessions. While active learning has been identified and discussed extensively in information literacy literature (Finley, Skarl, Cox, & VanderPol, 2005) the style of session described above was a "passive learning experience" (Houlson, 2007). Time constraints limited the potential for active learning.

Towards the end of 2010 we were facing a crisis: the tools that we expected students to use were a selection from a collection of around 300 information databases, the library catalogue, an image database, various subject guides, electronic reading lists, and an institutional repository of research. We had not managed to bring these together in a way that empowered students and academic staff to locate the right source for their information needs at the right time. This Herculean task of reform was made somewhat harder by the politics and ownership of IT within the University. The library had limited control over the way its resources and services were presented through the student portal. We were also conscious that during this period the information landscape was being transformed by the availability of tools such as Google Scholar, open repositories of scholarly publications and Wikipedia. In addition, we had little in the way of spare time or local expertise to work through these issues. In a sense our information literacy teaching was being shaped by the past rather than looking to the future.

The journey from content to process

Certain key drivers allowed us as an academic library to reassess the way in which we delivered information literacy teaching. The university focus on the student experience, employability, and graduate attributes were all important elements.

In early 2009 Learning and Information Services (LIS) developed an Information Literacy Framework in order to underpin the University's Learning,

Teaching and Assessment strategy. The goals of the framework are to "identify and articulate those information skills which a graduate, postgraduate, or researcher needs to develop to equip them to become autonomous learners and to enhance their employability within an information rich society, and to embed these skills in the student experience" (Sheffield Hallam University, 2009).

There were also specific local initiatives that fed into the work of the information literacy group. One required us to respond to the differing needs of a large influx of Net Generation students each September taking a range of undergraduate business related courses. Our starting premise in re-examining our approach to information literacy development for these students was that they needed to understand and appreciate the importance of these skills before they would be able to incorporate them into their academic mindset. We designed teaching sessions aimed at raising their awareness of the skills they would need for university and which would be transferable to future employment. Students "must first understand and appreciate the importance of information literacy … before they will incorporate information literacy skills into their academic mindset" (Brown, Murphy and Nanny, 2003). We had to shift from being satisfied with systems that librarians know how to navigate to ones that are intuitive to our students and non-library staff.

Finally, we acknowledged that we needed a technological solution to consolidate the vast array of resources under one roof. Our initial exploration and evaluation of our existing subject guides with a view to their replacement had stalled when we realised the practicalities of bringing all our resources together. We therefore needed to design and create a new library resources portal that contained the rich, academic information sources that students and academic staff needed; we called this the Library Gateway[1] .

Developing the Library Gateway involved librarians from Subject, Virtual Learning Centre (VLC) and Systems teams working together. Within LIS the Systems team is largely responsible for specification, procurement, implementation, and running of the library systems. The VLC team focuses more on how these systems should be designed and implemented to enhance and facilitate an effective experience for the users. We sought feedback from academics and students to ensure that our plan to bring together our information into one interface was a positive contribution to enhancing their experience. The first version of the Library Gateway ticked a lot of boxes in terms of our aims but we still felt we were focusing too much on the content, albeit linked from one place.

In its first year we monitored and measured use of the Library Gateway. Although it solved a number of problems, we were aware it still needed work. We held focus groups for students, academic and library staff, and conducted online and face-to-face surveys of students about their use of the Library

---

1   Available at: http://library.shu.ac.uk

Gateway. We asked them which bits they used and what they didn't like: "better layout!", "declutter", "make it easier to navigate", "it is so complicated I often give up before I have found what I am searching for." It was clear we still needed to address the 'clutter' issue and improve the user experience, particularly with regards to where they should start their searching. Their comments informed the direction we then took.

As well as launching the Library Gateway we also redesigned our online information literacy tutorial: we developed a new system called re: Search[2] to replace InfoQuest. This new online information literacy tutorial focused much more on the process of searching and evaluating information resources.

Implementation of web-scale discovery

At this point web discovery tools came on the scene (Breeding, 2012) and we saw another opportunity to improve the user experience of our Library Gateway. The procurement group included staff from the Systems team, VLC team, and faculty teams; academic staff and students were also consulted. Four different products were evaluated and after many presentations and extensive discussions among the wider staff group, we chose Summon from Serials Solutions.

The Systems team worked on the integration of our information resources, the library management system, link resolvers and authentication. The VLC team concentrated on the user interface. Through the process that informed our thinking and design we addressed issues of usability and graphic design. We also sought tools that would enable integration and offer good mobile and off-campus access. For example, for design we were inspired by Edward Tufte's principles (Tufte, 2001). We already had expertise in web 2.0 tools and their integration into library systems but we needed to improve usability and for this we drew on the work of Jakob Nielson and Hoa Loranger, (Nielson, 2000, Nielsen and Loranger, 2006) and held focus groups.

Throughout this development we liaised with our colleagues in the department to ensure that we were maintaining compatibility with the university's e-learning approach, our information literacy group, and faculty support teams. The VLC team developed tools and standards for other staff to follow such as guidelines on producing and storing screencasts. We had an editorial overview and maintained the highest standards for what we and others were producing to ensure it was relevant, timely, up to date, and accessible.

This work revealed other aspects of our information resources user interface that needed attention. The introduction of the web-scale discovery tool had served as a catalyst for us to critically analyse every aspect of our user in-

---

2   Available at: http://alacarte2.shu.ac.uk/subject-guide/7-About-re-Search

terfaces. Our research informed the decisions we made to streamline the presentation of all our resources: subject guides, online help, screencasts, and online information literacy tutorial.

However, to achieve our goals we did need some further skills and policy development. We already had some expertise in creating basic HTML pages but more was necessary. To achieve a modern look and feel for our resources we undertook research into best practice for CSS[3] and new web standards such as HTML 5[4].

Our raised skills allowed us to also develop and test a mobile version of the refreshed Library Gateway (Figure 1). It was important that we created something that did not need to be delivered through an 'App Store' or similar, so we created a web optimised version to ensure it worked on the vast majority of the handheld devices most commonly used by our students.

In the past we had paid some attention to user statistics but this had generally been to count how many times a particular database had been accessed, to ascertain how popular a given resource might be. Again we felt this demonstrated a focus on content. To support the work we were doing, we integrated Google Analytics into all of the online resources that allowed it. This gave us much richer information regarding how people were accessing our resources, and enabled us to identify the devices they were using, along with technical information such as web browser type and screen resolution. This hard data enabled us to make evidence-based rather than intuitive decisions. We also used software that allowed us to monitor which parts of the Library Gateway were being used in real time, such as mouse hovers and active clicks, thus enabling us to focus on the user experience.

We also purchased new software on which to host our Subject Guides. We chose LibGuides, from Springshare, and created guidelines for subject librarians regarding their structure. This allowed them to contribute their expertise, whilst framing this within the context of what we considered was a first class user experience.

Librarians as facilitators of learning

We had consulted widely to inform our redesign and our introduction of the web-scale discovery platform but we faced a challenge in selling the concept to all those who support students both in information skills teaching sessions and at the library Helpdesk. The Helpdesk staff include professional librarians who design and teach information literacy skills, library assistants, and IT Help staff.

---

3   www.w3.org/TR/CSS
4   http://dev.w3.org/html5/spec/Overview.html

Figure 1 : Mobile Library Gateway[5].

While our rethink had been prompted by developments in library technology and information literacy teaching not all of our 120 Helpdesk staff are as engaged with these concepts as we are and we realised that training sessions for the new interface would need to communicate the principles behind the redesign and web-scale discovery software as much as being a "how to do it" session. We were mindful that most staff would agree with Vaughn's suggestion that "connecting users with the information they seek is one of the central pillars of our profession." (Vaughn, 2011). Naturally staff are proud of the range of resources they know about and their skilled searching techniques. However, we wanted them to be moving away from the approach of knowing about hundreds of databases and the complexities of searching them with a variety of Boolean operations.

We were also facing a problem that arose during the closed beta trial of Summon; subject librarians found their searches were frustrating and producing unexpected results. Other institutions had reported immediate benefits such as a massive increase in the number of full text downloads. During this testing phase, we stumbled on a concept that for us began to explain the unexpected results and also help us with our staff development. This concept is "Shoshin", or "beginner's mind" and stems from the dichotomy that exists between the beginner's and the expert's mind. It is taken from Zen Buddhism, and was popularised by the Zen master Shunryu Suzuki in his 1970 book "Zen Mind, Beginners Mind." in which he suggests "The mind of the beginner is empty,

---

5   Available at: http://m.library.shu.ac.uk

free of the habits of the expert, ready to accept, to doubt, and open to all the possibilities" (p13).

When we applied this concept to the way we were testing the web-scale discovery system it became apparent why our results were dissatisfying. We were testing using carefully constructed search terms and phrases – mirroring the way we had previously taught information literacy. Once we stepped away from being the expert, and treated the system as a beginner might, the results were more meaningful. The connections between results were clearer and the relevance to the initial search was more obvious. This approach made it appear there were more relevant results rather than fewer. The expert mind focuses on the content, the beginner mind focuses on how the content is experienced. As Suzuki suggests "In the beginner's mind there are many possibilities, but in the expert's there are few." (1970; p 21). Once we had embraced this concept our role as facilitators of learning in this context was much easier to define and act on.

It also gave us a focus for our summer staff development half day which was dedicated to the introduction and demonstration of the new web-scale discovery system in the context of our new Library Gateway. The training objectives for the day were to:

- communicate the concept and principles
- demonstrate its use
- allow hands-on practice (with support available)
- gather FAQs
- develop confidence and competence
- identify issues for future work

We didn't undertake a formal evaluation of existing skills for two reasons. Firstly, there is a core set of skills required for staff working on the Helpdesk. We were therefore able to assume certain standards of skill in supporting students with their information seeking. Secondly, for the purposes of training in the new approach we were not really calling on prior knowledge. Our aim was to demonstrate how the redesign and web-scale discovery system encourage a different type of support approach. One that better reflects the way students undertake searching and concentrating more on developing their critical and evaluative skills.

The concept of Shoshin also facilitated our engagement with academics. Although we had consulted with them during the tendering process, we wanted to ensure that they were confident in promoting the new web-scale discovery system to their students. At first, we encountered a significant amount of feedback that suggested the new system was 'dumbing down' the information resources. There was also consternation that familiar ways of working had disappeared. We tackled these issues in two distinct ways. Firstly we suggested that the faculty subject teams concentrated on the Shoshin notion when talking to academics about Library Search. Making the academics understand that for their students it was an excellent starting point was key. Also, highlighting that the Library Gateway was a portfolio of first class academic resources and that they should be viewed in conjunction with each other helped demonstrate the benefits of our approach. We also created help guides that explained how to replicate previous behaviour with the new resources. If academics had a particular database they required, we ensured that these were easy to locate.

Refreshed library gateway as a hub

At the start of the 2011/2012 academic year we were in a position to officially launch the refreshed Library Gateway, which included prominent positioning of Library Search, as we had named our implementation of Summon (Figure 2). The prominence given to Library Search within the Gateway is indicative of the shift in focus from content to user experience. The Library Gateway is the hub of the package of resources that are available to students and staff at SHU. It is designed to allow easy access to the vast range of resources available to students and offers online help and contact options for those users that require more assistance. For most subjects, the Library Gateway is also one of the fundamental building blocks of information literacy teaching.

Lessons learned

We have encountered a number of learned lessons throughout this process. Firstly, library staff will include a mix of people from a variety of professional backgrounds. Staff development therefore has to be tailored to suit the specific group that you are working with; we found that the key element is to constantly contextualise how the processes we are engaging with will help and benefit the users. Given that academic librarians generally have a one shot session with students, it is crucial that the curriculum for these sessions is carefully crafted to ensure that users are familiar with navigation and exploring resources, rather than focussing on specific content or database. Empowering the academic librarian through encouraging the shift from expert mind to beginners mind is crucial in this area.

Designing interfaces has to be done with the user in mind. For example, link farms are not an appropriate way to guide students to the resources that they need. We also found that designing systems and interfaces to suit librarians is the best way to alienate new and returning students. However, there is often a need for library staff to quickly access specific tools such as an ISBN search facility. These options should obviously be made available, but not on the front page of the library website.

Figure 2 : Refreshed Library Gateway, launched January 2012.

We quickly discovered that making changes to interfaces without advance warning or explaining why the changes have been made is the fastest way to annoy students and academic staff! It also frustrates academic librarians who have prepared screenshots and developed self-help material. Providing a central repository of up to date screenshots and other material is one way to solve this.

The introduction of new systems and new ways of searching is as much of a political issue as it is a technical one. However, working together to build what users need, and then educating library staff as to why it's been done in this way is the best way to create usable library systems. We are using feedback from teaching sessions to inform staff development. Finally, the message that "we are not our patrons" is essential in staff development and training.

Conclusions

We are now in a position where we are able to confidently promote our web-scale discovery system, Library Search, as the departure point for information searches. In our information literacy teaching this approach also allows us to move from explaining the mechanics of search to focusing on evaluating search results. There are times when students will want a quick search, times when they will need basic information literacy, and times when they need subject specific information, and there are times when they simply want to talk to someone. The shift in focus from content to a focus on a first class user experience enabled us to design our interfaces and our interactions to allow this to happen. We feel that the more intuitive design alongside the staff training we did when we introduced the new interface will achieve this. Justifying changes to systems needs to be a user driven process, not one driven by historical technologies, practices and ideals.

Acknowledgements.

We would like to thank our colleagues in Learning and Information Services without whom this work could not have been achieved, but any weaknesses in the paper are the sole responsibility of the authors.

References

Breeding, M. (2012). Library web-scale. *Computers in Libraries*, Jan/Feb, 19-21.

Brown, C., Murphy, T.J., & Nanny, M. (2003). Turning techno-savvy into info-savvy: authentically integrating information literacy into the college curriculum. *Journal of Academic Librarianship,* 29(6), 386-398

CIBER. (2008). *Information behaviour of the researcher of the future : a CIBER briefing paper.* London: University College London. Retrieved from the JISC website: www.jisc.ac.uk/media/documents/programmes/reppres/gg_final_keynote_11012008.pdf

Finley, P., Skarl, S., Cox, J., & VanderPol, D. (2005). Enhancing library instruction with peer planning. *Reference Services Review*, 33(1), 112-122.

Honey, P., & Mumford, A. (1992). *The manual of learning styles.* Maidenhead: Peter Honey Publications.

Houlson, V. (2007). Getting results from one-shot instruction: a workshop for first-year students. *College and Undergraduate Libraries,* 14(1), 89-108.

Milne. A.J. (2006). Designing blended learning space to the student experience. In D. Oblinger (Ed.), *Learning spaces.* Washington, D.C. : Educause.

Nielsen, J. (2000). *Designing web usability.* Indianapolis : New Riders.

Nielsen, J., & Loranger, H. (2006). *Prioritizing web usability.* Indianapolis : New Riders.

Oblinger, D., & Oblinger, J.L. (2005). *Educating the Net Generation.* Boulder : Educause

Sheffield Hallam University. (2009). *Information literacy framework.* Unpublished report. (Available on request from the authors).

Suzuki, S. (1970). *Zen mind, beginner's mind.* Tokyo: John Weatherhill.

Tufte, E.R. (2001). *The visual display of quantitative information.* Cheshire : Graphics Press

Vaughn, J. (2011).*Web-scale discovery.* [American Libraries blog]. Retrieved from: www.americanlibrariesmagazine.org/columns/dispatches-field/web-scale-discovery.

Information Literacy and Knowledge Management Tools for First Year Students

Sharon Favaro
Digital Services Librarian/Assistant Professor, Seton Hall University Libraries, USA
Sharon.Favaro@shu.edu

Abstract

With advances in technology, there is cause for a re-examination of the definition of information literacy. How does this impact first year students? It is proposed to include knowledge management tools in information literacy instruction to give first year students the foundation needed to understand the entire lifecycle of knowledge and to become successful lifelong learners. This paper examines the definition of information literacy as it relates to the 21st century information landscape and how to respond to the changes through applying knowledge management tools to teach first year students information literacy.

Introduction

The information landscape is constantly evolving due to rapid development in technology thus driving changes in research workflow practices and putting new demands on skills within the workforce. With emerging technologies to collaborate, communicate, share and manage information, it is imperative that students are prepared with the skill-set needed to be successful within the university and the workforce thus possessing lifelearning skills. It is crucial that students are given the foundation needed in the first year of college. This can be accomplished by building a framework through knowledge management tools for first year students. A new model is proposed to teach information literacy (IL) to first-year students by including knowledge management tools. Due to the changes in the 21st century information landscape, the definition of information literacy should be re-examined with specific emphasis on the skills needed for first year students.

Defining information literacy for the 21st century

Review of current information literacy definitions

There are several definitions of information literacy. A few of the most common ones are as follows. Information literacy is "the set of skills needed to find, retrieve, analyze, and use information", according to the Association of College and Research Libraries (ACRL, 2011). The Chartered Institute of Library and Information Professionals (CILIP) expands on the definition of information literacy as "a need for information, the resources available, how to find information, the need to evaluate results, how to work with or exploit results, ethics and responsibility of use, how to communicate or share your findings and how to manage your findings". Similar to CILIP, the Joint Information Services Committee (JISC) combines information literacy and IT skills to form i-skills "the ability to identify, assess, retrieve, evaluate, adapt, organise and communicate information within an iterative context of review and reflection" (Investing in staff skills, 2005). The NHS Education for Scotland definition is "An information literate person can recognise an information need and is able to apply the set of transferable skills, attitudes and behaviours needed to find, retrieve, assess, manage and apply information in any situation, throughout life."

Is there a need for changing how we think about information literacy?

Recently, library and information science articles have called for a "re-examining" of the definition of information literacy. The concept of literacy is changing due to digital technologies (Koltay, 2011). Emerging technology is having a huge impact on information literacy and what it means to be information literate. This raises the question of a need for changing the information literacy definition to navigate today's information landscape. Mackey and Jacobson (2011), review the definition of IL with incorporation of new media: "Metaliteracy is an overarching and self-referential framework that integrates emerging technologies and unifies multiple literacy types. This redefinition of information literacy expands the scope of generally understood information competencies and places a particular emphasis on producing and sharing information in participatory digital environments". Marcum (2002), calls for a "refocused" way of teaching information literacy with an emphasis on learning and socialtechnical fluency. Tuominen, Savolaien, and Tajia (2005) state "that understanding the interplay between knowledge formation, workplace learning, and information technologies is crucial for the success of information literacy initiatives and knowledge management as one of the key components to promote company-wide knowledge creation and sharing".

Role of technology in re-shaping research practice

New technologies are re-shaping research practices. One conducts research in a fast paced complex environment where information is much more abundant. "Massive technological changes in the area of research, knowledge production, publishing and communication are influencing the way research is done and the functions of the research library in supporting and facilitating research and learning" (DEFF, 2009). As a consequence, it is important to instill in students early on how to evaluate information within the library and freely available information outside of the library's digital walls. It is not only important to teach students how to critically evaluate information but also how to navigate the entire life-cycle of knowledge.

Challenges for learners in connecting library resources and new technology

There many disconnects between library resources and the research process. In a 2010 report from the University of Minnesota Libraries "searchers should be able to discover access, and interact with a digital resource as a seamless process. Types of interaction can include adding personalized data, e.g., annotations; creating and sharing ad-hoc collections; repurposing content in new ways (as rights allow); or enhancing access points for other searchers." However that is not the case, as a graduate student writes (Lawson, 2009), "lack of connections between my notes on my sources and my broader dissertation outline" cites not having a middle-layer to connect these resources together. A digital humanities study conducted by Reiger (2010), found a lack of awareness of tools and a need for training.

Librarians are very familiar with the difficulties users face on a daily basis while interacting with the library and research tools to complete assignments (Favaro, 2011). Students may have trouble locating the library resources online due to poor web design, silo-ed systems, lack of full text, lack of integration with tools, and in some cases, difficulty seeking out help from librarians when not on campus (Favaro, 2011). In addition, students are encountered (undergraduates and graduates) who are lacking skills in information technology use such as improper file management (ranging from a lost flash drive, incompatible software, or trying to save documents to the library's information commons computer), using online citation managers or lack of citation manager use, hardware failure with no back copies, organizing annotations, and managing information. Another observation is that many times first year students come with diverse backgrounds in library skills from high school. This ranges from not having a high school library, being where there is a library with only physical format material, to having access to both online information and physical format. First year student information literacy instruction needs to bridge the gap from high school to college.

Need for changing information literacy for first year students

It is vital that first year students are given a framework to understand the entire lifecycle of research early on. Everyday our society is inundated with information; not only do students need to understand how to find, search and retrieve, and evaluate information but how to manage information, share and collaborate, and ethically use to create new knowledge. In order to support this structure, it is necessary to have a new definition of information literacy. Through examining the literature there needs to be greater understanding of the definition of information as it applies to 21st century skills. Emphasis should be on teaching the learner the entire life cycle of research. The role of technology is changing research workflows and creating a demand for new types of skills sets within the workforce. There is a need for changing first year student information literacy instruction classes to encompass knowledge management tools.

Redefining information literacy

Due to the rapidly changing information environment, it is appropriate for a new definition of information literacy to provide students with the skills needed for the 21st century. A new definition for information literacy was put forth by Swan (2011) as the ability "to find, retrieve, analyze, synthesize, share and use information from a variety of media sources". Building on Swan's definition, it is appropriate to incorporate collaborating, organising, managing information alongside its ethical use. This inclusion leads to the adapted definition of information literacy being: to find, retrieve, synthesize, organize and manage information, collaborate, share, and use information from a variety of media sources ethically. Learners should be taught the entire life cycle of knowledge. This is important not only for their time as student but within the workforce and lifelong learning.

Knowledge management within libraries

In order to create a model for this new definition of information literacy, knowledge management needs to be incorporated to support it. Knowledge management is defined as the managing of information and the creation and sharing of information throughout a group. Traditionally, knowledge management within libraries has been for internal library operations. Jantz (2001) and Gandhi (2004) describe use of knowledge management for reference services, whereas Shanhong (2009) writes "knowledge management in libraries is to promote relationship in and between libraries, between library and user, to strengthen knowledge internet working and to quicken knowledge flow". According to Dillon (2002), in order to understand knowledge management, we must understand "how to create it, to store it, or to manipulate it to achieve some purpose".

Knowledge management tools are defined as technologies "which enhance and enable knowledge generation, codification, and transfer" and are "designed to ease the burden of work and to allow resources to be applied efficiently to the tasks for which they are most suited" (Ruggles, 1997). These tools are of particular importance for libraries. Jantz (2001) believes knowledge management tools could help transform the library into a more efficient knowledge-sharing organization because knowledge management involves the reusing and recycling of knowledge (Ralph and Tijerino, 2009).

Knowledge management for instruction

Rather than only using knowledge management for internal library operations, there is an opportunity to apply these knowledge management skills to library instruction to teach students. It is especially important to teach these skills to our first year students in order to give them a foundation to build on when understanding the life cycle of research practices. Knowledge management tools could also be used to teach first year students how to manage, share, and create new information. Snyman and Rooi (2006) discuss facilitating knowledge management skills within libraries "librarians understand the information seeking behaviour of users, which gives them an advantage over those people who deal exclusively with the technology of information because they add human value to information". In addition librarians have the ability to extend the reach of information literacy training beyond students to include academic staff within the university, "enhancing the ability of all employees of the university to create, capture, organise, store, access, share, use, publish and understand information." This builds a foundation for first-year students to integrate such tools and practices for their research to be used during their time as an undergraduate and transferred to workforce skills.

Prior knowledge and knowledge management tools

It is a major transition for first year students to move from the high school library to the college library. The research skill set needed for college is quite greater than the skills used in high school, thus it is import to bridge the gap. Building on prior-knowledge is a way to incorporate knowledge management tools into information literacy instruction. Prior knowledge is based on a learner's domain-specific knowledge (Mayer, 2005). New experiences are integrated into these organized thought patterns and establish the basis upon which learners make inferences about new and future events in an attempt to maintain a stable worldview (Ackerson, Flick, and Lederman, 2000; Meyer

2004). Students are able to make meaningful connections between what they already know and are being asked to learn (Driscoll 2005).

Based on empirical research there is an indication that first year students could use prior knowledge of knowledge management tools. In a study from Project Information Literacy, iSchool University of Washington, a large scale study involving undergraduate students from 25 colleges in the United States focusing on information seeking behavior in the digital age, it was found that students were using the following tools: highlighting text 62%, citation management 55%, Google Docs 48%, online forums 26%, Flickr 24%, wikis 18%, blogging 14%, virtual research environments 14%, and one in ten students used social booking marking (Head and Eisenberg, 2010). Such tools consist of online document storage, annotation tools, and citation tools as well as social media. Another study issued by the Pew Research Center in 2011 (Madden and Zickuhr, 2011) reported 83% of the young American adults aged 18-29 surveyed are using social networking (Facebook, LinkedIn, MySpace). Some of the common tasks in these applications are to create, share, and manage information which all could be applied to the use of knowledge management tools. First year student information literacy classes can build on prior-knowledge to use these tools for the research process.

Creating a learning environment based on constructivism for first year student instruction

Information literacy can be related to the learners' prior knowledge through skills the learner is already familiar with from using such tools as Facebook, Wikipedia, and Google. This will aid in schema acquisition thus aiding in building a mental model for representation which assists faster recall in long-term memory thus reducing cognitive load. Students are sharing, managing, searching, evaluating, and creating information. All of these processes can be related to information literacy instruction. An example of what this would look like is using Google, as generally students are familiar with Google and in some cases this might be where they start a search. This could be used in class as a compare and contrast by having students start searching by using Google and switch it to Google Scholar using the same search terms. Next instruct students on how to set preferences within Google Scholar to allow for access to the library's resources and citation export. By relating searching within the library to a familiar resource helps to reduce cognitive load and allows the student to build on prior knowledge.

To further assist first year students with the transition, it is necessary to create a learning environment to build schema and mental representations of the research life cycle. This can be accomplished by using a constructivist approach. Constructivism broadly defined says "only the active learner is successful; learning from examples or by doing enable learners to achieve deep levels of understanding; learning with understanding is what is desired, not rote learning; and the social structure of the learning environment is important" Driscoll (2005), or simply put learning by doing. By incorporating knowledge management tools into instruction this will give students the framework needed to put information literacy instruction into context. Listed below are examples of types of tools that could be used (but not limited to any specific tool) to assist in instruction:

- Google Docs[1]: create, share, collaborate, review, manage
  Google docs is a free web-based product, allowing users to easily collaborate through sharing documents, editing, and chat all in real time within the document. It allows for document storage and management, color coding and keeping information online and accessible anywhere.
- Citavi[2]: reference management, knowledge organization, and writing tool
  Citavi is a reference and knowledge management tool to help users with research tasks: information seeking, knowledge organization, project management, document storage, writing tool, and group work. It is possible to conduct searching of library resources within Citavi or to export resources to Citavi from within some library resources.
- Scrivener[3] : writing tool
  Scrivener is a writing tool allowing users to organize content through the use of story boards, outlining, and managing collections for the entire writing process.
- Zotero[4]: citation management
  Zotero is a freely available citation manager allowing for not only the management of citiations but also document storage, notes, and sharing of resources. It also allows the user to maintain ownership after graduating from the university.
- Scrible[5]: annotation
  Scrible is freely available tool allowing for annotating webpages, storing and retrieving annotations and sharing.

Conclusion

The definition of information literacy should be reviewed to determine its timeliness with 21st century demands in research practices as well as within

---

1   https://docs.google.com
2   www.citavi.com
3   www.literatureandlatte.com/scrivener.php
4   www.zotero.org
5   www.scrible.com

the workforce. More specifically as this pertains to first year students to enable them to be successful within the university and as lifelong learners. Further research should be conducted to integrate knowledge management tools into first year student instruction. Studies need to be done to determine the impact of prior-knowledge when using knowledge management tools on students' understanding of information literacy.

References

Akerson, V., Flick, L., & Lederman, N. (2000). The influence of primary children's ideas in science on teaching practice. *Journal of Research in Science Teaching*, 37(4), 363 – 385.

Association of College and Research Libraries. (2011). *Information literacy website*. Retrieved from ALA website: www.ala.org/ala/mgrps/divs/acrl/issues/infolit/index.cfm

DEFF Denmark's Electronic Research Library (2009). *The future of research and the research library*. Retrieved from DEFF website   : www.bibliotekogmedier.dk/fileadmin/publikationer/rapporter_oev rige/deff/the_future_research/index.htm

Dillon, M. (2002). Knowledge management: chimera or solution? *Portal: Libraries and the Academy*, 2 (2), 321-336.

Driscoll, M. (2005). *Psychology of learning for instruction,* 3rd ed., Boston : Pearson A and B.

Favaro, S. (2011). *Cloud library – a virtual personal collaborative work place for researchers*. Unpublished masters thesis. New York University. Retrieved from the New York University website: http://teinhardt.nyu.edu/alt/ect/ma/projects

Gandhi, S. (2004). Knowledge management and reference services. *Journal of Academic Librarianship*, 30(5), 368-381.

Head, A.J., & Eisenberg, M.B. (2010) *Truth be told: how college students evaluate and use information in the digital age*, Project Information Literacy Progress Report, University of Washington's Information School. Retrieved from the Project Information Literacy website : http://projectinfolit.org/pdfs/PIL_Fall2010_Survey_FullReport1.pdf

NHS Education for Scotland (n.d*) Information Literacy*. Retrieved the from NHS Education for Scotland website: www.infoliteracy.scot.nhs.uk/home.aspx

Investing in Staff i-Skills. (2005). Retrieved from the JISC website: www.jisc.ac.uk/media/documents/publications/sissinvesting.pdf

Jantz, R. (2001). Knowledge management in academic libraries: special tools and processes to support information professionals. *Reference Services Review*, 29(1), 33–39.

Koltay, T. (2011). The media and the literacies: media literacy, information literacy, digital literacy. *Media, Culture & Society*,33 (2), 211-221.

Lawson, K. M. (2009). *A proposal for a powerful new research tool – organizing information for dissertation writing, part 3 of 3*. Retrieved from: http://muninn.net/blog/2009/03/a-proposal-for-a-powerful-new-research-tool-organizing-information-for-dissertation-writing-part-3-of-3.html

Mackey, T. P., & Jacobson, T. E. (2011). Reframing information literacy as a metaliteracy. *College & Research Libraries*, 72(1), 62 -78.

Marcum, J.W. (2002). Rethinking information literacy. *The Library Quarterly*, 72(1), 1-26

Mayer, R. (2005). *The Cambridge handbook of multimedia learning.* Cambridge : Cambridge University Press.

Madden, M., & Zickuhr, K. (2011). *Pew Internet. 65% of online adults use social networking sites.* Retrieved from Pew Research Center website: www.pewinternet.org/~/media//Files/Reports/2011/PIP-SNS-Update-2011.pdf

Meyer, H. (2004). Novice and expert teachers' conceptions of learners' prior knowledge. *Science Education*, 88(6), 970 – 983.

Ralph, L., & Tijerino, C. (2009). Knowledge management and library culture. *College and Undergraduate Libraries*, 16(4), 329-337.

Rieger, O. Y. (2010). Framing digital humanities: the role of new media in humanities scholarship. *First Monday*, 15(10). Retrieved from the FirstMonday website: http://firstmonday.org/htbin/cgiwrap/bin/ojs/index.php/fm/article/view/3198/2628

Ruggles, R.L. (Ed.). (1997). *Knowledge management tools.* Boston: Butterworth-Heinemann.

Shanhong, T. (2000). *Knowledge management in libraries in the 21st century.* 66th IFLA Council and General Conference. Retrieved from the IFLA website: www.ifla.org/IV/ifla66/papers/057-110e.htm.

Swan, K. (2011). Technology and information literacy. *Journal of Information Fluency*, 1(1), 4-9.

Snyman, R., & Rooi, H. (2006). *Facilitating knowledge managent: opportunities for librarians in a changing world.* XVII Standing Conference of Eastern, Central & Southern Africa Library & Information Associations Proceedings, 58(3), 261 – 271. Retrieved from the Tanzania Library Association website: www.tla.or.tz/scecsal2006/Volume1.pdf#page=124

Tuominen, K., Savolainen, R., & Talja, S. (2005). Information literacy as a sociotechnical practice. *Library Quarterly*, 75(3), 329-345.

University of Minnesota Libraries. (2010). *Discoverability : phase 2 final report.* Retreived from the University of Minnesota website: http://conservancy.umn.edu/bitstream/99734/3/DiscoverabilityPhase2ReportFull.pdf

Forging Strong Links: Strategies for Building a Collaborative Information Literate Learning Community through the School Library

Elizabeth Greef
Head Librarian, St Andrew's Cathedral School, Sydney, Australia
egreef@sacs.nsw.edu.au

Abstract

Integrating information skills into the school curriculum is one of the prime focus areas of the teacher librarian and strong collaboration is a key to the library becoming a vital cog in the teaching and learning mission of a school. This is easily said, but how do we make it happen? What strategies can we use for building information literacy? How can we change our practice and develop skills to effect change? This paper will briefly consider definitions and models of information literacy and collaboration, particularly Montiel-Overall's work, including the theoretical and pedagogical underpinning of these ideas. As well as reflecting on the role and the mindset of the teacher librarian, a range of practical macro- and micro-strategies for effectively developing information literacy in collaboration with teaching staff will be presented, including technology, special learning needs, building a reading culture, literacy and instructional design. A self-diagnostic tool developed from this paper will be offered during the conference to enable each teacher librarian to evaluate opportunities for further developing information literacy through his/her library.

Introduction

> "We must raise the bar in our thinking; libraries and librarians enhance the total development of our society. If we do not seek to strengthen the link between libraries and the classrooms, the real losers will continue to be our students who miss access to current materials for information, recreational reading and team teaching by the class teacher and the librarians. We are also aware that we are living in an information-driven age where we must be on the cutting edge of technology. In light of this there must be a major paradigm shift by administrators,

classroom teachers and librarians especially those who are of the view that libraries and librarians are not as important as other educational institutions. The library should be an integral part of the school's reading programme and … collaboration should exist between the classroom teacher and the librarian for the creation of units and lessons that link content, information literacy and technology literacy" (Grant quoted in 'Libraries critical to development …, 2006).

We as teacher librarians are link people, connectors to making the paradigm shift towards an integrated curriculum and deeper learning happen for our students, our colleagues and our schools. We have influence but change is achieved through the support of the school principal, collaboration with others, belief in ourselves and a vision for the future.

The substantial body of recent research on the relationship between effective school libraries and student academic performance has validated significant factors, including collaboration between teacher librarians and classroom teachers (Lance, 2002; School libraries work!, 2008). Collaboration is a prime means of facilitating ongoing personal professional development; we learn from each other. It is also the key for a teacher librarian to bring about change, to work successfully in integrating information skills into the school curriculum and to become a vital cog in the teaching and learning and professional development (PD) cycles within the school. Teacher collective learning and shared work have a powerful impact on student learning (Leonard, 2002). What strategies can we use to make this happen? This paper examines definitions of collaborative practice, relevant research, the critical role of the teacher librarian, the underpinning pedagogy of learning communities, information literacy and constructivist learning. It presents a range of macro-strategies for developing collaboration to build information literacy and deeper student learning, and micro-strategies to enable the collaboration to occur in an effective and integrated way, arising from my professional practice and experience.

A definition of collaboration and how innovation develops through collaboration

The American Information Power initiative states: "Effective collaboration with teachers helps to create a vibrant and engaged community of learners, strengthens the whole school program as well as the library media program, and develops support for the school library media program throughout the whole school" (Information Power, 1998, quoted in Small, 2002) and can become contagious. Collaboration is based on "shared goals, a shared vision and a climate of trust and respect" (Muronago and Harada, quoted in Russell, 2001; Small, 2002). It is a strong 21st century trend and a vehicle for school renewal. Collaboration is embedded within the social constructivist learning theories of educators such as John Dewey and Lev Vygotsky (Montiel-Overall, 2005). In particular Vygotsky's concept of the "zone of proximal development" where more mature and capable people like teachers guide those who are less advanced within a socially constructed learning experience is significant (Montiel-Overall, 2005) and has been employed by Carol Kuhlthau in her Zones of Intervention within the Guided Inquiry process (Kuhlthau, Maniotes and Caspari, 2007). Collaboration creates a third space between people, a space from which creative synergy and ongoing professional development flow. Montiel-Overall's definition (2005, pp. 5-6) encapsulates educational collaboration well:

> "Collaboration is a trusting, working relationship between two or more equal participants involved in shared thinking, shared planning and shared creation of integrated instruction. Through a shared vision and shared objectives, student learning opportunities are created that integrate subject content and information literacy by co-planning, co-implementing, and co-evaluating students' progress throughout the instructional process in order to improve student learning in all areas of the curriculum".

Facets of collaboration

Collaboration is a complex concept as well as a process where we learn from each other. Montiel-Overall (2005) developed four models or facets to describe collaborative relationships:

Facet A: Coordination involves people exchanging information, sharing time, resources or students to help one another

Facet B: Cooperation/Partnership requires more commitment, responsibility and intensity; underpinned by a philosophy of teamwork and cooperation it may involve the school library in gathering resources to support the classroom or some joint instruction

Facet C: Integrated Instruction involves *"shared thinking, shared planning and shared creation of integrated instruction"*, an integration of both content and information skills instruction. Responsibility is shared in the creation of a meaningful learning experience and synergy develops, resulting in a richer learning activity

Facet D: Integrated Curriculum, where the process of Facet C is implemented across the entire curriculum with all teachers in the school planning, teaching and assessing a unit of work integrating subject content with library information literacy instruction.

Pedagogy underpinning collaboration in support of information literacy

Learning communities

Henri (in Henri & Asselin, 2005, p. 12) clarifies the significance of the learning community in relation to collaboration:

> "Community is something that transforms thinking within the school... Collaboration and collegiality are key measures of community well-being and are partial indicators of the existence of an information literate school community... In essence the information literate school community... places a significant priority on transforming information into knowledge and in turning knowledge into information..."

The effective principal is a critical factor in the learning community, inspiring the school with a common vision and promoting a consistent philosophy of education, encouraging collaborative partnerships and the sharing of expertise to enrich and optimise student learning (Henri 1988; Hay and Henri, 1995; Oberg and Henri, 2005). Recent research also validates the school library as an important instrument of school improvement (Hartzell, 2003). Six hallmarks of a learning community which dovetail well with the work of the school libraries are that, "the principal and teachers…:

- Create continuous learning opportunities
- Promote inquiry and dialogue
- Encourage collaboration and team learning
- Establish systems to capture and share learning
- Empower people towards a collective vision
- Connect the organisation to its environment"
  (Watkins & Marsick, 1993, cited in Henri & Asselin, 2005).

However, collaboration is neither valued nor sought by all teachers; it can even be seen as a threat.

Constructivist pedagogy and resource-based learning

Teacher librarians work within a constructivist framework in the belief that students learn best when they construct their own knowledge, creating new learning experiences which allow students to extend themselves and create and transform knowledge. Constructivism is a highly influential theory of cognitive growth and learning (Bartlett, 2005). The library is an environment that allows more independence and self-directed learning, and certain student-centred constructivist pedagogical strategies marry well with information skills such as problem-based learning, inquiry-based learning and project-based learning, optimised by collaborative practice (Robins et al, 2005).

Information literacy and deeper student learning

Information literacy is foundational to the concept of lifelong learning. An information age school needs "to be built on the centrality of information literacy" (Mackey and Jacobson, 2005, p. 1) because "information literacy is a meta-outcome in the learning process" (Ratteray, quoted in Mackey and Jacobson, 2005; p. 2). For years teacher librarians have used information literacy frameworks such as Kuhlthau's Guided Inquiry and Eisenberg & Berkowitz's Big Six to help students and colleagues understand the research process. However, the professional thinking is shifting to see this generic approach as often too limited and limiting for developing deep thinking and critical engagement with information (Todd, 2007). Todd encourages school libraries to become "intellectual hotbeds of discontent", places where debates can rage and active exploration of and deep engagement with ideas takes place, promoting the synthesis and transformation of ideas and knowledge.

Deeper student learning involves critical literacy skills of perceiving, interpreting, examining and critiquing information and using higher order thinking skills – connecting pieces of information, transforming and creating new knowledge and engaging in meaningful reflection. Limberg's research noted concerns in the study of information seeking which were not addressed explicitly by teachers through instruction, particularly critical reflection, formulation of questions, time management, critical evaluation of sources, analysis of information and synthesis of material (Limberg, 2005). Teacher librarians clearly need collaboratively to address students' deeper cognitive needs and higher order thinking skills (Todd, 2007).

Technology

Technology has transformed schools and opportunities for learning. Lee (Henri and Asselin, 2005, p. 15) asserts that the "key feature of a learning community is that it is networked", knowledge sharing is "the key force behind the learning organisation" (Hawamdeh, cited in Henri and Asselin, 2005, p. 15) but the factor which transforms and empowers the school as an online community is really "the way that schools use an educational rationale to drive …objectivity" (Henri and Asselin, 2005, p. 15); then the educational value of technology will be realised. Increasingly, Web 2.0 technologies facilitate collaborative knowledge construction and development of online communities and teacher librarians can guide and influence here.

Mindset and role of the teacher librarian

Information specialist – Teacher librarians are a critical factor within a collaborative school as they have a comprehensive, umbrella view of teaching and learning because of their whole school focus and highly developed information skills. Teacher librarians need to be "Renaissance" men and women with multiple skills bridging both arts and sciences. Despite all the evidence linking school libraries to raised student achievement, Todd believes that the primary underpinning factor in this process is the "transformational actions of the school librarian" (Todd, quoted in Kenney, 2006, p. 3).

Self-belief and readiness to meet the challenge – We must believe in ourselves and our professional value to our schools. Our role also demands humility because so much of what we do is in partnership and in support of others to propel the educational vision of our schools. We collaborate with subject content experts to provide the best learning environment for all our students in equal partnerships. We want to see positive change in our schools, intellectual growth in our students and increasing sophistication in their ability to access, organise, evaluate and transform information and to drive improvement. Valenza (2002; p. 2) argues that "a good librarian is one of the best educational bargains around". Flexibility, a willingness to take risks and a commitment to personal lifelong learning are fundamental to success.

Change agents to drive the paradigm shift – Teacher librarians need to be prepared to be change agents. Gandhi put it this way: "We must be the change we want to see in the world" (quoted in Rosenfeld, 2006; p. 63). We need to take on the risk ourselves, have a vision for change, look for strategic opportunities and negotiate and alleviate the concerns of others in the process of changing the school culture to bring others along with us. We need to identify the inhibitors or barriers to change and the enablers in order to move forward. The enablers need to be in place in each school and the inhibitors need to be addressed.

Advocacy – Related to the notion of being a change agent is that of advocacy. We need to "sell" the ideas of collaboration and information literacy, including promoting research linking effective school libraries and student academic improvement.

Transformational leadership – A transformational leader is relationship-oriented, enlisting others in a vision for learning and travelling on with them in the process, working from within and alongside in a positive, motivational and participatory way (Beare, Caldwell and Millikan, 1989). Research relating to teacher librarian leadership indicates that the positive effects of library programmess increase significantly if the role is expanded to include curriculum and leadership involvement well beyond the library (Lance, 2002, p. 2). Harada (2002) also notes integral links between collaboration and leadership.

Manager and program administrator – A major role of the teacher librarian is the responsible management of a large whole-school facility, a visible metaphor for the school's existence as a learning community, as well as the delivery of services and the development of effective reading and information literacy instructional programs.

INHIBITORS TO COLLABORATION	ENABLERS IN COLLABORATION
Lack of time	Team approach to teaching
Confusion of roles	Shared constructivist approach to learning
Poorly designed assignments	Shared commitment to lifelong learning
	Competence in developing learning strategies and activities
Kuhlthau, (1993, cited in Henri & Asselin, 2005)	
Resistance to moving beyond traditional roles	Flexible timetable
Lack of awareness of students' information needs	Principal support
Lack of institutional support for collaboration and information literacy	
Belief that teaching information literacy is the job of library staff	
Montiel-Overall (2005; Mackey & Jacobson 2005)	

Figure 1: Inhibitors and enablers

Vital attributes – A collaborative mindset requires the teacher librarian to be eminently approachable, willing to forge links and connections between people and with resources, and flexible application of a range of teaching and learning strategies to help cement the library's ability to make a difference in the school. Oberg (1999) regards vital qualities of the teacher librarian to be excellent communication skills, willingness to take initiative, confidence, leadership qualities, and being a risk taker. Montiel-Overall (2005) believes a willingness to share and establishing collegial and trusting relationships are very important.

Instructional partners with knowledge of our school's culture – Collaborative teaching can be seen as both expensive and high risk in terms of time, effort and changing one's practices; integrating technology increases the price and risk factor (Oberg, 1995). Oberg advises that teacher librarians develop knowledge of the current teaching practices of their schools, the school's culture and also the skills, knowledge and attitudes teachers bring to the collaborative table, to help make the process more painless.

Teachers with commitment to authentic student learning – We must consider our students and reinvent ourselves to meet the needs of the new generation. We need to see teaching as a political activity where we empower our students to become critically-informed, perceive underlying agendas and address issues such as "social justice, globalisation and ethical use of information" (Henri & Asselin, 2005, p. 5), transforming the school learning community into *collaboratories* (Lunsford and Bruce, quoted in Henri and Asselin, 2005, p. 5) which exhibit "values and practices already held by teacher librarians: shared inquiry, intentionality, active participation and contribution, access to shared resources, technologies and boundary crossings"

Mastery of technology – Use of information and communication technologies (ICT) is central to this concept and requires strong ICT skills. In schools teacher librarians are often the "human link between technology and knowledge" (Valenza, 2002, p. 3); therefore, we must be informed and up-to-date with both technology and pedagogical thinking to assist in technology integration.

Professional development – Collaboration with library colleagues is vital for professional development, providing encouragement and advice, helping us remain up-to-date and informed. Participating in active teacher librarian listservs like OZTL_NET (Australia) and LM_NET (USA) allows cross-pollination of ideas and offers enormous professional wisdom and insight. Professional development including conferences, one day events, professional journals and sharing ideas at a regional or local level, are useful for learning and keeping up with research findings. Collaboration can be taken to a higher level where a district group or school team sets up a common resource bank on a website or DVD. Teacher librarians are in a powerful position to provide PD to the school community especially on ICTs and information literacy.

Macro-strategies to create opportunities for collaboration

Inspecting the architecture of our learning community – Firstly, in creating opportunities for collaboration and building information literacy we need to know our teaching staff and their perceived needs, understand our school's culture and map the inhibitors and enablers to collaboration. Then we can attempt to address these, lobbying for the enabling aspects to be in place such as principal support and flexible scheduling and addressing the concerns recognised as inhibitors. If the school situation is already collaborative, we can offer our help as an instructional partner with a difficult topic or curriculum area by suggesting ideas and resources and planning and teaching a unit of work together. We need to take risks.

Connecting strategically with school priority areas – Strategic thinking is needed around integrating the library into the heart of the school. Identify the priorities and educational emphases of your school and think how the library can help meet these needs, improving the community for all its members. Priority areas may be integrating technology, differentiating the classroom, low literacy levels, lack of reading, addressing plagiarism, racial minorities, gender education, assessment, curriculum design, collaboration and information literacy.

Building collaboration around technology – All schools are becoming more technology-focused. A teacher librarian can be influential here. Set up or join the Technology Committee of your school; be a voice in a technology vision for the future. If appropriate, the committee could audit staff technology skills to gauge training needs across school faculties and create a training plan. Develop a three year plan including acquisition of technology, training and maintenance strategies. Investigate potential learning and content management systems and databases. Be informed; liaise with others to learn about useful new technology and integrating it. Develop competence in software applications; write or find simple instructions for students. Help integrate technology into teaching and learning. Take risks! Be the bridge/moral support/technology coach in the class to help teachers develop comfort and confidence in using new technology such as:

- Blogs as reading journals
- Forums, discussions on class-related issues
- Wikis; for notes, meetings, ideas and minutes
- Digital streaming software (ClickView)
- Subscription databases
- E-journals and E-books.

Work collaboratively with the subject teacher to design and teach units of work incorporating ICTs; for example, we have tried a year-long program with our English faculty in which we build information literacy skills integrated with ICTs around a reading program on historical fiction. Provide an electronic "toolbox" for the school community – PDF files with instructions on skills like citation, PowerPoint tips, developing a website, mind-mapping and using online databases. Learning management systems such as Moodle or Edmodo help in managing a digital learning environment (Terry and Spear, 2003), offering an online classroom to manage web-based projects, upload assignments, link websites, send messages, include instructional tutorials and integrate calendars with access from anywhere.

Developing a library website to centralise access to information resources – A school library website is a powerful tool for students and staff and also acts as an online advocate for the library and its services and can be a vehicle for PD. It offers centralized access for library resources such as the library catalogue, databases, instructional tutorials, reading lists, website hotlists and pathfinders, and can generate enthusiasm for the wealth of resources available (Terry and Speare, 2003). The library becomes one without walls, and with access from anywhere.

Building collaboration around curriculum – A curriculum committee which is a visionary think tank about the nature of teaching and learning, assessment for learning, professional development and strategies for dealing with plagiarism and fostering higher order information skills, is a rich and worthwhile forum for teacher librarian involvement. With our unique perspective we can share our insights and contribute to cutting-edge thinking in the school.

Building collaboration around special needs –We can help differentiate the curriculum for gifted learners by individual support and resource provision for extension and personal interest projects. Useful generic types of modifications such as templates and scaffolds can be put on the library website or staff material area for all teachers to access, to help them cater for the needs of those in their classes who need extension or modification. In collaborative instruction modifications can be more explicit scaffolding, simplified instructions, vocabulary, and employing lower levels of Bloom's Taxonomy oriented more towards fact-finding.

Building collaboration around reading culture – Reading is a foundational skill for all students. Negotiate the introduction of a reading program such as Literature Circles, Drop Everything and Read (DEAR) or a Wide Reading Challenge. Literature Circles, cycling through silent sustained reading, discussion groups and writing reflective responses, can result in substantive conversation and sets up a powerful ongoing dialogue about reading. Teacher librarians can create blogs for students to write their reading responses, develop book lists for levels and genres, promote reading through displays, competitions and book club websites and support "literary learning".

Building collaboration around literacy – Literacy is also a critical issue in schools. Rosenfeld (2006; p. 63) affirms the need for teacher librarians to be "literacy advocates". Join the Literacy Committee and integrate information literacy and digital literacy instruction. Develop publications with models – text types, citation, the information skills process, evaluating resources. At St Andrew's we developed several literacy programs including a PD file of strategies for teachers, *The L-Files. WOW (Working on writing)* targeted writing improvement across Year 9. A publication for Seniors is *CARS (Citation and referencing skills)*. The *RAW (Research and writing)* booklet uses the New South Wales Information Process as a scaffold, with strategies to assist guided inquiry across the curriculum:

DEFINING	concept maps, questions, understanding instructional words
LOCATING	list of library and other general resources, access points, pathfinder
SELECTING/	note-making and organisational
ORGANISING	strategies, evaluating websites
PRESENTING	PowerPoint and presentation tips; language use, essay writing, scaffolds
EVALUATING	self-evaluation

For years *RAW* became the foundation for collaboratively taught units of work in the library in Year 8.

Building influence around professional development – The literacy booklets provide PD in information and literacy skills for teachers and extend the library's influence in the school. The work of the school library often results in providing PD for teachers through collaboration. Teacher librarians are in a strong position to provide PD programmes in areas of literacy and technology, e.g. *Let's play* program at St Andrew's (an exploration of Web 2.0 for teachers), based on Helene Blowers '23 things'[1]:

Developing an information literacy continuum and collecting evidence – A graded continuum of information and technology skills lends credibilityto the process of collaboration and demonstrates clearly the intentional and incremental nature of the teacher librarian's interventions in developing skills in students. It provides substantial justification for the collaborative process and also provides a helpful guideline for teacher librarians and teachers in staging the introduction and consolidation of particular skills. It demonstrates that we as teacher librarians have a clear direction and mandate for developing information skills in students especially if integrated with syllabus documents. Library staff can also use curriculum mapping to keep a record of the collaboration that occurs with classroom teachers and the skills taught. Evidence-based practice is useful for collecting one's own evidence of differences the library may have made in teaching and learning (Todd, 2003).

Building collaboration around reducing plagiarism – We need to promote ethical scholarship and make it clear to students that they need to write in their own words. It is best to reduce plagiarism at the stage of instructional design. We can offer suggestions and interventions for rich tasks and construction of questions that allow little scope for plagiarism such as comparison/contrasting, taking an unusual angle on the question, group work, and explicit instruction in reference and citation skills, to foster more independent thinking and deeper learning.

Building collaboration through designing integrated units of work – Loertscher (2003) suggests that in planning units of work we use the relevant out-

---

1   http://sacsnet.sacs.nsw.edu.au/library/Teaching/SACSPDWeb2.0courseLetsplay.htm

comes/standards to set clear goals for students about what they need to learn, then draw upon the resources and technology of the library and beyond, collaborate with other staff and expect this will lead to a flow-on of collaborative experiences across the school; also the assessment of learning should take into account both product and process. Collaboration with teaching staff to create meaningful resource-based units of work provides the opportunity for a successful and graduated research experience, integrating information skills and technology, eliciting higher order thinking skills, minimising the opportunity for plagiarism and allowing students to embed and refine transferable purposeful skills – thinking, information skills, problem-solving and critical evaluation of resources. The classroom teacher brings understanding of students' abilities and weaknesses and expertise in the content to the partnership; the teacher librarian brings a thorough understanding of the information process and a variety of resources and strategies to help construct a successful research experience. Developing collaborative instruction around assessments is particularly helpful because this approach allows all students in the school to be taught information skills embedded in their subject content and staff to be mentored in these approaches. It also challenges the teacher librarian professionally to develop and communicate information skills.

Micro-strategies to support collaboration

The shape of the collaborative instruction process – Typical stages of collaborative planning involve discussion about the outcomes of the task, type, length, due date, areas of research, possible questions, and the model that will suit the task and maximize the achievement of the outcomes. A library impact statement can help to initiate this discussion. Formulation of the draft task with library staff ensuring sufficient resources at appropriate levels to meet the task requirements happens next; the draft unit is sent between the faculty and the library until it satisfies all stakeholders. The library staff assemble resources, copy worksheets, upload the task, electronic resources and links to the online class space, and book the library.

The teaching phase works as a partnership with the librarian usually explaining the task, the location of the resources and strategies for approaching aspects of the task, and the teacher adding whatever is needed to clarify. The introduction to the topic is essentially a motivational talk to inspire students to explore the ideas, to feel excited about learning and investigating and to link it to prior learning and the larger context. Narrative, interesting trivia or setting the task up as a mystery to be solved can heighten motivation. Reassuring students about the cyclic nature of the research process and universal feelings of uncertainty is helpful. Instructional interventions will be needed at times using modelling, guidance, explicit instruction, demonstration and questioning. Assessment and a final debrief, incorporating improvements for next time, are conducted together.

Useful prompts for planning – A planning folder with idea prompts is useful. This could include – sample units, Blooms Taxonomy wheel, continuum of information literacy and digital skills, syllabus documents, critical thinking strategies and multiple intelligence matrixes – as prompts to help us think more creatively and from a broader pedagogical standpoint.

Useful equipment resources for the library involved in collaborative instruction – A set of assignment shelves with relevant labels, e.g. Year 7 Middle Ages, is helpful for easy location of resources on closed reserve. Spare book trolleys are also desirable for moving relevant resources quickly to the allocated teaching area.

Ambience of the library – The school community needs to see the library and its services as useful and responsive, a means to success and higher achievement, with a welcoming, positive and stimulating ambience, which develops the whole person.

Conclusion

All that we do is for our students and our colleagues; we ourselves must continue to grow and "raise the bar" through refining our collaborative instruction to facilitate deeper learning. To reiterate:

> "We must raise the bar in our thinking; libraries and librarians enhance the total development of our society. If we do not seek to strengthen the link between libraries and the classrooms, the real losers will continue to be our students…" (Grant, 2006)

References

Bartlett, J. (2005). Curriculum integration and information literacy: developing independent learners. In *The information literate school community 2: issues of leadership*, J. Henri & M. Asselin (Eds). Wagga Wagga, NSW: Centre for Information Studies.

Beare, H., Caldwell, B.J., & Millikan, R.H. (1989). *Creating an excellent school*. London: Routledge.

Harada, V.H. (2002). Taking the lead in developing learning communities. *Knowledge Quest*, 31(2), 12-16.

Hartzell, G. (2003). Why should principals support school libraries? *Teacher Librarian*. 31(2), 21.

Hay, L., & Henri, J. (1995). Leadership for collaboration: making vision work. *61st IFLA General Conference – Conference Proceedings*, August 20-25, 1995. Retrieved from: www.ifla.org/IV/ifla61/61-hayl.htm.

Henri, J. (1988). *The school curriculum: a collaborative approach to learning*, 2nd ed. Wagga Wagga, NSW: Centre for Library Studies.

Henri, J., & Asselin, M. (Eds.). (2005). *The information literate school community 2: issues of leadership*. Wagga Wagga, NSW: Centre for Information Studies.

Kenney, B. (2006). Ross to the rescue! *School Library Journal*, 52(4), 44

Kuhlthau, C.C., Maniotes, L.K., & Caspari, A.K. (2007). *Guided inquiry: learning in the 21st century*. Westport, CT: Libraries Unlimited.

Lance, K.C. (2002). What research tells us about the importance of school libraries, *Knowledge Quest*, 31(1), 17-22.

Leonard, L. (2002). Schools as professional communities: addressing the collaborative challenge. *International Electronic Journal of Leadership in Learning*. 7(1). Retrieved from: www.ucalgary.ca/~iejll/volume6/leonard.html.

Libraries critical to development says education official. (2006). *SKNVibes*. Retrieved from: www.sknvibes.com/News/NewsDetails.cfm/2301.

Limberg, L. (2005). Informing information literacy education through empirical research. In *The information literate school community 2: Issues of leadership*, J. Henri & M. Asselin (eds). Wagga Wagga, NSW: Centre for Information Studies.

Loertscher, D. (2003). *Project achievement: brief guide and handout*. Salt Lake City, UT: Hi Willow. Retrieved from: www.txla.org/conference/SLSS/ProjectAchievement.pdf.

Mackey, T.P., & Jacobson, T.E. (2005). Information literacy: a collaborative endeavour. *College Teaching*, 53(4), 140.

Montiel-Overall, P. (2005). Toward a theory of collaboration for teachers and librarians, *School Library Media Research*, 8. Retrieved from: www.ala.org/ala/aasl/aaslpubsandjournals/slmrb/slmrcontents/volume82005/theory.htm.

Montiel-Overall, P. (2007). *Mixed methods research: developing a deeper understanding of teacher and librarian collaboration*. [PowerPoint]. Presentation at CISSL-ILILE Research Symposium, "Multiple Faces of Collaboration", May 17-18, 2007, Kent State University, Kent. Ohio. Retrieved from: www.libros.arizona.edu/TLClogo/TLCLOGO.htm

Oberg, D. (1995). High stakes: Technology and collaborative teaching. Information Technology Education Connection (ITEC) conference on schooling and the information super highway. Paper presented in *Cooperative planning and teaching model for the 21st century?* K. Strand (Ed.). Wagga Wagga, NSW: Charles Sturt University, Centre for Teacher Librarianship, June 3-15.

Oberg, D. (1999). Teaching the research process – for discovery and personal growth. *IFLA Bangkok 1999 Conference Proceedings*. Paper presented at 65th IFLA Council and General Conference, Bangkok, Thailand, 20-28 August. Retrieved from: www.ifla.org/IV/ifla65/papers/078-119e.htm.

Oberg, D., & Henri, J. (2005). The leadership role of the principal in the information literate school community. In *The information literate school community 2: Issues of leadership*, J. Henri & M. Asselin (eds). Wagga Wagga, NSW: Centre for Information Studies.

Robins, J. et al. (2005). Beyond the bird unit. *Teacher Librarian*, 33(2), 8

Rosenfeld, E. (2006). Teacher-librarians supporting student learning. *Teacher Librarian*, 33(3), 63. Available from: www.redorbit.com/news/education/397057/teacherlibrarians_supporting_student_learning/index.html

Russell, S. (2002). Teachers and library media specialists: collaborative relationships. *Teacher Library Media Specialist*, 29(5), 35-38.

School libraries work! 3rd edn. (2008). Scholastic. Retrieved from: www2.scholastic.com/content/collateral_resources/pdf/s/slw3_2008.pdf

Small, R. (2002). Developing a collaborative culture. *The best of ERIC, ALA*. Retrieved from: www.ala.org/ala/aasl/aaslpubsandjournals/slmrb/editorschoiceb/bestoferic/besteric.htm #developing.

Small, R. (2002). Collaboration: Where does it begin? *Teacher Librarian*, 29(5), 8-11.

Terry, M., & Spear, D. (2003). Connecting the classroom and the library. *MultiMedia Schools*, 09-01-2003. Retrieved from: www.infotoday.com/MMSchools/sep03/terry_spear.shtml.

Todd, R. (2003), Irrefutable evidence. *School Library Journal*, 49(4), 51.

Todd, R. (2007). *Leading learning through the school library: a guided inquiry approach.* Seminar at Cockle Bay, Darling Harbour, Sydney, 2 March.

Valenza, J.K. (2002). School librarians: a field guide to an evolving species. *Classroom Connect Newsletter*, 8(7). Retrieved from: www.classroom.com/community/connection/connectednewsletter/librarians.jhtml.

Librarians – Moving from Being 'The Elephant in the Room' to Becoming Central to the Learning Process

David V. Loertscher
San Jose State University
reader.david@gmail.com
and
Blanche Woolls
San Jose State University
blanche.woolls@sjsu.edu

Abstract

This paper reports the results of interviews with students in one U.S. school district's elementary, middle, and high schools, and explores two ways: Book to Cloud and Knowledge Building Centres which place librarians "On the Road to Information Literacy." It acknowledges librarians in all types of libraries as people who, in real time, are facilitating learning and knowledge building. They are essential elements in the learning space. The paper will present the concept of the librarian at the centre of learning, address the perceptions students have of librarians in their learning lives, demonstrate strategies that put the librarian at the centre of learning and immerse and embed the librarian into the learning experience. Most librarians would agree that they have seemed to be elephants in the room. They have been considered outside the sphere of learning for much too long. Patrons at all levels are using Google in their attempts to locate information lacking any awareness of the quality of what they find or how to find even better information. They bypass the librarian in their attempts at learning and knowledge building. This paper shows librarians how to use tools familiar to patrons to emerge from being the silent and often ignored yet essential elephant in the room.

Introduction

For centuries before the emergence of the Internet, the library with its collection of manuscripts or books was the major source of information in a school, community, or campus. No one could be knowledgeable in the learned sense by ignoring the collection of the library. It was the jewel of a university such as Harvard; the centre of intellectual and cultural life in a city as in the New York Public Library or for a nation with the British Museum and the Bibliotheque Nationale de France. Scholars throughout the world would seek out a treasured collection in which to do research. How well prepared scholars were to answer their research questions often depended upon receiving instruction from the librarian, although librarians were not always acknowledged as part of the process. They might be described as the "elephant in the room," someone who is there, but not really visible.

The advent of the Internet has democratized information which is now accessible from a connected device anywhere and at any time. Suddenly there is a perception that the Internet is the library of the world and Wikipedia the encyclopedia of choice, library users bypass their library preferring Google. In comparison, faced with financial difficulties, libraries have lost staff and other resources. In the face of these challenges, many librarians are now proposing a total re-envisioning of the mission of the library. R. David Lankes (2011) has proposed that the new role of the librarian is the creation of knowledge as opposed to the storage and retrieval of information.

One response within education has been to look at the physical library space and to align technology and reference services in a Learning Commons, for example Loertscher, Koechlin and Zwaan (2011) proposed the replacement of the school library and computer lab with a Learning Commons. This vision, called the iCentre in Australia (Hough, 2011), was defined by Hay (2010) as "… the central facility within the school where information, technology, learning, and teaching needs are supported by qualified information and technology specialists".

The Learning Commons concept has become quite common in academic libraries in Canada and the U.S. and is gaining momentum in other countries as well. In the U.S. this is perceived as an information commons which combines open computing resources into the library space with added comfortable seating to encourage collaborative work. Integrating access to other institutional services as well means the library becomes as much a service commons as an information commons, but not necessarily a *learning* commons.

Where this has been mirrored in public libraries, patrons of all ages appreciate access to the Internet, access to connective devices, a place where they can connect their own devices, and all types of advice in troubleshooting problems with all of the various technologies. Those lacking access or devices at home depend on these services and expect that they will be present for walk-in access.

How will these changes in the mission of the library change the position and impact librarians have in this very different information world? While laudable and useful, providing basic services, whether in the area of technology or reference, are not central to either informal or formal learning. Knowledge creation requires more than a supportive role; it pushes the librarian into the role of teacher, mentor, coach, in ways that emphasize outcomes rather than inputs. No matter the type of library, the Learning Commons we advocate is both a physical and a virtual environment. It is a commons because it is "owned" in a participatory environment by the patrons and is the centre of both teaching and learning for the school or any other type of community. It plays a role in the new arena discussed by David Weinberger in his book *Too Big To Know* (2011), where the smartest person in the room is the room.

Finding out what students want

Much has been said about a new generation of young people who have grown up with constant access to the Internet. They are said to behave quite differently in this information and technology rich world than the generation before them. The authors of this paper alongside sixty other school library scholars and practitioners assembled in Minneapolis, Minnesota in September of 2011 asking themselves about the information and technology habits of young people and its impact on the concept of the library. This location was chosen because the school district technology and library staff had been making major progress in incorporating technology and information skills with students throughout all grade levels.

The research group was privileged to be able to interviews students at all levels. Gaining access to interview students is no longer easy in the U.S. The number of tests required by governmental units takes a great deal of time away from classroom, and any additional non-required testing is simply not allowed.

Administrators in this suburban school district cautioned the group that they were not allowed to ask direct questions; district employees had to do that; but, the researchers could be present, smile, and record the answers to the interview questions and make clarifications. Researchers worked in pairs, some in elementary schools, others in a middle school and others in designated classrooms in the high school in which the meeting was being held. The researchers conducted a total of 22 interviews of individual students. The researchers could not draw a random sample of students across the district, so they made no claim that the conclusions were representative of all students, only of those who were available and willing to be interviewed in the schools at the time of the research.

During the interviews, the researchers asked two questions:

- Describe your use of technology both at home and at school and how technology helps you.
- Describe a favorite project you have done at school telling about those who helped you, and what you learned.

The researchers recorded answers using a Google Form on a computer so all results appeared on the results spreadsheet immediately and could be seen instantly on a Google Spreadsheet back at headquarters[1]

With this technology, the group of scholars could analyze responses immediately. Dr. Ross Todd of Rutgers University led the original synthesis activity at the close of the conference. Both authors reviewed the findings in preparation for writing this paper and they are discussed below in terms of technology, assistance, and learning.

Technology

Throughout the grade levels, students have access to a variety of devices both at school and at home, including computers of all types, cell phones, iPads, iPods, xbox, flip cams, smart boards, document cameras, e-readers, Gameboy and MP3 among others. It is apparent that they have wide access to the Internet. No one complained about filtering (limiting access to Internet sites considered harmful to youth), which is a requirement at some schools. They feel comfortable in using technology and want more and better devices to boost their efficiency. All know that technology is an essential part of their learning and realize that the culture that surrounds technology is very collaborative. The students understand that technology is a means to learn and build their knowledge and expertise. Gender did not seem to be a factor in the use of technology devices or tools.

Assistance

Across the grade levels, students recognize the help they receive from peers, family, teachers, and various information sources they can access. Their librarians seemed to be invisible to these students even though the researchers knew that the teacher librarians in all the schools were exemplary and had facilitated technology access, use of information, and the creation of multimedia products.

Learning

The students have most enthusiasm when describing an authentic learning task. They show a level of detail when they talk about the project, including product and process, that indicates a level of recall specific to authentic learning tasks. They realized that they were creating their own knowledge through active participation in a project. They seemed to be more metacognitive and talked about their learning process when engaged in authentic learning tasks.

---

1   See:https://docs.google.com/spreadsheet/
    ccc?key=0AnflIXlSMo2_dDlFQXJlQjJZaVRJRVMxOHlab3NNRFE#gid=0

Students who participate in well-constructed projects are likely to remember their chances to learn from a time they were in third grade right through to experiences in high school. Finally, they realize a sense of competition and wish to do well in collaborative projects.

After listening to the analysis and synthesis of the findings, other observations were made by both the director of technology and the district library supervisor who both recognized the progress that had been made in the past few years through the infusion of technology and access to that technology throughout the district. While proud of their achievements in boosting learning through technology, both recognized that they are, as professionals, in a perpetual beta state and that they must constantly make progress by listening to the students and the best ideas from the faculty to continue their progress. All conference participants were impressed by the district leaders who really understand and promote the effective use of information and technology in learning. The entire group discussed the invisibility of the librarian to the students in the study. Why? The researchers knew that all students recognized the improvements in technology and its role in learning but did not sense the contribution of those who had made this possible.

What skills do librarians need?

Promotional skills

If the patrons of your library are like the students in this study, they are appreciative and recognize the influence that access to technology has in their learning experiences. However, they may not know from whence that advantage has come. For example, we all may appreciate our access to electricity but its provision is assumed and the installers belong to a category of "they" or just "it." Who is that helpful person behind the reference desk? Is "help" a central part of learning or just a means to the real mental effort and accomplishment? Why would a teacher be recognized but a librarian not? The researchers could only speculate but recognized that the implications of invisibility are dangerous in times of financial exigency experienced by many organizations across the globe.

Teaching skills

The concept of a *learning* commons rather than a *service* commons may be a key element where librarians are able to go beyond the provision of information or tools or equipment and actually engage alongside teachers in the use of that information to develop such things as better decisions, deep understanding and the recognition of quality information. The building of technical skills can bring efficiency into the learning process and, most importantly, the actual engagement in the conversation, thinking, creating, sharing and reflection on what has been learned alongside the skills required to boost that learning.

Technology skills

Assistance with using new devices to find information may also be a key element. The expansion of technologies allows librarians to help their clientele use both the technology tools and gain the skills necessary to choose from the ever expanding range of resources they find. The next step is to get that patron to tell others about the help given and to encourage their going to the library.

In a large part of the world access to mobile and other technological devices has made Internet access common and improving all the time. Every group of patrons or potential patrons is routinely embracing new tools and devices as ways of connecting, collaborating, creating, and learning. They are no longer content to be passive consumers of information or resources collected and distributed by libraries. This generation of students attending basic education schools and moving into colleges and universities gravitates instantly to any convenient resource they feel helps them accomplish their task. Thus, they will bypass the library if it does not respond to their needs. Librarians of all types need to adapt quickly to a perpetual beta world if they are to remain players in the lives of their patrons and command the investment from their sponsoring institutions.

How do librarians gain these skills?

What do librarians need to do to "adapt quickly?" A first step here is to determine if librarians themselves are digital natives or digital immigrants. Sweeny (2005) considers academic library students are "digital natives" because they have grown up with technology, while most librarians are "digital immigrants" or adults who learned technologies much later. This knowledge requires action in order to carve out an indispensable role at the centre of teaching and learning. Librarians must experiment more and refine their thinking to accomplish this. There have been some responses to this skills gap.

Academic Librarian Response

As reported by Quinney, Quinn and Galbraith (2010), academic librarians at the Harold B. Lee Library of Brigham Young Library, recognized that "undergraduates, as members of the Millennial Generation, are proficient in Web 2.0 technology, and expect to apply these technologies in their coursework – including scholarly research" (p. 205). However, to do this, they had to make sure their librarians could overcome the gap in their technology knowledge.

This was delivered through a program titled "Technology Challenge," a self-directed training program where staff spent at least fifteen minutes each day learning the new technology skills essential to their work. Their training was then evaluated through before and after surveys. These academic librarians realized that students need Librarians 2.0, librarians who are able to help those students familiar with Web 2.0.

Public Librarian Response

The public library in its beginning years in the U.S. was called the "people's college", as it provided lifelong learning and education for those who could not attend institutions of higher learning. The role of the librarian was as an intermediary to help adults find information in card catalogues (and then later online public access catalogues) and to answer reference questions by accessing databases rather than teaching the patron to conduct the search. This has changed as we enter an era where anyone, anywhere, and at any time can learn what they want or need to learn, often for free, and without requiring a stamp of approval from any organization.

Blowers (2007) reported the development of a core competency program by the technology staff in the Public Library of Charlotte and Mecklenburg County of North Carolina that "keeps workers afloat by providing them with the technology skills they need to support the change that has already occurred" (p.11). They then created "Learning 2.0", a "discovery learning program" where librarians could learn these new technologies on their own. "Through the learning and knowledge-exchanging process, self-proclaimed technology novices became experienced Learning 2.0 tutors to fellow staff" (p.15). Gerding (2011) tells us that, while not the people's college, "Libraries are community centers…being the only place with free public computers and Internet access and, moreover, free technology training" (p.43). She describes in detail how to connect people and knowledge through guidelines for technology training that will be helpful to any librarian with this goal.

New tools place librarians at the centre

In order to open our collections and resources to patrons on a 24/7 basis librarians need to use existing tools in a new way, in particular social networking tools can be used to promote services and to get participation from patrons:

Virtual Learning Commons

Librarians of all types can create their own Virtual Learning Commons, a digital space where both librarians and patrons are building and creating a learning community. An example of this is being built by school library management students at San Jose State University who are creating a sample school Virtual Learning Commons with five portals:

- an Information Commons where access to all types of resources predominates
- a Knowledge Building Centre which features learning experiences from all over the school
- the Reading Culture portal with literacy initiatives from across the school
- Social Culture, which is a living school yearbook created by many groups and individuals such as clubs, sports, events, performances, awards. This can also easily be broadcast to parents
- an Experimental Learning Centre where all school improvement resides.

These students are using Google Sites to create their Virtual Learning Commons because it allows them to authorize "authors" in each of the portals and can be viewed widely or privately as the group decides. Google Apps for Education can be used by any educational institution throughout the world for free and in a safe environment and includes collaborative tools where learners anywhere can build, write, create, present or store products and information.

Knowledge Building Centres

Using a Google Site, the librarian and teacher/professor construct a virtual room housing a topical exploration. The class may be studying persons, places, issues, or trying to solve a problem or a challenge together. In this environment, everyone concerned with the learning experience can participate. By the very nature of the tool, instructors, librarians, consulting experts, or other mentors are in the room alongside the teacher and collaborating with the learners. The instructors/mentors plan, teach, and assess the entire experience as partners because the structure of the room encourages that kind of collaboration. This presence is a major role change for librarians who previously may have assisted in a learning experience only once or briefly. It transforms librarians into co-teachers alongside the class instructor. Examples of such collaborative experiences created by students at San Jose State University[2]

In the academic library setting, subject librarians could start this process with the instructors who have been most active in having the librarian participate in the teaching/learning process in the past. Students at this level could become far more interested in the content if they were involved in this process as has been shown by the students at San Jose. While they are creating a vir-

---

2   See   https://docs.google.com/spreadsheet/ccc?key=0AkkdWYq2f0WvdENEZmpJa0NyTHF0
MzJndktIejV3dkE&hl=en#gid=0

tual library, they are adding their expertise to the process which helps them build new learning into the experience. An engineering class building a bridge could use this to identify potential problems in a group's proposed design. Students in journalism could plan a month's journal content including the amount of space allocated to advertising. Art history students could plan an exhibition and select paintings from museums all over the world to place on view. The process might encourage collaboration from professors who would learn more about the library's resources in creating the assignment. If the actual "assignment" became the property of the students, even more learning would occur. While these examples apply directly to institutions charged with teaching students, it also fits activities within the public library, for example, a book discussion group would be available without the need for weekly meetings as each participant could add their knowledge of the background for the book, the other writings of the author, what was happening at the time the book covered. It would provide a simple move to Book2Cloud.

Book2Cloud

A second example of using Google to transform learning is the use of Book2Cloud for learning experiences that concentrate on the mastery of complex texts. The instructor may have selected a poem, speech, short story, play, or novel as the centrepiece of a learning experience and wants students to develop deep understanding of that text and use it to build, think, and create some new product. If you search for Book2Cloud on Google, you will find a website that explains the construction of, and gives examples of text-based learning environments. One U.S. example is the Gettysburg Address by President Abraham Lincoln during the U.S. Civil War. Using the features of a Google Site, the speech is divided up into phrases around which individuals or groups can curate or collect information or multimedia from the Internet to assist in the understanding of the phase at hand.

After curating around each phrase, the group pieces together their personal understanding in order to build a much deeper and collaborative understanding of the text far beyond a simple reading or explanation could produce. The responsibility of the teacher and librarian in the room of the Book2Cloud is to mentor the construction of that understanding in a constructivist environment rather than in a behaviorist directive environment. Such a construction can happen for both non-copyrighted and copyrighted texts. When copyright free, the actual text can be posted on the Book2Cloud website. When copyrighted, the website refers to a book in hand or a digital text purchased for use by the class. Either way, everyone is building, constructing, thinking, and learning how to learn better with the encouragement of a collaborative environment that makes both personal expertise and collaborative intelligence a natural way of constructing meaning.

An expanded role for the librarian

In the examples given, the librarian steps beyond being a supplier of information to the position of co-teacher alongside the classroom instructor. Together, the content expert and the "learning how to learn" expert use their skills to promote deep understating. For all librarians, traditional information literacy skills and reference skills are not enough. Intervening occasionally in a learning experience is not enough. Teaching the finding of information is not enough; it is the use of that information in what the learner knows and is able to do that is paramount. Such a shift, we propose, brings the library or Learning Commons as we envision it to the indispensable centre of teaching and learning in all types of libraries, the place where librarians should have been for centuries.

What's next?

For the immediate future, the authors invite readers to join them in the creation and fostering of the Learning Commons concept described in this paper. The authors have set up a website which details much more information[3] about the Learning Commons concept. A community has been set up[4] that focuses on children and teen learning experiences, but librarians of all kinds can get ideas to adapt to their situations. You may also wish to search for the Learning Commons Facebook page where scholars and practitioners are discussing ideas and giving tips on constructing the Learning Commons environment, or contact the authors for additional information.

Finally, whether a Learning Commons approach is taken, using cloud computing or establishing a knowledge building centre, we challenge all librarians to experiment and share the best ideas that work in the various cultures and countries on the Internet. Technologies will change, but with a learning community, we can take advantage of emerging tools that promote, develop, and provide opportunities for our profession to turn myth into reality. In this proactive role, providing opportunities for learning, the elephant steps out onto the stage in full view of everyone.

References

Blowers, H., & Reed, L. (2007) The C's of our sea change: plans for training staff, from core competencies to learning 2.0. *Computers in Libraries,* 27(2), 10-15.

---

3   https://sites.google.com/site/iflalearningcommons2012
4   https://sites.google.com/site/schoollearningcommons

Gerding, S. (2011). Transforming public library patron technology training. In The transforming public library technology infrastructure. *Library Technology Reports* 47(6), 43-49.

Hay, L. (2010). Developing an information paradigm approach to build and support the home-school. In M. Lee and G. Finger (Eds.). *Developing a networked school community: a guide to realising the vision.* (pp 143-158). Camberwell, Victoria : Australian Council for Educational Research.

Hough, M. (2011). "Libraries as iCentres: helping schools face the future." *School Library Monthly,* 27(7), 8-11.

Lankes, R. D. (2011). *The atlas of new librarianship.* Cambridge, MA : MIT Press and ACRL. (Available at: www.newlibrarianship.org/wordpress)

Loertscher, D. V., Koechlin, C., & Zwann, S. (2011). *The new Learning Commons : where learners win!. Reinventing school libraries and computer labs.* 2nd ed. Salt Lake City : Hi Willow Research and Publishing. (Available at: http:// lmcsource.com)

Quinney, K. A., Smith, S. D., & Galbraith, Q. (2010). Bridging the gap: self-directed staff technology training. *Information Technology and Libraries*, 29(4), 205-13.

Sweeny, R. T. (2005). Reinventing library buildings and services for the Millennial Generation," *Library Administration & Management,* 19(4), 170.

Weinberger, D. (2011). *Too big to know: rethinking knowledge now that the facts aren't the facts, experts are everywhere, and the smartest person in the room is the room.* New York: Basic Books.

Academic Integration of Information Literacy at the Durban University of Technology in Preparing for Lifelong Learners

Shirlene Neerputh
Durban University of Technology Library, Durban, South Africa
Neerputs@dut.ac.za

Abstract

The mission of Durban University of Technology (DUT) is to create lifelong learners in South Africa as well as to ensure preparedness for the world of work. The mission of DUT Library is a student centred service that enables teaching, learning and research, and encourages lifelong learning by: acquiring information resources; providing information skills training; ensuring equitable access to information and facilities; using appropriate technology and skilled staff, and engaging in resource sharing and community outreach. The paper presents an Information Literacy (IL) strategy for promoting lifelong learning. A powerful collaborative IL model between subject librarians and academics, underpinned by an institutional commitment for valuing the research process is outlined. An IL model for academic integration is presented across all six faculties in the university. The paper proposes IL as a mainstreamed module in academic integration for undergraduates and postgraduates. This paper provides insight about: DUT Library's role in IL instruction; the university curriculum renewal project aimed at creating lifelong learners; the role of subject librarians leading instructional change; the role and experience of faculty members as they design assignments and modify courses to include IL; web based learning as a student centred learning tool, and the adoption of blended learning styles. The paper advocates for a changed purpose of academic libraries as integrated partners in fulfilling the mission of teaching, learning and research in universities. It is of value in highlighting academic integration of libraries in promoting lifelong learning in South Africa.

Introduction

The Durban University of Technology (DUT) is one of six Universities of Technology in South Africa. DUT is situated in the heart of KwaZulu-Natal province, in the city of eThekwini (Durban) in South Africa. The institution is a member of the International Association of Universities and a multi-campus University of Technology that offers undergraduate and postgraduate programmes across six faculties:

- Engineering and the Built Environment;
- Art and Design;
- Accounting and Informatics;
- Applied Sciences;
- Health Sciences;
- Management Science.

The vision of the Durban University of Technology is to be a preferred university for developing leadership in technology and productive citizenship. The mission of the university is to achieve:

- A teaching and learning environment that values and supports the university community;
- Promoting excellence in learning and teaching, technology transfer and applied research;
- External engagement that promotes innovation and entrepreneurship through collaboration and partnership.

Library Mission

The services of DUT Library are designed to support and enhance the University's core business of teaching, learning and research. The Library's mission is to be a student centred library that enhances learning, teaching and research. The key goals of the library are:

- Embedding library activities in teaching, learning and research;
- Developing information skills for lifelong learning;
- Providing equitable access to information facilities;
- Engaging in flexible delivery modes, and;
- Improve the quality of library services in accordance with best practices.

The literature indicates that a library which is actively and directly involved in advancing all aspects of the mission of higher education teaching, learning and research plays a vital role in lifelong learning. However, librarians have rarely been treated as colleagues by teaching faculty, and thus had little impact on the curriculum. For a teaching library to succeed close collaboration between librarians and the faculty is necessary to develop a powerful library which helps the institution adapt to the changing needs of society (Esterhuizen and Kuhn, 2010; Faber, 1999). This paper portrays the role that subject librarians can play in lifelong learning.

Information services

The DUT Library information services unit comprises fifteen information professionals and one librarian for training and professional development. This team of information professionals subscribe to the DUT Library Service Charter in executing their prime duties within a student centred approach. Their core tasks are:

- Embedding information literacy in curricula and research;
- Collection development and management;
- Other services as applicable to a student centred library e.g. Open Access initiatives, virtual access to the library resources, use of discovery tools, online reference management software, anti-plagiarism, writing centres and knowledge commons facilities.

DUT subject librarians are acutely aware of the Library's strategic changes, from having a support role to playing a proactive role in teaching, learning and research in the university. Gilchrist (2007, p.2) and Esterhuize and Kuhn (2010) state that a small percentage of faculty integrate instructional opportunities embedded in the library's facilities and collections. This situation persists in spite of the fact that the library's educational role, and specifically a library's instruction program, now forms a significant spoke, if not indeed the hub, of many college library missions (Bangert, 1997; Dewey, 2001; Hardesty, 2004; Jordan, 1997 in Gilchrist, 2007). This significant spoke is situated within the DUT context and the library mission has embraced lifelong learning.

Subject librarians competencies

DUT subject librarians have gained valuable teaching and learning experience via the IL program. Each subject librarian must be confident and competent in IL teaching and it's interconnections to curricula. Selematsela and du Toit (2007) identified the technical skills for instruction librarians as: the promotion of IL to the institution; organising IL programs; the presentation of appropriate

IL instruction skills; the course design and development of IL programs in collaboration with academics; the continuous evaluation of IL programs; keeping updated with e-learning and electronic resources; learning methodology and pedagogy.

Library management hosts regular meetings with the information services team to map out IL teaching, e-learning strategies and coaching opportunities for new subject librarians. Teaching and learning workshops are factored into the library skills plan at the beginning of each year. These workshops provide additional opportunities to share or review best practices of teaching IL, in particular: using new technologies; interpersonal skills such as attentive listening, negotiation skills, presentation skills; and creating interactive classes. The training librarian assists the subject librarian in designing IL specific tutorials; fun or interactive templates or lesson plans which are housed on the Library shared folder; and enables sharing of good practices in IL teaching.

Workshops are conducted by the University's Centre for Excellence in Teaching and Learning (CELT) to continuously improve subject librarian pedagogic competencies. The workshops focus on: how to handle large classes; how to plan and design IL lessons; assessment practices; and effective learning strategies including blended learning. Subject librarians are expected to be competent in designing and collaborating on the Blackboard platform to embed IL into the curricula. CELT often invites subject librarians to faculty based learning workshops, which denotes the level of professional acceptance and commitment the subject librarians have to promoting teaching and learning. These workshops are effective in two ways – it provides networking/collaborative opportunities for subject librarians to work with academics in the faculty, secondly to engage both parties in enhancing teaching and learning in DUT.

Knowing our students and staff

The Library aims to get to know students and staff needs. Subject librarians annually collect statistics and formulate Faculty and Departmental profiles for providing quality information services. Professional peer relations and liaisons between the subject librarians and academics have escalated. Subject librarians participate in Faculty board meetings, they form part of the quality review process or curriculum renewal meetings and are often invited to departmental meetings or conduct library training/presentations in the faculty.

The library also uses the South African Students Satisfaction Survey, and / or student data garnered from the Centre for Quality Assurance and Promotion, to re-think the library's strategy in promoting lifelong learning in the university. The survey revealed that students are: unfamiliar with using library resources because of their socio-economic backgrounds; do not know how to reference sources; have no knowledge of using a computer; prefer using mobile phones for information; and prefer web-based tutorials. This data has an impact on the way that the library configures programs and services to meet student needs.

Subject librarians conduct an overview analysis of students by interrogating the enrolment statistics per annum and conducting ice breaking exercises in the first IL class. For example: what tradition and culture does one belong to? (Hindu's, Zulu's, Xhosas, Islam); students being part of a game – drawing or naming five important things in a university; or students who belong to different regions in KwaZulu-Natal.

DUT information literacy strategy

DUT Library strategically positioned information literacy (IL) at the forefront of developing graduate preparedness. The objective of mainstreaming information literacy is to create a proactive intervention in equipping all students with IL skills, to improve the throughput rate and create lifelong learners. Information literacy is defined as "the ability of learners to access, use and evaluate information from different sources, in order to enhance learning, solve problems and generate new knowledge" (South African National Council for Library and Information Services, 2001,p.1). The IL program of the DUT Library aims to instill in our students and staff the skills to:

- Be critically aware of information and knowledge;
- Interrogate the myriad of information resources;
- Evaluate and apply information appropriately;
- Undertake research;
- Observe academic integrity.

The IL program takes a two pronged approach aimed at (1) students and (2) academics across all six faculties in the university. The Information Literacy Framework is underpinned by the Association of College and Research Libraries (ACRL) outcomes for lifelong learning. These initiatives play an important role in transforming the act of learning across the six faculties in the university. Dale and Holland (2006); Webb (2006) and Corrall (2007) refer to the formal recognition of information literacy as the basis of lifelong learning in universities. The DUT program is formalised with most faculty positioning IL in the teaching calendar. Statistics and feedback from faculty show that there is a strong correlation between students attending information literacy classes and academic success. This issue is flagged purposefully and reported on at all Library Committee and Faculty Board meetings. Feetham (2006) and Dale, Beard and Holland (2011) highlight that Wolff (1995) believes "that the next stage of development for the library is to serve as a full partner in transforming the act of learning."

"The main point is the library needs to be taken out of its confining role as support service and be seen as a central element in any institution's response to the learner of the future and the next challenge is that technology and the information explosion will affect not only the quantity of information available and our access to it but the very definitions of knowledge and learning … learning will change as will process – what does it mean to prepare students for a future where there will always be more readily accessible information on any topic than can be mastered?

…where the content as well as the underlying foundational principles of the disciplines … may change at least once (if not more often) during the individual lifetime?" (Wolff, 1995; p.88)

Academics and subject librarian collaborate to integrate basic information skills into the curriculum at a "point of need" approach for undergraduates (Esterhuizen and Kuhn, 2010). This is done in DUT by:

- Planning and curriculum preparation undertaken jointly by the subject librarian and the academic;
- IL lessons included in the lecture timetable for each programme;
- IL integrated into the curriculum. Academics select a topic for library research using the IL competency approach;
- IL test / assignment marks are incorporated into the course year marks, in most cases the subject librarian initiates this assessment practice.

The role of faculty in mainstreaming IL

In examining the teaching roles for academic librarians, the literature has suggested that the new learning-centred focus of higher education offers librarians increased opportunities to play a forceful, dynamic role in collaboratively designing and developing learning strategies (Gilchrist, 2007). The fact that process-learning and learning-centred pedagogies directly correlate with the unique instructional strengths of the library provides an opportunity for academic libraries to assume instructional leadership roles at new and increased levels. With the overarching and interdisciplinary nature of library programs, the hours and structure of the library building, the instructional savvy of librarians, and the diverse types of information resources as framing and supportive elements, libraries are well positioned to exercise leadership and accomplish this transformation (Gilchrist, 2007). Pedagogically, organizationally, philosophically, and physically libraries have the potential to bring to the instructional table many of the devices and skills necessary to assist an institution in adopting more of these recommended, mutually developed, and effective instructional strategies.

An embedded DUT IL program in curricula, has the potential to generate new ideas in a subject discipline from current and prior knowledge. DUT's subject librarians have to intensify their efforts in the faculty to explore ways of seeking out and generating new ideas in subject content via academics research interests. The reward will be an increased number of research publications in the university. Subject librarian / postgraduate training help create an enabling environment in the current IL teaching and learning strategy for academics.

Academics act as advocates for lifelong learning. The advanced model (constitutes advanced subject discipline specific training with enhanced features such as user profiles, setting up alerts, research tools available within the databases, use of web-based learning programs, knowledge of plagiarism and software) forms part of the library strategy to ensure that each academic per faculty are exposed to the IL program in DUT. The library has adopted this approach to strategically gain the attention of academics for successful IL integration and to teach academics in need of information literacy development. Many of DUT academics are currently pursuing additional qualifications and engaged in research, which provides a need to equip academics with IL skills. Deans also request such training to be conducted in their departments.

Academics skilled in IL may become the Library's champion and ambassadors for both embedding IL in the curricula, as well as ensuring high student IL class attendance. DUT Library recognises academics at a formal award ceremony during Library Week celebrations that are held annually, by awarding an information literacy champion certificate and gift, for commitment and dedication to the IL program.

Partnerships and collaboration

A number of authors (Kakkonen and Virrankoski, 2010; Dale and Holland, 2006; Dale, Beard and Holland, 2011; Gilchrist, 2007; Esterhuizen and Kuhn, 2010) advocate that subject librarians must engage with the teaching, learning and research environments, and team-teach, taking the academic integration to a higher level in the university. New academics are introduced to the IL model at the Human Resources Induction Programme. The library partners with Faculty and the DUT Centre for Excellence in Learning and Teaching (CELT) to promote IL programmes across the university. The library works closely with CELT-Academic Development Unit and the E-Learning team, to teach IL competencies as well as offer hands-on interactive sessions. An interactive professional style of teaching encourages full participation, and fosters recognition for the IL program in the university.

Evaluations show that these interventions are valued by academics. IL mainstreamed statistics for 2009 to 2011 reveal that the faculties have adopted and recognize the importance of the library in contributing to teaching, learning and research in the university. The 2011 statistics reveal that eighty-five percent of DUT academic departments subscribed to an embedded IL program for all first year students. Partnerships are established between subject librarians and academics to assess students on: how well they know the library; how to reference using the DUT Harvard referencing style; and how to retrieve different sources of materials for their assignments. This is done via class interventions, class surveys and the inclusion of library related questions in assignments and exam papers. A high degree of integration is evident when academics partner with the subject librarian and incorporate library related questions in the exam paper.

The Library collaborated institutionally in embedding the IL program into a formal module called the first year student experience pilot project. This project was transformed into the General Education component for undergraduates in 2011. This module, initiated by executive management, is shaped by international models for graduate preparedness and lifelong learning. This module attempts to build critical thinking, lifelong learning, graduate preparedness in South African society (encompassing local history, information literacy, liberal arts and humanities, non-violence and HIV and Aids being some of the electives on offer) for students. The library is an active player in the General Education module. The General Education module will be credit bearing, and expected to be formalised in the 2013 teaching and learning radar in DUT.

Undergraduates

DUT adopted a three step model in IL aimed at full integration from the first to third year levels of study. The first year IL model encapsulates the following: teaching students topic analysis of their assignment or research projects; how to search the library catalogue; referencing techniques as required by the discipline; evaluation of information and plagiarism. A writing program is included in the IL programme to enhance graduate preparedness. The second year and third year undergraduates are given advanced training as determined by academics and faculty needs. The DUT information literacy programme is pitched at "point of need" basis, promoting faculty buy-in and graduate preparedness, as asserted by Gilchrist (2007); Kakkonen and Virrankoski, (2010) and Esterhuizen and Kuhn (2010). DUT subject librarians teach the following:

- Topic analysis and selecting relative tools for research work;
- Advanced OPAC / discovery skills;
- Endnote referencing techniques;
- Comparing and evaluating internet websites;

- Overview of research methodologies / proposal writing and literature searches and;
- Generic writing skills and awareness of Turnitin.

Postgraduates

The IL programme for teaching and training postgraduates (sometimes interwoven with the Research Office programs) comprises: how to conduct a good literature review; processes involved in research; referencing and EndNote; and the use of Turnitin. The library will continue to assert the integrative model of IL in postgraduate induction and research workshops. Presently, there is faculty based demand for this type of IL teaching.

IL teaching strategy

The information literacy program is underpinned by an effective teaching strategy aimed at optimizing learning for DUT students. Benjamin Bloom identified three domains of educational activities (2011):

- Cognitive: mental skills (knowledge);
- Affective: growth in feelings or emotional areas (attitude);
- Psychomotor: manual or physical skills (skills).

The above taxonomy of learning behaviours is construed as the goals of the learning process. Subject librarians apply Bloom's taxonomy of learning in the IL program.

In teaching IL, DUT graduates will meet IL international competency standards. This is based on the Association of College and Research Libraries (2000) information literacy competency standards for higher education which require an information literate individual to be able to:

1. Determine the scope of information required;
2. Access the required information effectively and efficiently;
3. Evaluate critically the information and its sources and incorporate this new information into her or his existing knowledge base;
4. Use information effectively in his or her studies and work;
5. Understand the economic, legal and social issues pertaining to the use of information, and to access and use information ethically and legally (Kakkonen and Virrankoski, 2010).

Farber (1999) stated that the college library is a vital part of the undergraduate experience. This is true for the DUT library experience. Since the library expresses the philosophy of education and the distinctive characteristics of the college, its role should be to "bring students, faculty and books together" in ways that would encourage learning, intensive scholarship, and casual browsing (Faber 1999; p.2). Therefore every first year student is given the opportunity to undergo an IL program.

With the changing role of the subject librarian, Dale, Holland and Mattews (2006) emphasize that subject librarians are ideally placed to implement the IL program in the university. "If lifelong learning is the true goal of IL education, information specialists are ideally placed to impart skills that go beyond the ostensibly limited relevance (from a student's perspective) of academic assignments" (Shenton and Fitzgibbons, 2010; p.2). The IL program is administered with prior faculty liaisons and conducted at a point of need. This means the collaboration with faculty creates an IL program interwoven into student academic needs.

The DUT three tier model ascribes to Harrison and Rourke's view that (2006; p.3) libraries should "embed IL outcomes into the curriculum at the program level, enhancing all levels of an undergraduate education". The goal is to move students from "novice" library users, through the IL pillars to become "proficient" or even "expert" users of information / researchers. The teaching strategy is also dictated by the allocation of time slots granted by faculty and methodologies involved in facilitating learning. To enhance learning, subject librarians employ different modes of teaching; such as: brainstorming; chalk and talk; presentation and discussion of specific lessons; and exploration methods of placing students in sub-teams. Team teaching is part of the strategy to formalize the IL program across the university. Subject librarians are involved in varying degrees of assessments and evaluation practices, in the absence of a national South African standard for IL assessment.

Promoting Blended Learning

Farber (1999; p.180) aptly stated that "a point of entry for libraries to aid learning through technology lies first in aiding students and faculty to manoeuvre onto the information superhighway .... [Librarians] can offer useful filters to students and faculty in need of them .... Clearly, this filtering must be done intelligently .... But who better suited to the task than those who understand both the available resources and the needs of the client--the librarians?"

Blended learning is part of the subject librarians approach to assist students who are "techno savvy" and those that are not so. A hands-on practical experience in the library e-zone, together with OPAC (Online Public Access Catalogue) database training and written practical exercises, form part of the interactive training. The *Research it Right* tutorial hosted on the library web page offers a way of promoting blended learning in the university. It is designed to teach users IL competencies online, as well as to test learners' abilities via an online assessment tool. This tutorial was designed to encourage the 'google generation' to access the IL program and includes a referencing tutorial that aims to promote academic integrity at DUT. Dale, Beard and Holland (2011; p.41) stated that students are choosing the internet for their citation referencing, "they are not choosing to access guides to help them create their own citations but the even easier option of having the citation put together for them".

Some academics in DUT are communicating with their students via Facebook and Twitter. The Library will embrace institutional social networking tools to communicate with students and host links to IL online programmes. A cautious approach is planned for the implementation of social networks for DUT students because of online logistics. Perhaps the DUT4Life e-mail system will provide for online communications and effective learning solutions for the millennium generation.

Blackboard version 9.1 and Moodle are online learning management systems that have given the library impetus to be involved in e-learning. IL Blackboard classroom is in the design stage for universal university use. Blackboard provides an excellent opportunity for collaborative teaching and learning.

Challenges

Some of the millennium challenges facing academic libraries today in DUT are: students who have never used computers before; subject librarians often do not have enough time to teach basic computer skills in addition to IL skills; the classes have a diverse student population; diverse socio-economic backgrounds and varying levels of school experiences in a class group. The "Google generation" of DUT students want to navigate their way to information sources without evaluating the sources or understanding content,even disobeying academic integrity. Subject librarians observations reveal: that students need help with computers in their first level of study regardless of whether they are mobile phone savvy; some of them have never been exposed to assignments, projects and referencing in school, so they are clueless regarding research; but most students are eager to learn and want all the help that they can get in the library. It is recommended that computer literacy be taught prior to an IL class or incorporated into this program.

Impact on student learning

Library committee reports compiled by the Academic Services Manager revealed that many academics commented on improved student assignments. Students became aware of plagiarism and how to evaluate information, and they have learnt how to reference using the Harvard system. The lecturers' positive comments and e-mails regarding the visible changes in student works, especially with referencing are indications of the impact of the IL program. Good results after assessing IL exercises administered during the IL programme of all lessons show an increased understanding of the use, access and evaluation of information.

Evaluation and monitoring

Quality permeates the DUT IL instruction methodology. Library management drives the quality agenda by means of: subject librarian audits; continuous evaluation of teaching and learning methodologies; and quarterly reports on the IL teaching. DUT Library adheres to a process of staff development and training that fosters good practices and professionalism in IL teaching and the learning process.

The Academic Services Manager has developed IL teaching in Blackboard to offer leadership and mentorship for the information services team in DUT. The online IL programme incorporates interactive technologies, web links and other current IL trends interfacing effective teaching and learning in universities and colleges nationally or internationally. The assessment practices for IL (formative and summative) will be posted on this web based learning management tool for subject librarians to emulate and customise in designing and delivering the library IL program.

Surveys are conducted to ascertain IL awareness among academics and impact of the program in curricula. The 2011 survey conducted via Survey-Monkey revealed that most academics subscribed to the model of academic integration.

Assessment

Formative and summative assessments constitute a vital part of the IL program. Academics are encouraged to give feedback on tasks or activities conducted by the library to improve student learning. Reflective writing (thinking about how you are conducting your work / tasks, your progress, what problems you are experiencing and how you can improve) or activity based tasks such as games, constitute formative practices in DUT IL programS.

Summative assessments conducted in the form of a test, examination or project forms part of IL. Assessments are conducted at the discretion of the academic and are not uniform across the IL offering per faculty. The assessment of IL skills is integrated into subject specific assignments and projects where a percentage of the mark is assigned to IL. Alternatively, the IL assessment takes the form of an assignment that both the lecturer and the subject librarian design and assess, giving equal weighting to library and curricula content. Summative assessment is preferred, as it denotes serious integration of IL into the curriculum and values the role of the subject librarian in promoting teaching, learning and research in the university.

Conclusion

DUT library embraces becoming student centred and supporting the objective of lifelong learning in the university. The library continues to evaluate and review the IL program in light of media and IL, garnering relevance for graduate preparedness by way of extending to information technologies to encompass learning, critical thinking and interpretative skills. This paper outlined an embedded IL model with subject librarians being a powerful collaborative partner with faculty in promoting teaching, learning and research in DUT. The IL program is integral for students wanting to exploit their potential for lifelong learning.

Acknowledgements

The author acknowledges the work of Library Management and the Information Services Team in promoting IL in DUT.

References

Association of College and Research Libraries. (2000). *Information Literacy Competency Standards for Higher Education.* American Library Association, Chicago.Retrieved from: www.ala.org/acrl/standards/informationliteracycompetency.

Brewer, J. M., Hook, S. J., Simmons-Welburn, J., & Williams, K. (2004). Libraries: dealing with the future now. *Academic Research Library.* June (234), 1-9.

Corall, S., & Keates, J. (2011). The subject librarian and the Virtual Learning Environment: a study of UK universities. *Electronic Library and Information Systems,* 45(1)**,** 29-49.

Dale, P., & Holland, M. (Eds.) (2006). *Subject Librarians: engaging with the learning and teaching environment.* Aldershot :Ashgate.

Dale, P., Beard, J., & Holland, M. (Eds.). (2011). *University libraries and digital environments.* Aldershot : Ashgate.

Durban University of Technology. *Information Literacy Learner Guide.* (2012). Unpublished. Durban University of Technology.

Durban University of Technology. *DUT Library Strategic Plan.* (2012) Unpublished. Durban University of Technology.

Esterhuizen, E.M, & Kuhn, R. (2010). Committee of Higher Education Libraries in South Africa (CHELSA) draft guidelines on Information Literacy: paving the way to a South African national framework. *Innovation*, 41. Retrieved from: www.ajol.info/index.php/innovation/article/view/63630

Faber, E. (1999). College libraries and the teaching/learning process: a 25-year reflection. *Journal of Academic Librarianship,* 25 (3),171-185.

Faber, E. (1999). Faculty-librarian cooperation: a personal retrospective, *Reference Services Review,* 27(3), 229 – 234.

Feetham, M. (2006). The subject specialist in higher education – a review of the literature. In P. Dale & M. Holland (Eds.), *Subject librarians: engaging with the learning and teaching environment* (pp. 3-17). Aldershot : Ashgate.

Gilchrist, D. L. (2007). *Academic libraries at the centre of instructional change: librarian and faculty experience in library leadership in transformation of teaching and learning.* Unpublished PhD Dissertation, Oregon State University, United States.

Harrison, J., & Rourke, L. (2006). The benefits of buy-in: integrating information literacy into each year of an academic program. *Reference Services Review*, 34(4), 599-606.

Kakkonen, A., & Virrankoski, A. (2010). Implementation of the Finnish university libraries national information literacy recommendation into academic studies at the Kumpula Science Library, University of Helsinki. *New Library World, 111*(11/12), 493-502.

Selematsela, D. N. S., & du Toit, A.S.A. (2007). Competency profile for librarians teaching information literacy. *South African Journal of Library and Information Science*, 73(2), 119-129.

Shenton, A. K., & Fitzgibbons, M. (2010). Making information literacy relevant. *Library Review,* 59(3), 165-174.

South Africa. (2001). National Council for Library and Information Services, Act 6 of 2001. Pretoria

Webb, J., Gannon-Lary, P., & Bent, M. (2006). *Providing effective library services for research*. London : Facet

Wolff, R. (1995). Using the accreditation process to transform the mission of the library. *New Directions for Higher Education,* 90, 77-91.

Engineering Students' Information Literacy Instruction and Blended Learning Course Design – A Case Study

Antti Rousi
Aalto University Library, Otaniemi, Finland
antti.m.rousi@aalto.fi

Virpi Palmgren
Aalto University Library, Otaniemi, Finland
virpi.palmgren@aalto.fi

Kirsi Heino
Aalto University Library, Otaniemi, Finland
kirsi.heino@aalto.fi

Abstract

This study focuses on the benefits derived from a blended learning course design in an engineering students' information literacy course. The results of this study are also discussed within the context of professional development of the Aalto University Library's information specialists working with information literacy instruction. This study draws from the experiences of the graduate engineering students participating in the Aalto University Otaniemi Campus Library's "Tools for Master's thesis" course. The data of this study were gathered by an online survey. The students connected a variety of different learning tasks with either the promotion of their personal inquiry, with sharing of experiences and practices or with the promotion of their overall learning. The engineering students also identified four positive ways in which the participation in the classroom enhanced the participation in the online environments. Respectively, the students identified four ways in which the participation in the online environments enhanced classroom participation. According to this study it seems possible to generate a single environment enhancing fusion of both classroom and online environment learning tasks in information literacy instruction. The blended learning approach seems to generate new ways of both thinking and realizing engineering students' information literacy instruction.

Introduction

University students are on the path of lifelong learning and graduate students are at the crossroads of their future careers professionally or academically oriented. Aalto University Library addresses the needs of the graduate engineering students by providing them with information literacy courses at the beginning of their master's thesis projects. This study focuses on the benefits derived from the blended learning approach in a graduate engineering students' information literacy course. The results of this study are also discussed within the context of professional development of the Aalto University Library's information specialists working with information literacy instruction. The purpose of this exploratory case study is to promote critical thought and improvement of current information literacy instruction practices.

Information literacy (IL) is one of the new literacy concepts which, when derived from the tradition of information science, may be defined to focus on the skills of seeking, acquiring, evaluating and applying of information (Bawden, 2001). Information literacy is also associated with deep and transferable learning (Andretta, 2007). The myriad of skills to which the concept of information literacy refers to have been more precisely defined by for example American Library Association (2000) and SCONUL Working Group on Information Literacy (2011).

Garrison and Vaughan (2008) define blended learning as a course design which fuses together face-to-face and online learning experiences in a manner which optimizes student engagement. The advantage of asynchronous online learning lies in the reflection not possible in the fast and free flowing face-to-face environments (Garrison and Vaughan, 2008). Respectively, face-to-face environments allow immediate and familiar forms of communication which promote, for example, idea generation, emotional support and sense of community (Vaughan and Garrison, 2005). The challenge of creating a single component enhancing fusion of both textual and verbal communication lies at the heart of blended learning approach (Garrison and Vaughan, 2008). Since all teaching can be in essence presented as an integration of both communication methods and didactic models, the concept of blended learning has been criticized for vagueness. However, within it lies the valuable aim to purposefully integrate different didactic elements with the most suitable communication methods and technology (Levonen, Joutsenvirta and Parikka, 2009).

Despite the growing body of literature concerning e-learning in IL instruction (e.g., Anderson and May, 2010; Zhang, Watson and Banfield, 2007) and literature focusing on the demands which the e-learning methods pose on the library personnel (e.g., Comba, 2009; Allan, 2002), only a few recent studies have studied the blended learning methods within the context of IL instruction (e.g., Galvin, 2011; Anderson and May, 2010). Thus, it is of importance to study different course settings and the enhancing or non-enhancing effects between the online and classroom assignments provided within IL context. By presenting a concrete example of a course design, by contemplating on the students' feedback and by discussing the demands of this approach, this study aims to promote critical thought and continuing improvement of teaching methods used in IL instruction.

The paper is structured as follows. The first section examines of the context of this case study. The second section examines the used methodology. The third section focuses on the results derived from the survey and the last section elaborates the findings of this study and their implications on the professional development of the Aalto University Library's personnel working with IL instruction.

Case study context

This case study draws on the experiences of the engineering students participating in the Aalto University Otaniemi Campus Library's "Tools for Master's thesis" course. The course is especially designed to suit the needs of graduate engineering students who work on their Master's theses. The engineering students are a challenging group of users due to their often diverse and multidisciplinary information needs (see e.g. Rodriques, 2001;Tenopir and King, 2004; Ward 2005).

The participants of the "Tools for Master's thesis" course come from all of the four technical schools (i.e., School of Chemical Technology, School of Electrical Engineering, School of Engineering and School of Science) of Aalto University. Participating in the "Tools for Master's thesis" course is voluntary for the students and they receive 3 ECTS-credits from successfully completing the course.

The course is an example of curriculum integrated IL instruction as defined by Grafstein (2002). A feature of this study is the assessment of the used IL instruction methods through their experienced applicability to the subject specific task of an engineering student's master's thesis. The "Tools for Master's thesis" course curriculum included the following themes:

- planning the Master's thesis project
- the use of concept map -tools in research work
- examination of different study techniques
- scientific information-seeking
- scientific writing
- creativity and research work
- advice from the recently graduated.

An information specialist of the Aalto University Otaniemi Campus Library is responsible for both planning and realizing the course. Traditionally the information specialists in the Otaniemi Campus Library have held a Master of Science (Tech) degree. The classroom learning tasks were developed in collaboration with the Aalto University's Strategic Support for Research and Education Unit. The online learning tasks were developed in collaboration with the IT personnel of the library and through participating in national development activities organized by Aalto University's Professional Development Unit. The course was first conducted during spring semester 2008 and from therefore on the course has been conducted four times a year.

Both classroom and online tasks were further developed in collaboration with the student participants, as they experienced problems with, for example, the online assignments or suggested contents for the classroom learning tasks. In the courses held during 2011, the use of Ning online social networking site, varied group work in the classroom, different online exercises and varied lecture topics were all included as ways of mediating the course contents to the participants.

The course duration was seven weeks during which seven lectures were given. The lecture derived online assignments (i.e., discussions on the Ning social networking site or the concept map exercise) were obligatory and complemented each lecture. The obligatory online assignments were designed so that participating in them did not require participation in the corresponding classroom environment exercises. The obligatory online exercise on information-seeking worked independently from the lectures and included detailed instruction. Within all of the learning tasks of the course, the direction and guidance of an information specialist or a visiting lecturer was present. Personal tutoring concerning information retrieval was also offered to the students, but the students were not obliged to participate in them.

In order to produce a research setting, the following two dimensions derived from the work of Garrison and Vaughan (2008) were used to create a theoretical framework. The first dimension classifies the used mediators based on their approach in utilizing the social aspects of the community in knowledge constructing. Mediators were classified either as directed towards utilizing the social aspects of the community, like interaction and free play of discourse, or as directed towards an individual inquiry emphasizing personal responsibility and choice. The second dimension classified the used mediators either as based on asynchronous text-based communication (i.e. online environment) or based on synchronous verbal communication (i.e. classroom environment).

The combination of both a mediator and content is referred to as a learning task. This framework allows the examination of a blended learning course design throughout its dimensions. An overview of the learning tasks of the "Tools for Master's thesis" course is presented in Figure 1.

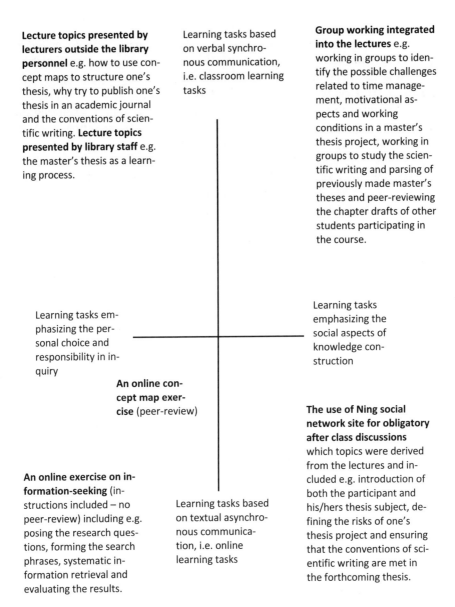

Lecture topics presented by lecturers outside the library personnel e.g. how to use concept maps to structure one's thesis, why try to publish one's thesis in an academic journal and the conventions of scientific writing. Lecture topics presented by library staff e.g. the master's thesis as a learning process.

Learning tasks based on verbal synchronous communication, i.e. classroom learning tasks

Group working integrated into the lectures e.g. working in groups to identify the possible challenges related to time management, motivational aspects and working conditions in a master's thesis project, working in groups to study the scientific writing and parsing of previously made master's theses and peer-reviewing the chapter drafts of other students participating in the course.

Learning tasks emphasizing the personal choice and responsibility in inquiry

Learning tasks emphasizing the social aspects of knowledge construction

An online concept map exercise (peer-review)

The use of Ning social network site for obligatory after class discussions which topics were derived from the lectures and included e.g. introduction of both the participant and his/hers thesis subject, defining the risks of one's thesis project and ensuring that the conventions of scientific writing are met in the forthcoming thesis.

An online exercise on information-seeking (instructions included – no peer-review) including e.g. posing the research questions, forming the search phrases, systematic information retrieval and evaluating the results.

Learning tasks based on textual asynchronous communication, i.e. online learning tasks

Figure 1: Overview of the "Tools for Master's thesis" course learning tasks presented through dimensions of personal inquiry/social knowledge constructing and of verbal/textual communication.

Methodology

The data were collected from two "Tools for Master's thesis" courses held during autumn term 2011. The study was conducted by an online survey which all of the students who completed either one of the two courses were asked to fill afterwards. This study could be described as an action-research oriented case study since formative evaluation and theory building give in to exploring the connections between community specific phenomena (about action-research, see Patton 2002).

The purpose of the survey was to examine how the students perceived and described the value driven from this blended learning course design to their Master's thesis projects and how they experienced the possible enhancing or non-enhancing effects between the differentiated learning tasks. The survey design was a mixture of both questions based on the subjective continuum scales and open-ended questions. Most often the respondents were asked to clarify their answers on subjective continuum scale based questions through the open-ended ones. No demographic data about the respondents were gathered due to the exploratory nature of the study. The survey was created with Webropol[tm] software. See Appendix 1 for the detailed structure of the survey.

Out of the 76 engineering students who completed either one of the fall 2011 courses successfully, 16 students answered the voluntary survey. The latter forms a response rate of 21% for the survey. Because of the low N number of the study, the classification of the responses into, for example, different degree programs produces no generalizable results.

The numeric data from the subjective continuum scale based questions were analyzed with Microsoft Excel[tm] software. The data from the open-ended questions were scrutinized through content analysis in order to seek the predominating phrases or concepts (Patton, 2002). The found predominating phrases or concepts were then quantified and turned into graphs with Microsoft Excel[tm] software.

The following limitation of this study needs to be acknowledged. This study is context-specific and its results are derived from a specific course setting. It remains open whether, for example, the same enhancing or non-enhancing effects between classroom and online environments may be assumed to happen in different course contexts or settings. Furthermore, the assessment of individual learning tasks, for example the assessment of the concept map exercise, might differ if it was to be realized in a classroom environment.

Results

When examining the students motives to participate in the "Tools for Master's thesis"course, the wish to seek overall support in the Master's thesis projects was present in the answers of 11 respondents (Q1, N=16). Out of these 11 respondents, 3 stated specifically that they wished support in *writing* of their Master's thesis. Peer-support and motivational encouragement were wished only by one respondent each. Five respondents stated that the reason for their course enrollment were the methodology module ECTS-credits derived from the course.

The concept map exercise, lecture content and the online exercise on information-seeking were seen by the respondents as the top three tasks that activated them to proceed with their personal inquiry (see Figure 2). When the respondents were asked to further elaborate their answers, they responded as follows. The concept map exercise was seen as significant for the purpose of examining the intended thesis subject and presenting this examination in an understandable form. The content of the lectures were in many cases seen to promote and support the process of writing one's own master's thesis. The reasons why the online exercise in information-seeking was seen to promote personal inquiry were not expressed.

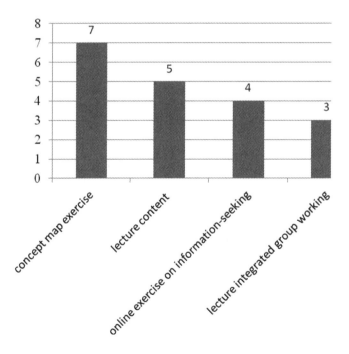

Figure 2: Which of the learning tasks of the course activated you to proceed with your own personal inquiry (Q3, N=16).

Lecture integrated group working and the discussions on Ning social network site were seen as the top learning tasks that activated the respondents to share insights and practices with other participants (see Figure 3). The answers to this question were seldom justified or explained in the open-ended answers. However, phrases such as 'sharing of experiences' and 'examining the Master's thesis project in its different phases' were present in most of the answers. Two of the respondents clarified that the use of Ning social network site allowed more profound reflection about the subject compared to the fast-paced group working in the classroom environment.

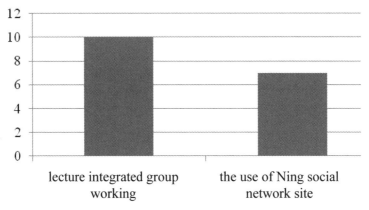

Figure 3: Which of the learning tasks of the course activated you to share insights and practices with other participants (Q4, N=16).

The respondents saw the classroom learning tasks as the most significant tasks when considering their overall learning (see Figure 4). This is an intriguing result. Even though the online learning tasks were seen by the respondents as significant in activating them to proceed with their personal inquiry, their overall impact on the learning of the respondents seems to be lower than of the classroom learning tasks. Unfortunately, when the respondents were asked to further elaborate the latter answers, they were seldom soundly justified. Three of the respondents mentioned concepts and phrases such as 'peer-support' and 'utilizing the ideas and insights of others'. One of the respondents interestingly phrased his/her answer as "the teaching in the classroom environment, since during the classes you forced to learn and to think about the subject." Since the online learning tasks were designed so that they required no participation in the classroom, this result can only be partly explained by the derivative and complementary nature of the online exercises.

When examining the experienced enhancing effects between online and classroom tasks, the respondents consistently viewed the classroom tasks more important for the sake of meaningfully participating in the online tasks than vice versa (see Figure 4). 69% of the respondents considered classroom tasks either very important or important for the sake of meaningfully participating in the online tasks. Respectively, 38% of the respondents considered participation in the online tasks important for the sake of meaningfully participating in the classroom tasks.

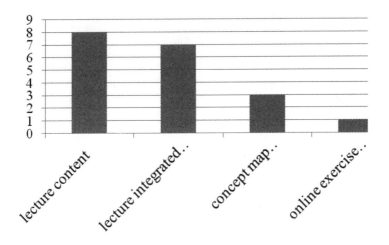

Figure 4: Which of the tasks of the course were the most significant for your overall learning. The answer 'classroom environment' (in two responses) was calculated as both lecture content and lecture integrated group working

When the respondents were asked to more thoroughly elaborate why the participation in the classroom environment was significant for the sake of meaningfully participating in the online environment, the most frequently stated reason was orientation and interest gathering for the forthcoming online exercises (see Figure 6). Other reasons stated were the use of the fast-paced and open interaction to pre-examine the given subject, the use of face-to-face contacts to gather interest for the forthcoming collaborative work in the online environment and personal learning styles. Only one respondent stated that participating in the classroom environment was not important for the sake of meaningfully participating in the online tasks.

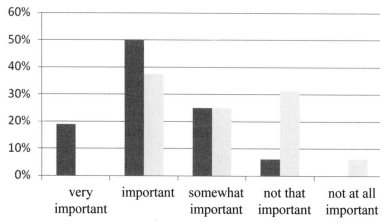

Figure 5: Assess the importance of participating in the classroom environment for the sake of meaningfully participating in the online environment – explain your answer briefly (Q8, N=16). One of the answers produced no concepts due to the misapprehension of the question:

- The light bar denotes "assess the importance of participating in the online environment for the sake of meaningfully participating in the classroom environment"
- The dark bar denotes "assess the importance of participating in the classroom environment for the sake of meaningfully participating in the online environment"

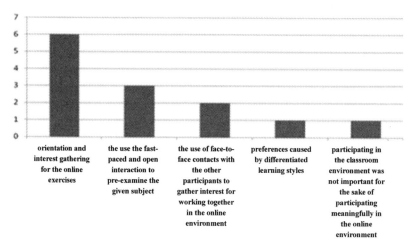

Figure 6: Assess the importance of participating in the classroom environment for the sake of meaningfully participating in the online environment – explain your answer briefly (Q8, N=16). One of the answers produced no concepts due to the misapprehension of the question.

Respectively, when the respondents were asked to elaborate on the reasons why participating in the online environments was important for the sake of meaningfully participating in the classroom environment, the most frequently stated reason was that the online learning tasks allowed more in-depth and detailed reflection of the topic (see Figure 7). Other reasons stated were that the online exercises broadened interaction originated in the classroom, the awareness about the forthcoming online exercises produced interest and orientation to participate in the classroom and, in the case of the concept map exercise, the online exercises turned theory into practice. Three of the respondents viewed that participating in the online environments was not important for the sake of meaningfully participating in the classroom.

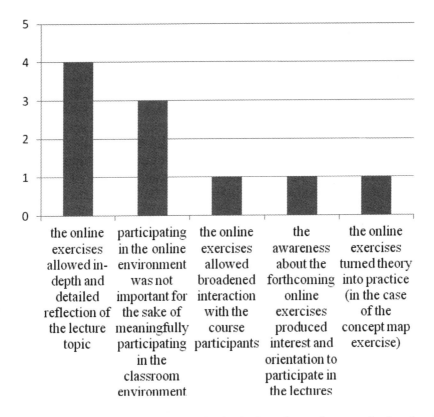

Figure 7: Assess the importance of participating in the online environment for the sake of meaningfully participating in the classroom environment – explain your answer briefly (Q10, N=16). Two of the answers produced no concepts due to the misapprehension of the question.

The respondents were also asked to elaborate on the amount of interaction produced by the course. This examination was two-fold and included both interaction with other participants and interaction with the lecturers. Total of 62% of the respondents saw that the "Tools for Master's thesis"-course produced a significant amount more or somewhat more interaction with the other course participants than the courses which they had previously attended (see Figure 8). Total of 51% of the respondents saw also that the course produced similarly more interaction with the lecturers than the previously attended courses.

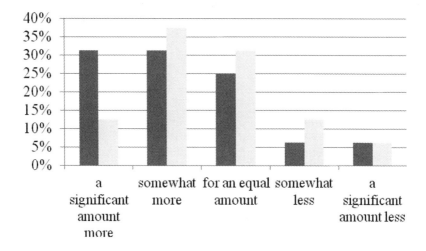

Figure 8: The perceived amount of interaction produced by the course:

–   The light bar denotes "when compared to your previous experience, this course produced interaction with the course lecturers"
–   The dark bar denotes "when compared to your previous experiences, this course produced interaction with other participants"

Discussion

The variety of different learning tasks connected with either the promotion of personal inquiry (see Figure 1), with the promotion of sharing experiences with other participants (see Figure 2) or with the promotion of the overall learning of the participants (see Figure 3) seems to posit a pro blended learning argument. When the latter results are combined with the perceived amount of interaction produced by the course (see Figure 7), it seems evident that the graduate engineering students benefitted from the blended learning course design in their IL instruction course. See Appendix 2 for that overall assessment of the course and its differentiated learning tasks.

Through the results of this study it seems also evident that both online and classroom environment learning tasks can be set to have enhancing effects on each others also in IL instruction. The respondents identified four ways in which the participation in the classroom environment enhanced the participation in the online environment. The most frequently stated enhancing effect in this scenario was the orientation and interest gathering for the forthcoming online exercises. Other reasons stated were the use of the fast-paced and open interaction to pre-examine the given subject, the use of face-to-face contacts to gather interest for the forthcoming collaborative work in the online environment and personal learning styles.

The respondents also identified four ways in which the participation in the online environments enhanced the participation in the classroom environment. The most frequently stated enhanced effect in this scenario was that online learning tasks allowed more in-depth and detailed reflection of the subject than the fast-paced classroom environment. Other reasons stated were that the online exercises broadened interaction originated in the classroom, the awareness about the forthcoming online exercises produced interest and orientation to participate in the classroom and, in the case of the concept map exercise, the online exercises turned theory into practice.

The findings of this study are in line with the blended learning literature (see e.g. Garrison and Vaughan, 2008). The blended learning approach changes the focus of the IL research from comparing the characteristics of the classroom and online environments (see e.g. Zhang, Watson and Banfield, 2007) to studying the possible enhancing fusions between them. The theoretical framework of this study, which was based on the dimensions of personal inquiry/social knowledge construction and verbal/textual communication, seemed to work as way of categorizing different IL related learning tasks. This framework was derived from the work of Garrison and Vaughan (2008).

Through the results of this study the following targets of development of both our course design and our IL pedagogy can be set forth. More diversified online learning tasks could be designed based more closely on the online-to-classroom and classroom-to-online learning effects presented by the students. Especially the learning tasks based on use of the Ning social network site and the online exercise on information-seeking could be improved to increasingly promote the engineering students' self-directed learning in this significant environment of their information behaviour.

When elaborating the results in the context of IL pedagogy, our experiences about the blended learning course design correspond with, for example, the following remarks from the blended learning literature. The blended learning approach implicates that teacher has the ability to differentiate between tasks that benefit from the asynchronous reflection from the tasks that profit from the fast-paced synchronous discourse produced in the classroom (Garrison and Vaughan, 2008, p. 33). Cognitive presence of either the teacher and/or other course participants helps students to view online assignments as worthwhile and therefore they are an important factor in creating meaningful online learning tasks (Garrison and Vaughan, 2008). Promoting and fostering critical discourse becomes also an essential task in both environments (Garrison & Vaughan, 2008). Since students tend to view classroom and online learning environments differently (Garrison and Vaughan, 2008), the participants in the blended learning courses might need to be assured that the online learning tasks are not mere add-ons but allow, for example, asynchronous in-depth and detailed examination of the content to which they are first introduced in the classroom environment.

Conclusion

The results of this study and our experiences with the "Tools for Master's thesis"-course encourages us in the Aalto University Library to further examine the possibilities of blended learning course designs. The professional development, including the previously mentioned targets of development, of the Aalto University Library staff is supported by the Aalto University's Service Career System. Also, Aalto University Library's partnerships with, for example, Aalto University's Strategic Support for Research and Education Unit have proven very fertile for our IL instruction (for more about supporting information literacy programs through partnerships, see Laverty, 2006).

This study seems to have touched a number of areas which should be investigated further. Different types of frameworks for evaluating blended learning IL course designs should be investigated and applied to research. The high perceived importance of the classroom learning tasks for the sake of the overall learning of the IL course participants needs also further examination. Most importantly however, the empirical base of this important area of research needs to be expanded within IL context. The potential of the blended learning course design seems to be evident as the horizon of different electronic resources continues to expand.

References

Allan, B. (2002). *E-learning and teaching in library and information services.* London: Facet

American Library Association. (2000). *Information literacy competency standards for higher education.* Retrieved from the ALA website:
www.ala.org/acrl/sites/ala.org.acrl/files/content/standards/standards.pdf

Andretta, S. (2007). Phenomenography: a conceptual framework for information literacy education. *Aslib Proceedings: New Information Perspectives,* 59 (2), 152-168.

Bawden, D. (2001). Information and digital libraries: a review of concepts. *Journal of Documentation,* 57(2), 218-259.

Comba, V. (2009). E-tutorships and e-learning – re-skilling librarians for interactive communication in virtual environments. In: J. Varlejs & G. Walton (Eds.), *Strategies for regenerating the library and information profession* (pp.279-288). IFLA Publication Series 139. München: Saur

Conklin, T., & Musser, L. (2001). (Eds.) *EngineeringlLibraries: building collections and delivering services.* New York: Haworth Information

Garrison, D.R., & Vaughan, N.D. (2008). *Blended learning in higher education – framework, principles and guidelines.* San Francisco, CA: Jossey-Bass.

Grafstein, A. (2002). A discipline-based approach to information literacy. *Journal of Academic Librarianship,* 28(4), 197-204.

Laverty, C. (2006). Educational technology – harnessing new tools to support information literacy. In: P. Genoni & G. Walton (Eds.), *Continuing professional development – preparing for new roles in libraries: a voyage of discovery* (pp. 83-89). München: Saur.

Levonen, J., Joutsenvirta, T., & Parikka, R. (2009). Blended learning – katsaus sulautuvaan yliopisto-opetukseen. In T. Joutsenvirta & A. Kukkonen (Eds.), *Sulautuva opetus – uusi tapa opiskella ja opettaa.* Helsinki: Palmenia.

Patton, M.Q. (2002). *Qualitative research and evaluation methods.* 3rd ed. Thousand Oaks: Sage.

Rodriques, R. (2001). Industry expectations of the new engineer. In T. Conkling & L. Musser (Eds.), *Engineering libraries: building collections and delivering services* (pp. 179-188). New York: Haworth Information.

SCONUL Working Group on Information Literacy. (2011). The SCONUL seven pillars of information literacy – core model for higher education. Retrieved from the SCONUL web site: www.sconul.ac.uk/groups/information_literacy/publications/coremodel.pdf

Tenopir, C., & King, D.W. (2004). Communication patterns of engineers. New Jersey: IEEE Press.

Vaughan, N., & Garrison, D.R. (2005). Creating cognitive presence in a blended faculty development community. *Internet and Higher Education,* 8, 1-12.

Ward, M. (2005). Information and the engineer. In R. MacLeod & J. Corlett (Eds.), *Information sources in engineering* (pp. 1-24). München: Saur

Zhang, L., Watson, M., & Banfield, L. (2007). The efficacy of computer-assisted instruction versus face-to-face instruction in academic libraries – a systematic review. *Journal of Academic Librarianship,* 33 (4), 478-484.

APPENDIX 1: Online survey used in study

The purpose of this survey is to gather student feedback from the "Tools for Master's thesis" course. By answering the following questions you will help the Aalto University Library to improve its information literacy instruction. It takes about 15 minutes to fill the survey and it is voluntary to do so. All given responses are kept anonymous and confidential. The data gathered from the survey is accessible only to the persons responsible for realizing the course. The persons realizing the course might use the data in academic publications and presentations. More information considering the survey can be acquired from either information specialist Virpi Palmgren (contact information) or information specialist Antti Rousi (contact information).

1 What was your motivation to enroll to this voluntary course? Did you have any expectations about the course?

2 Assess the value derived from "Tools for the master's thesis"-course to your master's thesis project

	excellent	very good	good	adequate	poor
Assess the value derived from the course as a whole	☐	☐	☐	☐	☐
Assess the value derived from the lecture contents	☐	☐	☐	☐	☐
Assess the value derived from the lecture integrated group working	☐	☐	☐	☐	☐
Assess the value derived from the online exercise on information-seeking	☐	☐	☐	☐	☐
Assess the value derived from the concept map exercise	☐	☐	☐	☐	☐
Assess the value derived from the use of Ning online social network site	☐	☐	☐	☐	☐

3 Which of the above activated you to proceed with your personal inquiry? How?

4 Which of the above activated you to share insights and practices with the other participants? How?

5 Which of the above were the most significant for your overall learning? Why?

6 Which of the above did not promote your learning?

7 Assess the importance of participating in the classroom environment for the sake of meaningfully participating in the online environments

very important	important	somewhat important	not that important	not at all important
☐	☐	☐	☐	☐

8 Explain briefly your previous answer

9 Assess the importance of participating in the online environments for the sake of meaningfully participating in the online environment

very important	important	somewhat important	not that important	not at all important
☐	☐	☐	☐	☐

10 Explain briefly your previous answer

11 When compared to your previous experiences, the course produced interaction

	a significant amount more	somewhat more	for an equal amount	somewhat less	a significant amount les
with other participants	☐	☐	☐	☐	☐
with the lecturers	☐	☐	☐	☐	☐

(The rest of the survey structure and the examination of its results are omitted)

APPENDIX 2: Assessment of course and learning tasks

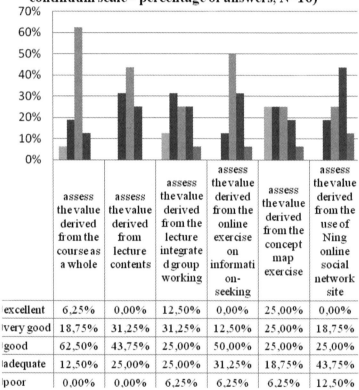

Assess the value derived from "Tools for the master's thesis"-course to your master's thesis project (a question based on subjective continuum scale - percentage of answers, N=16)

	assess the value derived from the course as a whole	assess the value derived from lecture contents	assess the value derived from the lecture integrated group working	assess the value derived from the online exercise on information-seeking	assess the value derived from the concept map exercise	assess the value derived from the use of Ning online social network site
excellent	6,25%	0,00%	12,50%	0,00%	25,00%	0,00%
very good	18,75%	31,25%	31,25%	12,50%	25,00%	18,75%
good	62,50%	43,75%	25,00%	50,00%	25,00%	25,00%
adequate	12,50%	25,00%	25,00%	31,25%	18,75%	43,75%
poor	0,00%	0,00%	6,25%	6,25%	6,25%	12,50%

Student Literacy for Succeeding in a Pervasive Digital Environment

Win Shih

Director, Integrated Library Systems, University of Southern California
winyuans@usc.edu

Abstract

Today's net-generation college students were weaned on multimedia, regularly viewing, sharing and loading video with YouTube and other social networking sites. At University of Southern California (USC), students across curriculum are producing video for their assignments and class assignments. Faculty in diverse disciplines now assign projects requiring some manner of video feed. Not surprisingly, we're seeing universities across the nation considering video production and related skill sets as part of their undergraduate core curricula (Young, 2011). Today's growing digital environment, new education programs are merging traditional information and research skills with IT fluency, digital and multimedia literacies demanding more-and-more knowledge of emerging technologies. A successful literacy education requires collaborative efforts from stakeholders including librarians, information technologists, faculty members, and media specialists on campus. This paper will first define the scope of digital and other technical literacies and their collective impact upon current higher education. Based on our home example, we'll discuss how USC Librarians corroborate with other campus colleagues in developing a coordinated, discipline-oriented literacy program meeting the pedagogical goals of the new undergraduate curricula. Furthermore, we will also talk about how to empower a culture of learning and innovation among faculty and graduate students. Marshall McLuhan stated half-a-century ago, "the medium is the message." Digital literacy is becoming integral to higher education and contributes to students' success in technology-enriched environments.

Towards a digital nation and citizenship

It was just 20 years ago when the first Web page was launched (Blum, 2011). Today, the Internet has become such an integral part of our daily life that more than 96% of working Americans use new communications technologies (i.e.

going online, using email, or owning a smart phone) as part of their daily life (Pew Research Center, 2008). While U.S. domestic online transactions in 2009 were estimated at a total of $3.3 trillion annually (U.S. Census Bureau, 2011). This turbulent wave of digital technology evolution will continue to advance the nation toward its next technological frontier. It is critical to prepare US citizens' online skills necessary for today's evolving workplace.

In the U.S. at the national level, President Obama noted the skills crucial for all Americans to navigate the Information Age by declaring October 2009 as National Information Literacy Awareness Month. In his proclamation, he pointed out a new type of literacy that "requires competency with communication technologies, including computers and mobile devices that can help in our day-to-day decision making." Furthermore, he urged all educators and institutions of learning to equip our students with, "the ability to seek, find, and decipher information [which] can be applied to countless life decisions, whether financial, medical, educational, or technical" (Obama, 2009).

The 2010 National Broadband Plan sets a concrete federal government agenda on developing a robust internet access infrastructure for Americans. It recognizes the importance and training needs of digital literacy as an essential skill for civic engagement, educational success, and economic growth in the digital age (Clark and Visser, 2011). Subsequently, a digital literacy initiative[1] website, aimed at helping Americans build their online skills, was launched by Commerce Department's National Telecommunications and Information Administration (NTIA) in 2011. Partnered with nine other federal agencies, the web portal offers resources and tools to teach and help develop computer and online skills (White House, 2011). NTIA has also developed a partnership with the American Library Association and the Institute of Museum and Library Services (IMLS) to promote the use of this portal by the nation's 16,600 public libraries.

Another leading agency at the federal level that advocates a digital literacy program is the Institute of Museum and Library Services (IMLS). It is an independent federal agency that support libraries and museums. Its 2012-2016 Strategic Plan, titled "Creating a nation of learners," is based on the 21st Century Skills Framework for Libraries and Museums and includes a set of necessary skills needed to support productive participation in the 21st century workforce. Adapted from a concept by the Partnership for 21st Century Skills[2], a non-profit coalition, the Framework delineates a set of nine literacy skills. These are: basic literacy; civic literacy; environmental literacy; health literacy; information literacy; information, communication, and technology (ICT) literacy; medical literacy; scientific and numerical literacy; and visual literacy (Institute of Museum and Library Services, 2009; p. 3). To assist libraries and museums, the Framework also includes detailed implementation plans, guide-

---

1   http://DigitalLiteracy.gov
2   www.p21.org

lines, self-assessment tools, case studies, policy analysis and skills definition, as well as an online assessment site[3]

Working with a new generation of learners

In the higher education arena, today's net-generation students were weaned on multimedia, regularly viewing, sharing and loading video with YouTube and other social networking sites. With constantly evolving technologies and new tools as well as overflows of information presented in various formats, higher education institutions are in an exciting and challenging era to work with the new generation of learners.

EDUCAUSE, a professional organization that promotes the use of information technology in higher education, explored the top challenges in teaching and learning with technology in 2008. Through surveys, focus group study, and community vote, it identified "Developing 21st century literacies (information, digital, and visual) among students and faculty" as one of the top five challenges in the next two to three years (EDUCAUSE, 2009).

Another leading barometer that identifies emerging technologies impacting learning, teaching, and creative inquiry in higher education is the annual Horizon Report, a collaborative project between EDUCAUSE Learning and Initiative[4] and the New Media Consortium[5]. Since 2008, digital media literacy has been consistently identified as one of the critical challenges for the next five years in the annual Horizon Report. The key issues pointed out in these reports include (New Media Consortium, 2008-2012):

- A rising need for formal training programs in information, visual, digital media, and technological literacy as well as in how to create meaningful content with new tools for the students in every discipline;
- Shortage of training in the supporting skills and techniques of digital media literacy in teacher education programs;
- Lack of training and expectation for faculty to develop media literacy skills;
- Lack of new and expanded definitions of what skills constitute digital literacy;
- The need to update the curricula and assessment rubrics for applying these new competencies;
- Rapid technological shift and change is outpacing curriculum development and skill acquisition by faculty members.

---

3   http://imls21stcenturyskills.org
4   www.educause.edu/eli
5   www.nmc.org/

As new technology, media, and tools emerge, concerns of their conversion with existing tools and the needs to incorporate them in current literacy education have been discussed by Jones-Kavalier and Flannigan (2006); Craig (2011); Weiner (2010); and Lippincott (2007). Discussion on specific digital and media literacy includes visual literacy (Bleed, 2005; Metros and Wollsey, 2006); mobile literacy (Yarmey, 2011; Futhey, 2011; Parry, 2011); and social media literacy (Rheingold, 2010).

In the academic library setting, "Project Information Literacy" at the Information School at the University of Washington is a large scale and on-going research project studying college students' information seeking behaviors, competencies, and the challenges in conducting research. Since 2008, the project has conducted surveys and interviews of more than 8,000 college students on 25 campuses across the U.S. The latest report, published in 2011, makes the following recommendations for educators, librarians, and administrators based on their findings (Head and Eisenberg, 2011):

- Assessing the library's role as refuge;
- Designing mobile apps to support new study practices;
- Exploring the viability of social media one course at a time;
- Learning beyond self-styled techniques for managing IT devices.

Digital literacy at the university of Southern California

The University

Located in Los Angeles, the University of Southern California[6] (USC), established in 1880, is now one of the world's leading private research universities, and a member of the Association of Research Libraries[7] (ARL). With a strong tradition of integrating liberal and professional education, USC fosters a vibrant culture of public service and encourages students to traverse academic as well as geographic boundaries in their pursuit of knowledge. With a total student population of 37,000, USC enrolls more international students (8,000+) than any other American university.

The Library service

USC has 23 libraries and information centers[8] as well as the USC Digital Library[9]. USC Libraries owns 4.1 million print volumes, more than half-a-

---

6   www.usc.edu/
7   http://arl.org/
8   www.usc.edu/libraries/locations/
9   http://digitallibrary.usc.edu/

million electronic books and journals; fueled by an annual budget of approximately $40.2 million and a staff of 250 professionals.

Digital Literacy

At University of Southern California, students across curricula are producing video for their projects and class assignments. Faculty from diverse disciplines now assign projects requiring some manner of video feed. Unsurprisingly therefore, we're also seeing universities across the nation considering video production and related skill sets as part of their undergraduate core curricula (Young, 2011).

USC began integrating digital literacy into its curricula when filmmaker George Lucas met with Professor Elizabeth Daley, now Dean of the School of Cinematic Arts, about incorporating "the language of sound and music" into its curricula in the late 1990s. As a result, the Institute for Multimedia Literacy[10] (IML) was born in 1998 to develop educational programs and models of teaching and scholarship based upon the usage and development of new digital media technologies and applications. (Daley, 2003)

Over the years, the IML initiative has grown from offering courses incorporating work in multimedia for non-cinema majors to establishing three undergraduate programs:

1. Honors in Multimedia Scholarship: equips students with a conceptual and technical foundation for multimedia scholarship and for expressing ideas through images, sound, video, text, networks, games and interactivity.
2. Minor in Digital Studies: students explore the rich potential of digital media for critical analysis and creative discovery.
3. The "Multimedia Across the College" program: pairing multimedia labs with upper division courses, undergraduates work with images, sound and text to create multimedia class projects.

Concomitantly, two state-of-the-art multimedia labs were built to strengthen and facilitate these programs.

Over time, IML has successfully shifted its financial dependence from research grants to tuition-based funding. The number of faculty involved and the students enrolled in IML-sponsored programs continues to mature steadily. Affiliated courses have likewise been conducted at Caltech and University of California, Berkeley.

USC leadership fully recognizes the importance of multimedia literacy in a student's learning experience. In 2010, an IML Advisory Committee was es-

---

10   http://iml.usc.edu/

tablished by the Provost with a mandate to make recommendations for extending the role and scope of IML. Committee membership constitutes faculty representatives from several academic programs, campus information technology services, and USC Libraries. In their 2011 final report, the committee offered the following recommendations to the University:

- Continue to expand rigorous and credible IML-based academic programs and courses;
- Make multimedia coursework a requirement in all undergraduate core curricula, with emphasis on cultivating high levels of skill sets and deep knowledge in understanding and utilizing digital information and multimedia technologies;
- The "Multimedia Across the College" program should be expanded to all colleges and schools;
- IML should provide training programs and facilitation to faculty members who are interested in incorporating a multimedia component into their courses;
- IML should also develop resources for integrating multimedia literacies into capstone courses and projects;
- IML must take a leadership role in advocating multimedia literacy and form partnerships with academic and supporting units on campus, including the Center for Scholarly Technology, USC Libraries, the Center for Excellence in Teaching, and USC research institutes; in tandem with academe's germane individuals: IT professionals, researchers, and faculty with expertise in multimedia literacy;
- IML should continue to lead research in *digital literacy* on campus; provide consultation to faculty members; identify opportunities, and proactively seek grant support;
- IML ought to develop resources for integrating multimedia literacy into USC Library's Information Literacy offerings.

Moreover in 2010, the Committee on Academic Programs and Teaching, which advises the Provost about multi-school curricula and undergraduate curricular issues and policies, published a set of ten recommendations concerning the University's global connections and engagement. Among these were: Developing a program to assist students and faculty in gaining fluency with new forms of digital communication. The Committee sees *"digital literacy* as an essential tool to giving USC students and faculty a competitive edge in a global world." (University of Southern California, 2011a)

The new USC Strategic Plan, released in December 2011, further incorporated digital and multimedia skills into the student learning process. Under the section, "Transforming Education for a Rapidly Changing World," the plan promulgates:

"New technologies demand new literacies and modes of academic inquiry that students must master. This is particularly true of digital and multimedia literacy. USC is a national leader in the study of new literacies and new media with its strengths in cinematic arts, the humanities, communications, visual and cultural studies, advertising, and new technologies. Competence in new media is, in many ways, an extension of traditional forms of literacy. An appreciation of this connection can instill respect for intellectual depth and rigor". (University of Southern California, 2011b)

In addition to the Institute for Multimedia Literacy, the Information Technology Program[11] in the USC Viterbi School of Engineering offers credit courses in multimedia, 3D animation, and introductory courses on user experience, Internet technologies, and mobile application development. ITP furthermore offers major and minor programs on video game programming, web development, 3D animation and special effects, along with video game production.

Examples of Multimedia Usage in College Courses

The following instances demonstrate how USC instructors are incorporating state-of-the-art multimedia in their core class curricula to enhance the learning experiences of our students.

French 352, Modern French Culture
Taught by Professor Danielle Mihram, this course studies the major intellectual, artistic and sociopolitical trends which have shaped French culture from the Revolution to Present Day, and is conducted entirely in French. Dr. Mihram, who is a librarian as well as teaching faculty in the Department of French and Italian, requires a multimedia group project, in addition to regular quizzes, blog postings, oral presentations and a research paper. The multimedia project accounts for 15% of the final grade, and requires students to explore a topic by producing a 2 to 3 minute "Video Essay." This group project *encourages* students to work collaboratively (as a *team*) and *creatively* – by constructing a coherent, scholarly expression and argument vis-à-vis *engaging audial-visual media*. The video essay not only tests conceptual understanding of a research topic, the French language and its idiomatic expression, but also student ability and skill in handling multi-media technologies. To aid students in acquiring the necessary research and multimedia skills, D. Mihram provides:
   - Library Instruction;
   - A course blog;[12]

---

11   http://itp.usc.edu/
12   http://modernfrenchcultures2012.blogspot.com/

- A comprehensive, online subject resource[13] in the use of LibGuides;
- Multimedia Workshops: A teaching assistant, funded by IML, works with Dr. Mihram to conduct four sessions of multimedia training outside regular class hours. These hands-on workshops develop the conceptual and technical foundations for multimedia scholarship. Students learn necessary skills and tools to complete their group project. Pedagogic content includes image scanning, Windows Movie Maker, iPhoto, Adobe Photoshop and Audacity for audio editing. Students also learn best research practice, how to inculcate both Internet and library resources for optimum presentation efficacy, in addition to competently critiquing and evaluating the multimedia works of others.

EDHP 593A Higher and Postsecondary Education Seminar, Capstone Project
Students from Masters of Education in Education Counseling, Postsecondary Administration and Student Affairs are required to complete a Capstone Project during their final year. The project requires them to create a personal Website: highlighting their experiences in the program, reflecting their professional philosophy and competencies, and illustrating their growth and development throughout their Masters Studies. This Website will also serve as each student's "e-portfolio" for job search and/or career advancement, and includes their mission statement, fieldwork, coursework, résumé, along with internship experience.

To develop their e-portfolio, students select from the following hosting services: Google Site, WordPress, or Weebly. Students are given a checklist of tasks to perform, working with a facilitator in developing their site. They also receive oral and written feedback from their thesis committee, advisors and classmates[14].

POSC 248 / WRIT 140 General Education, International Human Rights / Writing 140, Collaborative Presentation Project.
One of the assignments of this class is to develop a Web photo presentation with handouts, using Picasa or Prezi software, in groups of four. To prepare their slides, students are asked to review Edward Tufte's The Cognitive Style of PowerPoint as a guide. Team members work outside class to develop their presentation strategy and to prepare their slides and handouts. Each member contributes three "digital slides" and one page of handout. Each team group is allocated 15 minutes to present their final project to the class.

---

13   http://libguides.usc.edu/French351
14   Sample e-portfolio sites include: https://sites.google.com/site/ykopeleva/; www.wix.com/ataka0/capstone#!; https://sites.google.com/site/meganenc/; http://marcuskohl.weebly.com/; www.rickinhighered.com/.

USC Libraries' Instructional Services

USC Libraries has created an active information literacy program and developed close partnerships with key academic departments (Bahavar, Hanel, Howell and Xiao, 2011). During 2009-10 Fiscal Year, USC Libraries proffered 1,326 instructional sessions with 21,596 participants. To assist students in accessing and making the most of our rich collections, librarians have developed online guides, instructional websites and tutorials, in addition to traditional classroom-based instruction and training. USC Libraries' Instructional Services has further partnered with the Writing Center, the Engineering Writing Program, Freshman Academy, Ph. D. Summer Institute, American Language Institute, and the USC Language Academy to provide specific literacy programs.

Among the 23 USC libraries and information centers, the Leavey Library is a 24/7 technology-enhanced facility that strongly supports students' multimedia needs. The state-of-the-art Information Commons is equipped with 39 iMacs, 140 PCs, two hands-on interactive computer learning classrooms, 35 collaborative workrooms equipped with a PC, white board, high-speed network connections, audio/visual area with 18 viewing workstations, video conferencing rooms, and an auditorium. The Multimedia Commons is facilitated with higher-end workstations (iMacs and PCs), scanning and other technology and audio-visual equipment. All these workstations come with multimedia productivity software. The Library itself provides extensive multimedia equipment for checkout, including digital cameras, camcorders, digital audio records, headsets, pen tablets, microphones, and an LCD data projector. USC Library's video collection now contains more than 4,000 DVD titles, including foreign-language, documentary, independent and instructional films.

Librarians at USC are acutely aware of the trends and imperatives in offering training and support to our patrons regarding effectively working with digital resources. As stated clearly in USC Libraries' 2011-2013 Strategic Plan, the goal of "Integration with our Community" is "to become more thoroughly and systematically integrated into the research programs, teaching curricula and learning activities of our users," who arrive with diverse study habits, varied *media literacies* and disparate research methodology practices. (University of Southern California Libraries, 2011)

As pointed out in recommendations to USC's IML Advisory Committee, there are numerous stakeholders involved in the multimedia-literacy effort, including Libraries, Information Technology Services, IML, ITP, the Center for Excellence in Teaching, Annenberg School of Communications and Journalism, and USC Research Institutes. A concerted and coordinated effort will minimize unnecessary overlap and confusion, while maximizing our limited resources.

In summation, higher learning simply makes *profoundly wise educational sense*, when lab facilities, production equipment, common software programs, and digital portfolio archival systems, buttressed by training and support services – *the tools of digital literacy* – are standardized across campuses and academic programs – locally, nationally, and – at the dawn of the 21st century – globally.

Conclusion

There's no going back. Today's mushrooming digital environment and newest educational programs are merging traditional information and research skills with IT fluency, digital and multimedia literacies, thenceforth demanding evermore knowledge of emerging technologies.

Information literacy is the overarching term and concept encompassing all – traditional and emerging literacies – including digital literacy. Information literacy is now the domain and responsibility of all educators and is applicable to all disciplines. A successful "information-literate education" requires corroborative efforts and support from chief higher-learning stakeholders – including top administration, librarians, information technologists, faculty members, key academic advisors and media specialists university-wide.

Marshall McLuhan stated half-a-century ago, "the medium is the message." "The Digital Age" is a major harbinger of that message. Digital literacy is becoming integral to higher education and contributes to student success in technology-driven environments. As Lippincott superbly points out in her article, the campus community needs to develop a "coordinated, discipline-oriented literacy program," to cultivate a "convergence of literacies and frame a discussion of literacies in the context of *academic* work, rather than in the context of organizational structure." (Lippincott, 2007, p. 17)

References

Bahavar, S., Hanel, N., Howell, K., & Xiao, N. (2011). The University of Southern California's campus-wide strategies to reach international students. In P. A. Jackson & P. Sullivan (Eds.), *International Students and Academic Libraries: Initiatives for Success* (pp. 213-231). Chicago, IL : American Library Association.

Bawden, D. (2001). Progress in documentation--information and digital literacies: a review of concepts. *Journal of Documentation, 57*(2), 218-259.

Bleed, R. (2005). *Visual literacy in higher education.* Retrieved from EDUCAUSE website: http://net.educause.edu/ir/library/pdf/ELI4001.pdf

Blum, M. (2011). *20 years ago today: the first website is published.* Retrieved from WIRED website: www.wired.com/geekdad/2011/08/world-wide-web-20-years/

Clark, L., & Visser, M. (2011). Digital literacy takes center stage. *Library Technology Reports, 47*(6), 38-42.

Craig, K. (2011). The Ouroboros; or, how "digital" and "humanities" will shape each other in the near future. *EDUCAUSE Review*, 46(5), 58-59. Retrieved from: www.educause.edu/ir/library/pdf/ERM1157.pdf

Daley, E. (2003). Expanding the concept of literacy. *EDUCAUSE Review*, 38(2), 32-40. Retrieved from: http://net.educause.edu/ir/library/pdf/ffp0306s.pdf

DigitalLiteracy.gov. (2011). *Digital literacy initiative fact sheet*. Retrieved from: www.digitalliteracy.gov/sites/digitalliteracy.gov/files/Digital_Literacy_Fact_Sheet_05 1311.pdf

EDCAUSE. (2009). *The EDUCAUSE top teaching and learning challenges*. Retrieved from EDUCAUSE Learning Initiative website: www.educause.edu/eli/Challenges

Futhey, T. (2011). Embracing change: an interview with Tracy Futhey. 46(2), 47-58. Retrieved from: www.educause.edu/ir/library/pdf/ERM1126.pdf

Head, A.J., & Eisenberg, M.B. (2011). *Balancing act: how college students manage technology while in the library during crunch time*. Seattle, WA: The Information School, University of Washington. Retrieved from: http://projectinfolit.org/pdfs/PIL_Fall2011_TechStudy_FullReport1.2.pdf

Institute of Museum and Library Services. (2009). Museums, libraries, and 21st century skills. Retrieved from Institute of Museum and Library Services website: www.imls.gov/assets/1/AssetManager/21stCenturySkills.pdf~

Jones-Kavalier, B.R., & Flannigan, S.L. (2006). Connecting the digital dots: literacy of the 21st century. EDUCAUSE Quarterly, 29(2), 8-10. Retrieved from: www.educause.edu/ir/library/pdf/EQM0621.pdf

Lippincott, J.K. (2007). Student content creators: convergence of literacies. *EDUCAUSE Review*, 42(5), 16-17. Retrieved from: www.educause.edu/ir/library/pdf/ERM07610.pdf

Metros, S., & Woolsey, K. (2006). Visual literacy: an institutional imperative. *EDUCAUSE Review*, 41(3), 80-81. Retrieved from: www.educause.edu/ir/library/pdf/ERM0638.pdf

New Media Consortium. (2008-2012). *New Horizon Report*. Retrieved from New Media Consortium website: www.nmc.org/publications

Obama, B. (2009). National Information Literacy Awareness Month, 2009. Retrieved from the White House website: www.whitehouse.gov/assets/documents/2009literacy_prc_rel.pdf

Parry, D. (2011). On teaching mobile literacy. *EDUCAUSE Review*, 46(2), 14-18. Retrieved from: net.educause.edu/ir/library/pdf/ERM1120.pdf

Pew Internet and American Life Project, Most Working Americans Now Use The Internet or Email at Their Jobs, Sept. 24, 2008. Retrieved from: www.pewinternet.org/Reports/2008/Networked-Workers/1-Summary-of-Findings.aspx

Rheingold, H. (2010). Attention, and other 21st-century social media literacies. *EDUCAUSE Review*, 45(5), 14-24. Retrieved from: www.educause.edu/ir/library/pdf/ERM1050.pdf

University of Southern California, Committee on Academic Programs and Teaching (2010). *CAPT Report on Global Connections and Engagement*. Retrieved from University of Southern California website: http://strategic.usc.edu/CAPT%20on%20Global%20Connections%20and%20Engagem ent%20-%202010.pdf

University of Southern California. (2011a). *USC Strategic Vision: Matching Deeds to Ambitions*. Retrieved from University of Southern California website: http://strategic.usc.edu/USC%20Strategic%20Vision%20Dec%202011.pdf

University of Southern California Libraries. (2011b). *The Essential Library: The USC Libraries' Strategic Plan 2011-2013.* Retrieved from University of Southern California Libraries website: www.usc.edu/libraries/essential/integration/index.php

U.S. Census Bureau. (2011). E-Stats. Retrieved from U.S. Census Bureau website: www.census.gov/econ/estats/2009/2009reportfinal.pdf

Weiner, S.A. (2010). Information literacy: a neglected core competency. EDUCAUSE Quarterly, 33(1). Retrieved from: www.educause.edu/EDUCAUSE+Quarterly/EDUCAUSEQuarterlyMagazineVolum/InformationLiteracyANeglectedC/199382

White House. (2011). *Digital literacy initiative aims to help Americans build online skills.* Retrieved from the White House website: www.whitehouse.gov/blog/2011/05/13/digital-literacy-initiative-aims-help-americans-build-online-skills

Yarmey, K. (2011). Student information literacy in the mobile environment. *EDUCAUSE Quarterly*, 34(1). Retrieved from: www.educause.edu/EDUCAUSE+Quarterly/EDUCAUSEQuarterlyMagazineVolum/StudentInformationLiteracyinth/225860

Young, J. R. (2011, May 8). Across more classes, videos make the grade. *The Chronicle of Higher Education.* Retrieved from: chronicle.com/article/Across-More-Classes-Videos/127422/

Information Specialists as Facilitators of Learning on an Online Course on Information Skills Training. Case Study: Library Course for History Students in the Optima Learning Environment at The Pegasus Library

Tiina Sipola
Oulu University Library, Finland
tiina.sipola@oulu.fi

Abstract

This article discusses experiences with the first course on information skills delivered entirely online as e-teaching. The library course for history students was organised by the Pegasus Library at the University of Oulu during the autumn semester of 2011. The planning process was based on the socio-constructivist approach to learning, which posits that learning is an individual as well as social process of skill building and knowledge acquisition. We hoped to support the student learning process by activating their own inner dialogue and self-reflection. A selection of communication channels were created in the online environment with the intention of facilitating interaction between the students and information specialists, and also between the students themselves. We found that multifaceted interaction, together with explicit instructions, is especially important in keeping the students motivated in an online environment. The starting point for the design and implementation of an online course that supports the learning process is the pedagogical expertise of the information specialists and their view of how online tools can be utilised in a pedagogically meaningful way. The support of library management in the reinforcement of pedagogical expertise is essential for the support and development of the educational and teaching roles of university libraries.

Learning online pedagogics

Pedagogical skills of librarians and information specialists

Librarians and information specialists in university libraries need public performance, interaction, networking and pedagogical skills in addition to content expertise, since guidance and teaching are an important part of their job description. However, most of them have only very limited or no pedagogical studies at all behind them. And even today education is not among the most popular minor subjects for students of information studies. For example at the Department of Information Studies of the University of Oulu popular minor subjects are literature, philosophy, communication and history of science and ideas.

The design, implementation and assessment of teaching are seamlessly interwoven with each other when they are backed up by an understanding of conceptions of learning process and teaching methods and of their application to the teaching of information skills training – regardless of whether the teaching takes place in a classroom or online. An online course can easily turn into a teaching material repository without pedagogical activity, if an understanding of the theoretical background of teaching is missing.

An online learning environment offers exciting didactic methods for the teaching of information skills. These additions include online discussions and the sharing of information. An online environment makes it possible for students to learn from each other and opens up a lot of new perspectives for both the student and the information specialist: they can work together in the handling, learning and evaluation of information in various new ways. E-teaching promotes student-centred learning (Bonk and Cunningham, 1998; Hannafin, Hannafin and Gabbitas, 2009) as opposed to traditional classroom instruction, which tends to be more teacher-oriented and, as some studies suggest, less successful (Kahl and Venette, 2010).

When designing the library course for history students I benefited from the basic studies in education I have completed at the University of Oulu and of several courses on both online pedagogics and on the use of social media in teaching, which were included in my teacher's degree completed at Oulu University of Applied Sciences. During the studies I had the opportunity to specialize in university pedagogics and thus prepare for work in the university environment.

In this article I will detail the theoretical basis of learning on which we built the library course for history students, how the interaction between the information specialists and the students and between the students themselves developed and how the students performed throughout the course. Along the way I will present my thoughts on the importance of understanding the learning process for the successful implementation of an online course and of course for classroom instruction as well. Finally I will describe some opportunities that are available to information specialists at Oulu University Library for developing their teaching expertise.

History students as a test group

Prior to autumn 2011, the Pegasus Library[1], a unit of Oulu University Library[2], has offered courses on information skills in the form of classroom instruction. We wanted to offer the students the chance to complete these studies in an online environment and, at the same time, develop our own skills in online pedagogics. The students studying intermediate studies in history were the first to be given this opportunity because a one credit (according to European Credit Transfer and Accumulation Systems, ECTS[3]) library course is a mandatory part of their degrees. We reasoned that as the course was mandatory it would ensure that at least some of them would choose the online course option.

The structure of the library course in the optima learning environment

The planning process for the online version of the library course began in late spring 2011 and the first course was held between 1 November 2011 and 13 January 2012. The University of Oulu has widely adopted the Optima learning environment[4] and the students are already familiar with using it, so it was natural to utilise this platform for the course.

On the Optima homepage of the course we placed a diagram showing the course structure. The intention was to provide the students with a quick overview of the whole course. We also placed other important course information on the homepage, including the schedule, goals, content, ties to other studies, evaluation criteria and grading methods. Separate pages were added for instructions on how to use the various kinds of software and how to complete the assignments.

We used the course calendar and notice board in Optima to notify students of pertinent information. Notices could also be emailed to the students from the notice board. We created a discussion forum and implemented a chat option for real time conversation. Students could also make Skype calls to the information specialists and participate in two Adobe Connect Pro (ACP) online meetings. However, it was possible to complete the course by only using the Optima learning environment and not utilising the other possibilities.

The course material was divided into eight sections, which were made available to students in sequence according to the course schedule. The pro-

---

1   www.kirjasto.oulu.fi/index.php?id=529
2   www.kirjasto.oulu.fi/index.php?id=509
3   http://ec.europa.eu/education/lifelong-learning-policy/ects_en.htm
4   http://optima.discendum.com/

gression was logical: it began with the planning of the information search process, then moved on to Finnish databases and so forth. One of the sections focused on the reference management program RefWorks. At each stage the students reviewed and applied what they had previously learned. Each section included material with which the students had to familiarise themselves and assignments they needed to complete.

Each of the sections included information search assignments focusing on a given topic or, in some sections, on a topic freely chosen by the students. We also asked the students open questions related to the topics. The students submitted their assignments in a personal folder created for them in Optima and the information specialist then submitted written feedback for each assignment in the same folder. In order to receive credit for the course the students were required to complete all the assignments, participate in the mandatory forum discussion and respond to a feedback questionnaire online (Appendix 1).

All information specialists in the Pegasus Library participated in the design and implementation of the course, thus each individual student got instructions from several information specialists during their learning process.

Theoretical starting point

We elected the socio-constructivist approach to learning as the theoretical starting point for our online course (Al-Weher, 2004; Bonk and Cunningham, 1998). According to this learning theory, the students are active, motivated and responsible for their own learning. Previously acquired knowledge is taken into account with respect to both teaching and learning and the teaching is student-centred. Students shape information so that it is meaningful to them by actively constructing it both independently and in groups. Learning is seen as problem solving and critical thinking and as an active cognitive activity. The information specialist functions as facilitator who provides a favourable learning environment for the students.

It was clear from the start that a well-prepared and executed online course required more than just taking old classroom content and putting it online. It was necessary to create brand new learning situations and assignments. Producing content for Optima was the most familiar but also time-consuming phase in the process of creating an online course. Important questions from the pedagogical perspective were: how do we activate the students' previously acquired knowledge, what level of activity do we demand of the students in order to achieve good results and how do we link the subject matter to the needs of the history students so that they feel that their learning experiences have value? How do we strengthen the students' trust in their own abilities so that they apply what they have learned to new situations first during the online course and later on in their other studies? The constructive, facilitating role of the information specialist, referred to as scaffolded instruction by Bonk and Cunningham (1998), was also something we had to really think about. How do we avoid giving too complete solutions and advice and guide the students to find the answers themselves? How can we motivate the students? What sort of suggestions, hints, comments, explanations, questions and examples do we give to point the students in the right direction?

Motivation

In student-centred teaching the focus is on the student, whose job is to study. Motivated students find it easy to set goals for their studies, plan their studying process, structure the content that needs to be learned, practice regularly and be constantly watching and evaluating themselves. Motivated students are active participants in the learning process and they find the process to be so worthwhile that they are more likely to complete an online course than students who are not properly motivated. Sanna Juutinen (2011) has stated that motivation plays an especially large role in online courses, where the teacher is not physically present. This so called self-regulated learning (Zimmerman, 2001) is a good starting point for an effective learning process.

In practice, the history students participate in the library course as it is mandatory: they do not necessarily have a genuine interest in the subject matter. The students can choose between classroom and the online version of the course, but they have to choose one. It was a pleasant surprise to find that a total of 16 students signed up for the online course. Eight of the students were history majors and the rest were students of other history subjects like archaeology or museology. The library course was only mandatory for the eight history major students. We never asked why these students chose the online course over the regular one. Possible reasons might have included living or residing elsewhere, the idea that online courses are easier to complete, scheduling conflicts, and preferring e-learning to regular learning. Those students for whom the library course was not mandatory were perhaps genuinely interested in the content or just wanted to be awarded the one credit point.

We aimed to motivate the students further in various ways. We emphasised the facts that information seeking is a part of academic study skills and that it is also required in the professional arena. There was a link on the course material page to a playful music video titled Tää on tiedettä[5] (*This is Science*) on the University's Welcome to the Scientific Community page. The video's purpose was to highlight the unavoidable relationship between scientific activity and information skills and also to function as a kind of fun relief. We encouraged the students to self-regulate by suggesting that they reserve enough

---

5   www.oulu.fi/verkostovatti/materia/

time for their course work. We reminded students of upcoming milestones like the halfway point of the course by posting information on the notice board in Optima and actively notified them about the voluntary ACP meetings. We tried to inspire the students to take advantage of the course and look into the information searches they would need to conduct when researching their bachelor thesis topics. In order to clarify the students' understanding of their own abilities and to offer them potentially useful peer experiences, we encouraged the students to share their thoughts on the discussion forum and to talk to each other in the chat environment.

Interaction

Attention was paid to the interaction between students and information specialists and between the students themselves. We were cautiously optimistic in expecting lively interaction. The topic of the mandatory forum discussion was RefWorks. Each student had to make at least two posts: one on the usability of the program, and one on how the reference style of the History Department of the University of Oulu[6] worked in RefWorks. We expected the students to take the discussion seriously and post short, factually grounded messages and answer each other's questions, as well as "think aloud" and introduce new perspectives. In other words, the students were expected to share and produce information together. The role of the information specialist in the discussion was to make sure the discussion remained on-topic and no erroneous notions were formed. If necessary, the information specialist was to keep the discussion going. Free discussion on various related topics was also encouraged. The ideal size for an online discussion group is 9–14 students (Nevgi, Lindblom-Ylänne, and Kurhila, 2003), so the possibility for active discussion existed.

The students were also offered the opportunity to take part in two Adobe Connect Pro meetings, one of which was supposed to focus on RefWorks and the other on foreign databases like Historical Abstracts and Academic Search Premier. The students also had access to a real-time chat room and Skype, which offers the possibility to share screens besides free calls. Email was used for personal one-to-one correspondence. However, we aimed to minimise the use of email because it may cause a lot of extra work in an online course.

In our opinion the prerequisites for active, multifaceted interaction were in place. Information and feedback could be shared in multiple ways, both orally and in writing and with or without visual contact. It was also hoped that an actively communicating student group would in turn prove to be a resource for us information specialists.

---

6   www.oulu.fi/hutk/historia/en/

Evaluation and reflection

At the end of the course, the students were graded on the scale of pass/fail, which does not shed much light on actual learning results. However, throughout the course we constantly utilised formative evaluation to assess the students' results and learning processes (Wottawa and Pult, 2001). Students received personal written feedback on each assignment. Our goal was to let the students know what they were good at and what they needed to improve on. We gave them practical instructions to revise or completely redo assignments when necessary. For two sections a joint-feedback based on student-specific feedback was given and published for the whole group. Similar joint-feedback given on the online discussions summarised key content and strengthened the social atmosphere of the course.

In retrospect, the students should have been asked to set goals for their learning by themselves. We could have encouraged the students to "look back" and reflect more (Kansanen, 1995) on their own progress a bit more than we did. This would have helped them to be even more determined in directing their efforts at the goals and have better control over their learning process on every level. To further support the learning process, peer review could have been tried; the students could have evaluated some of each others' assignments according to given instructions. By implementing peer review it is also possible to ease the workload of an information specialist on an online course if necessary.

Understanding how students struggle with the various information search techniques and databases is important in assessing both the teaching and the learning process of the students. Leinonen (2008; p.35) mentions a so-called "expert's blind spot" and differentiates between pedagogical content knowledge and expert's content knowledge. From the perspective of the former, it is crucial to understand what needs to be stressed and what can be left out when teaching information skills to students. Could it be that excessive expertise makes a person blind to what is most important?

The quiet history student

In the next sections I will discuss the interaction between the information specialists and the students and between the students themselves. We found that in the online environment interaction with students of history was more lively than in a traditional classroom situation where it is very difficult to get any responses from the students at all. The online environment certainly makes lively interaction possible, especially if the information specialist's online social and instructional skills are strong.

Online discussions

Participation in the discussion about RefWorks on the Optima discussion forum was mandatory for the students. An information specialist began the discussion and gave the students short instructions. When we have asked students of history about a topic in a classroom setting, be it RefWorks or something else, we have hardly received any answers. In our online discussion we did receive some answers, although just to the extent of the two mandatory messages each student was required to write. In many of these messages students encouraged others to use the RefWorks program.

Chat

When students entered the chat they were first greeted with short instructions that told them that an information specialist would be present only on occasion, and that the chat discussions would not be saved. The students were encouraged to interact with each other freely in the chat environment. As it happened, not a single chat discussion was had between a student and an information specialist. It is possible that the students chatted with each other, but since the conversations were not saved there is no record of it.

Online Meetings with Adobe Connect Pro

Notifications about the two voluntary ACP meetings were posted on the front page of the course, the discussion forum and the notice board. The messages were also forwarded to the students' email addresses. Short instructions on how to use ACP were also placed on the front page of the course. Despite this, none of the students showed up for either ACP meeting. The reasons for this can only be guessed at, but one of them might be the students' unfamiliarity with ACP. The threshold to attend one's first ever online meeting might also be too high, especially if the meeting is optional.

Skype

For Skype calls, we offered the Skype name of one information specialist on the course's front page. Not a single Skype call was received. We asked the students in the feedback questionnaire at the end of the course whether they used Skype or not. Only three out of ten students said they did, which was rather surprising.

Email

Information specialists had to send several emails to students who had been asked to revise their assignment submissions on Optima, but who failed to do so in time. One student asked for a deadline extension via email. All ten students who ended up completing the course had to be reminded that the feedback questionnaire was a mandatory part of the course. The course was taught by several information specialists, each responsible for one to three sections. This made the workload of one individual reasonable when it came to email use. Still, using email meant extra work, because the information sent via email was also available in the online environment.

Study attainment

Sixteen students signed up for the course, four of whom never started studying. Two students only completed a few sections and then dropped out. Ten students completed the whole course and received a passing grade and the one credit point. Five of these students were history majors, the rest were students of other history subjects like museology or archaeology.

Why two students quit after completing some sections of the course is a challenging question. According to Sanna Juutinen (2011), the reasons can be many. It is possible that the students had a negative attitude towards e-learning, or that e-learning simply does not suit everyone. The reasons for quitting do not necessarily have anything to do with the system used, the content of the course, the teacher or the way the course is structured. The decision to quit might stem from the student's own feelings and views. Juutinen emphasises the meaning of interaction in e-learning. During an online course, the information specialist should attempt to convey positive emotional experiences to the students through active interaction. This might encourage the students to continue with the course even if it is a little difficult. When students participate in the different online activities, such as online discussions, their learning experience is enhanced.

The word 'mandatory' has a negative connotation to it, but it is an important aspect nonetheless. Without it many things would not get done, or at least not get done in time. Did the five history majors who completed the course only struggle through it because it was mandatory? And what motivated the other five students, for whom the course was optional? Maybe they realised the importance of information skills in their studies and thought that the course was interesting enough.

Bringing the students together as a group at the beginning of an online course makes them commit to finishing it. Maybe the next time we will ask students to briefly introduce themselves or hold a mandatory ACP meeting at the beginning of the course. Group assignments are also possible within the framework of the online environment e.g. forum discussions in small groups. It is possible to use the same educational methods in online learning as in classroom settings. For example collaborative learning might be worth trying. Incorporating online learning environments and social media into an online course offers a multitude of diverse learning and teaching opportunities.

Conclusions

This course gave us information specialists at the Pegasus Library new experiences in what it is like to function as a facilitator and resource in the learning process. We are quite pleased with our first online course. We feel we succeeded in compiling instructions that clearly explained the contents, structure and function of the course to the students. According to the feedback questionnaire learning results were good. Yet deeper learning outcomes could have been achieved. We probably followed the traditional teacher-centred model a little too closely. The students should have been allowed more room to figure out answers to questions. The course assignments should also be looked at more closely. Were there too many? Were some of them too detailed? Ideally, the assignments should help the students find connections between new information and their own experiences and ideas. Should we have made the course more optional by taking into account the students' own interests and so relied more on their critical thinking faculties and independent problem solving skills? All in all, focusing more on the student might prove beneficial to the learning process in the future.

From the perspective of the pedagogical implementation of an online course and especially of the student's learning process it could be beneficial to consider what are the benefits and disadvantages of having many information specialists participate in the implementation of an online course. Even though the workload related to preparing and marking the assignments is reduced, it is difficult to get an overall picture of the students' learning if the information specialist always changes when a new section begins. One alternative could be a system where the students are divided into smaller groups and each group is taken care of by an information specialist. This would provide more consistency for the students. However, this kind of arrangement can be problematic for the overall management of the course.

Could it also be necessary to consider if teaching skills are even more important than in-depth content knowledge? There's certain logic to the searching and evaluation of information, regardless of subject area, and easy-to-use database interfaces also guide the user through the search process. However in the end it is always the person in need of information who assesses the relevance of the search results.

At Oulu University Library the information specialists who participate in the teaching of information skills are not required to have studied pedagogics or education. Such studies are nevertheless recommended and information specialists have the opportunity to participate for example in in-house training courses aimed at the teaching staff, which are generally worth 1-3 credit points. The University of Oulu also offers a more extensive, 25 credit point study module in university pedagogics. In addition and as mentioned earlier Oulu University of Applied Sciences, School of Vocational Teacher Education[7] offers 60 credits teacher education during which one can focus on higher education or university pedagogics. In addition to the various courses and training it is worth keeping in mind that an important way to learn how to teach is to teach.

The need to deepen the pedagogical expertise of library professionals has been noted at the University of Oulu. The University offers degree students flexible study paths, giving them an opportunity to graduate as so-called pedagogical information specialists in the Degree Programme of Literacies[8], by combining studies in education and information studies. It remains to be seen whether this new kind of expertise has a positive effect on the status of the library professional field.

When information is in text form it is permanent. Our online course gave us an excellent teaching package. The material that we compiled can be used in many different ways, for example as supplementary material in classroom or face-to-face instruction. The material on Optima is also easy to update to match the needs of students from different fields and departments. By using the blended learning method it is possible to combine face-to-face instruction with computer-mediated instruction.

E-teaching offers interesting and inspiring possibilities. However, the online environment and social media should provide some extra value from a pedagogical perspective; they should not be used just for the sake of it. In addition to pedagogical know-how, e-teaching requires familiarity with matters of data security, copyrights, etc. The design and implementation of an online course requires time and resources, but it can also conserve them. After all is said and done, it is most important to provide different types of learners with flexible ways of completing their information skills studies and so moving toward the completion of their degrees. It is also important that the subject matter of the course lends itself to being taught in an online environment: information skills training is an excellent fit for the web.

---

7   www.oamk.fi/amok/english/
8   www.oulu.fi/yliopisto/opiskelu/opinnot/joustavat-opintopolut/lukutaitojen-asiantuntijuus-informaatiotutkimus

References

Al-Weher, M. (2004). The effect of a training course based on constructivism on student teachers' perceptions of the Teaching/Learning process. *Asia Pacific Journal of Teacher Education, 32*(2), 169-185.

Bonk, C. J., & Cunningham, D. J. (1998). Searching for learner-centered, constructivist, and sociocultural components of collaborative educational learning tools. *Electronic Collaborators: Learner-Centered Technologies for Literacy, Apprenticeship, and Discourse,* 25-50.

Hannafin, M., Hannafin, K., & Gabbitas, B. (2009). Re-examining cognition during student-centered, web-based learning. *Educational Technology Research & Development, 57*(6), 767-785. doi:10.1007/s11423-009-9117-x

Juutinen, S. (2011). *Emotional obstacles of e-learning.* Jyväskylä Studies in Computing, 145. Jyväskylä: University of Jyväskylä. Retrieved from: http://jyx.jyu.fi/dspace/bitstream/handle/123456789/37191/9789513945848.pdf?seque nce=1

Kahl, D. H.,Jr, & Venette, S. (2010). To lecture or let go: a comparative analysis of student speech outlines from teacher-centered and learner-centered classrooms. *Communication Teacher, 24*(3), 178-186.

Kansanen, P. (1995). *Discussions on some educational issues VI, (pp. 97-18) Research Report 145.* Department of Teacher Education. University of Helsinki.

Leinonen, A. M. (2008). *Ammatillinen opettajuus kansallisessa verkko-opetuksen kehittämishankkeessa.* Tampere: Tampere University Press.

Nevgi, A., Lindblom-Ylänne, S., & Kurhila, J. (2003). Yliopisto-opetusta verkossa. In *Yliopisto- ja korkeakouluopettajan käsikirja* (pp. 403-425).

Wottawa, H., & Pult, D. (2001). Educational evaluation: Overview. In N. J. Smelser, & P. B. Baltes (Eds.), *International encyclopedia of the social & behavioral sciences* (pp. 4255-4259). Oxford: Pergamon. doi:10.1016/B0-08-043076-7/02359-7.

Zimmerman, B. J. (2001). Self-regulated learning. In N. J. Smelser, & P. B. Baltes (Eds.), *International encyclopedia of the social & behavioral sciences* (pp. 13855-13859). Oxford: Pergamon. doi:10.1016/B0-08-043076-7/02465-7.

APPENDIX 1: Feedback questionnaire

The approved completion of the library course for history students required that the students filled out a feedback questionnaire in the Optima learning environment. The students who completed the course were asked the following 15 questions:

1. The course was equal to my expectations
2. The workload was reasonable
3. The schedule was reasonable
4. An online course is well suited for learning information skills
5. Interaction with the instructors was functional
6. I will make use of what I learned during the course in the future
7. The course included information important to me
8. My own work contribution was sufficient
9. I did not experience any technical difficulties during the course
10. I learned new things during the course
11. Other students gave me advice (in the chat or on the forum, for example)
12. I will recommend this online course to my peers
13. The feedback I received on my assignments was useful
14. After completing the course, my information skills are
15. Do you use Skype?

For questions 1-13 the students chose one of the following four options:

-   Strongly disagree
-   Somewhat disagree
-   Somewhat agree
-   Strongly agree

For question 14 the options were:

-   Good
-   Quite good
-   Somewhat uncertain
-   Poor

For question 15 the students answered yes or no.

The answers to the questions can be seen in the table below

QUESTION	Strongly disagree	Somewhat disagree	Somewhat agree	Strongly agree
The course was equal to my expectations	0	1	7	2
The workload was reasonable	0	1	7	2
The schedule was reasonable	0	1	4	5
An online course is well suited for learning information skills	0	1	2	7
Interaction with the instructors was functional	0	0	2	8
I will make use of what I learned during the course in the future	0	0	0	10
The course included information important to me	0	0	3	7
My own work contribution was sufficient	0	2	5	3
I did not experience any technical difficulties during the course	1	3	5	1
I learned new things during the course	0	0	2	8
Other students gave me advice (e.g. in the chat or on the forum)	0	4	3	1
I will recommend this online course to my peers	0	1	4	5
The feedback I received on my assignments was useful	0	0	5	5

QUESTION	Good	Quite good	Somewhat uncertain	Poor
After completing the course my information skills are	2	7	1	0

	Yes	No		
Did you use Skype?	3	7		

Wikipedia and Wikis as Forums of Information Literacy Instruction in Schools

Eero Sormunen
School of Information Sciences, University of Tampere, Finland
eero.sormunen@uta.fi

Heidi Eriksson
Upper Secondary Education, City of Tampere, Finland
heidi.eriksson@tampere.fi

Tuuli Kurkipää
Upper Secondary Education, City of Tampere, Finland
tuuli.kurkipaa@tampere.fi

Abstract

The City of Tampere and the University of Tampere are cooperating on the ongoing "Tieto haltuun" Information Literacy (IL) project to develop and study new types of IL learning assignments applying social media tools. The overall goal of the study was to learn how writing articles for Wikipedia (a public wiki) and for the school's own wiki can serve as a learning assignment in information literacy instruction. In this paper we report how a library visit as one element of the course programme affected students' information behaviour. We wanted to find out how a special IL session in the library can help students to expand the types of sources used. One aim was to investigate how students' tendency to write in their own words instead of copy-pasting and to cite sources appropriately instead of plagiarizing is associated with the type of sources used. Through the case courses we aimed to collect experiences of good practices in IL instruction organized as a collaborative effort on the part of librarians and teachers. We found that the IL session organized in the local library substantially increased the use of books as sources in writing the articles. The students used sources differently in differently designed assignments. The groups of students writing focused Wikipedia articles used more printed sources, wrote more in their own words and also summarised and synthesised more information from sources than the groups of students writing on more extensive topics for the school's wiki. The lessons learned from the project are discussed both from the teachers' and librarian's perspectives.

Introduction

In the school's Information Literacy (IL) instruction, writing based on sources searched by students themselves is a widely used type of learning assignment. The core of the task is for students to search and study multiple texts and compile another text. The goal is that students should read sources thoughtfully, construct knowledge on the given topic, and, drawing on that knowledge and available sources, compile a new text indicating what they have constructed and learned. Through this practical exercise students are expected to learn – in addition to subject content – to search, evaluate and use information effectively and ethically.

In the age of Wikipedia and Google, copy-pasting and plagiarism have become a widely recognized problem that makes it difficult to achieve the intended learning goals of IL assignments. Many students tend to transfer information mechanically from the sources into their own texts instead of transforming it in the cognitive process of knowledge construction (Limberg 1999; McGregor and Streitenberger, 2004; McGregor and Williamson, 2005). In the worst case, the student fails to achieve the learning goals in topical content as well as in information literacy.

For many librarians and teachers, the use of Google and Wikipedia is inappropriate information behaviour that students should grow out of (Achterman, 2005; Julien and Baker, 2009). However, others argue that Wikipedia is a useful forum for acquiring good information literacy practices (Jennings, 2009). We support the view that students' activity in the Web should be seen as an opportunity and that these forums should be used to enhance information literacy instruction.

"Tieto haltuun[1]" is a project that aims to enhance the IL skills of the upper secondary school students in the City of Tampere (age range from 16 to 18). Even though Wikipedia and other wikis are important modern day tools for finding, processing and publishing information, teachers and students typically do not master their principles well enough to exploit the opportunities they offer. The project librarian therefore took part in these courses teaching the students how to make a proper wiki article and how to seek and process the information for it.

The goal of our study was to find out in detail how students use printed and Web sources in writing their wiki / Wikipedia articles. In the pilot study, two classes – one in biology and one in geography – wrote Wikipedia articles. Only a general introduction to information seeking and Wikipedia authoring was included in the programme. In the main study, the students of a literature class wrote Wikipedia articles and the students of a history class wrote wiki ar-

---

1   "Tieto haltuun" is a Finnish slogan referring to gaining mastery of both information and knowledge.

ticles for their school wiki. This time an organized library visit was included in the course programme to ascertain how this intervention affects students' use of sources.

The "Tieto haltuun" project

The "Tieto haltuun" project was initiated in 2008 to improve teachers' and students' IL skills in Tampere upper secondary schools. The aim is to integrate IL skills into the school's curriculum. The students are also intended to be able to search for, process and produce information in their future studies in universities and colleges.

The project offers tuition in IL skills both for teachers and students. The information specialist designs the teaching according to the course objectives and topics. Usually the course assignments include portfolios or essays, for which the students have to seek, evaluate and use information independently. The lessons start with an introduction to basic information literacy, such as simple search skills and source criticism. The students are given examples of Web sites, books and other sources on where and how to find information on the topics of interest. For the rest of the lesson the students search their topics with the help of the information specialist.

In addition to the IL tuition the project endeavours to impart IL skills in the Tampere upper secondary school curriculum in all compulsory subjects. The information specialist takes part in maintaining and developing the school libraries. The project has promoted communication between schools and the City Library by organizing meetings and cooperation. For example, two librarians worked for a two-week period in a school library and together with the teaching staff developed new practices for IL.

The role of the researchers was to collect and analyse data from the case courses to learn more about students' information behaviour in source-based writing in general, and to give feedback specifically for the further development of information literacy instruction.

Wikis and wikipedia as forums of IL instruction

"A wiki is a website whose users can add, modify, or delete its content via a Web browser using a simplified markup language or a rich-text editor. Wikis are typically powered by wiki software and are often created collaboratively, by multiple users" (Wikipedia[2]).

---

2   http://en.wikipedia.org/wiki/Wiki

Wikipedia is a participatory encyclopaedia built on a wiki[3]. Anybody is invited to contribute by writing and editing articles as one of the Wikipedians. The authoring policy rests on three principles (1) Verifiability, (2) No Original Research and (3) Neutral Point of View (Huvila, 2010). Articles should not contain new information or interpretations that have not been published earlier in some reputable forum. The third principle reminds writers to present competing views or balance between them in controversial issues.

Some aspects of Wikipedia make it an authentic and meaningful framework for source-based writing assignments. Overall, students are familiar with the basics of Wikipedia because they search it regularly (Head and Eisenberg, 2010; Harouni, 2009). Students seem to trust Wikipedia because their everyday experiences are predominantly positive (Lim, 2009) and tend to use it uncritically (Harouni, 2009). Lim (2009) argues that students are aware of the quality problems of Wikipedia, but confused about how to deal with them. This tension calls for pedagogical interventions that help students to scrutinize the problems of information evaluation.

Sundin (2011) made an ethnographic study of the everyday practices of Wikipedia editors and found that the construction of knowledge and referencing external sources are fairly transparent processes. He concludes that this makes Wikipedia an excellent forum to discuss and demonstrate the credibility of information. Jennings (2009) compared the Wikipedia guidelines with the information literacy standard of ACRL (2000) and found that they overlap quite a lot. Basically, Wikipedia offers a framework for IL instruction that adheres to the IL standards.

Research questions

The programmes of the courses investigated in the pilot study did not include a library visit. The teachers were shocked by the students' almost exclusive use of Web sources. In the courses designed for the main study, the teachers decided to add a library session to the course programme to activate the use of printed materials. Thus our first research question is:

RQ1: How does a library visit as one element of the course programme affect the students' choices of sources?

Students' low engagement in working with sources and producing text of their own (high rate of copy-pasting) and in properly acknowledging the sources (plagiarism) are well known problems in students' assignments. The research

---

3   For the English version visit: http://en.wikipedia.org/wiki/Main_Page

suggests that poor information literacy practices are related to failure to design meaningful and manageable assignments (Kuhlthau, 2004; Limberg et al., 2008).

We investigated the extent of low engagement in the source-based writing in two classes and differently designed assignments by asking:

RQ2: How much do articles composed in differently profiled assignments contain sentences:

   a. Paraphrasing beyond copy-pasting?
   b. Summarising within and synthesising across sources?
   c. Plagiarising sources?
   d. Building arguments credibly on sources?

Copy-pasting and plagiarism are associated with a tendency to use Web sources instead of printed sources. We aimed to ascertain if low engagement in the writing process was related to the types of sources used:

RQ3: Is the use of printed and Web sources similar or different in terms of:

   a. Copy-pasting?
   b. Plagiarism?
   c. Summarising within and synthesizing across sources?
   d. Building arguments credibly on sources?

In addition, we collected reflections from the librarian and teachers on their roles in the project. These qualitative results are presented in the discussion section.

Methodology

Case courses

We started with a pilot study on two eight-week courses in an upper secondary school in the spring term 2010. Four groups of students participated in an eight-week geography course and seven groups in an eight-week biology course. Each group wrote an article for Wikipedia as part of the course programme. The main study was conducted during spring term 2011. Thirty students divided into ten groups completed a course in Finnish literature. Twenty-eight students divided into seven groups completed a course in Finnish history. The members were randomly assigned to the groups.

The original plan in the main study was that each group should write and upload an article into the Finnish edition of Wikipedia. However, the history teacher decided to use the school's wiki as the writing forum because she considered it more flexible in designing the assignment in extensive topics. On both courses the instructions to writers were designed to be as similar as possible to the Wikipedia conventions.

The groups of students selected topics for their articles from a list prepared by the teacher. In the literature course each group worked on one classic Finnish novel. The teacher checked in advance that Wikipedia did not contain a complete article on the novel. The students were required to read the novel first and write a personal literary essay on it before the group work on the source-based writing task started. In addition to the analysis of the novel itself, the students were required to write about the author and her/his works in general, about the reception of the novel in its day, and about the role of the author/work in Finnish literature.

On the history course, the teacher had prepared topics on Finnish history dealing with the period from the Civil War of 1918 to the beginning of the Winter War in 1939. The topics were quite extensive: The Civil War (1918), a dispute over the Finnish constitution (1918-19), economic development, the role of the left wing, the role of the right wing and foreign policy. The articles in the last four topics were intended to cover the period of 1918-39. For each topic, the teacher had listed sub-topics to help students to comprehend what themes the article should discuss.

In the literature class, the assignment was introduced during the second week of the course and the articles were completed in the sixth week. In the history class, the start was a week later and the end a week earlier than in the other class. The students of the literature class were given two weeks' extra time to read the novel and write the literary essay before approaching the source-based writing task.

The assignment was introduced, written guidelines were distributed, groups formed, and topics for the articles selected at the first session. The information specialist took part in the case courses, discussed the assignments with the teachers and taught the students how to make a proper wiki article and how to seek and process information for it. The second session was a visit to the nearby City Library. One 30- minute session was devoted to the library collections and services and another session to searching on the internet. The librarian was informed of the topics selected and had collected materials from the library collection for the students to look at. Time was also reserved for students to search in the library catalogue and directly browse in the collection. The teacher and the librarian gave the students hints and answered their questions. Most but not all students took part in the library visit.

After the visit to the library, the students worked in the next five (on the history course four) sessions in the computer classroom to search for information, to select and read sources found and to write texts for the articles under the teacher's supervision. On the history course, a substitute teacher was supervising the class in two sessions instead of the teacher in charge. We observed that the students worked less actively in the absence of their own teacher. Eventually many groups in the history class were badly behind schedule and completed their articles in a panic. On the literature course, the class had one extra session allocated for working in the computer classroom, the teacher constantly reminded them of the deadlines, and students worked and collaborated more actively in their groups.

Text transformation categories

The comparison between the sources and the texts written was based on a framework of text transformation categories composed in the main study (Sormunen, Heinström, Romu and Turunen, 2012). The dimensions applied in this study are the following:

- Degree of paraphrasing;
- Degree of synthesis;
- Credibility in building arguments on the basis of sources;
- Accuracy of citing.

The *degree of paraphrasing* indicates the extent to which the writer uses his/her own words in source-based writing (categories: *copy-paste / near copy-paste / paraphrased / own text*). The *degree of synthesis* measures the extent to which the writer connects pieces of information from different parts of a single source or from multiple sources (categories: *sentence / paragraph / source /multiple sources /combined with own text*). *Credibility* indicates how soundly the arguments evinced in a sentence rely on the evidence presented in the sources used (categories: *credible / ambiguous / error / weak source*). *Accuracy of citing* deals with the precision of linking the written sentence to the sources used (categories: *sentence / paragraph / article /other / plagiarism / cheating*). For detailed category definitions, see Sormunen et al. (2012).

Data collection

We collected all the articles written and sources used in them (also non-cited when identifiable) applying a method developed in our earlier studies (Sormunen and Lehtiö, 2011;Sormunen et al., 2012). Two second-year Master's degree students were recruited as research assistants. One of them was studying Finnish literature and the other history. All the articles were split into sentences and stored in MS-Word tables. For each sentence, the sources used were searched starting from the closest text citations and expanding to plagiarism

tests in the Web. If a substantial share of article sentences still lacked identified sources (> 10 %) we checked the textbooks available to students and the
materials mentioned by students in the interviews.

Plagiarism checking was done mainly by Wikipedia and Google searches.
To avoid problems of text variation caused by paraphrasing we selected up to
four "best" words from each sentence as keyword candidates for Wikipedia
searches. Queries were made by using all combinations of two keywords
(maximum of six queries if necessary). A similar procedure was applied in the
Google searches, but a set of five keyword candidates was used first. The queries were made by using all keywords and combinations of four keywords
(maximum five attempts). In each search result, a set of 20 first hits was
checked.

Articles and sources were only a small part of the data collected from
the process. We also interviewed groups of students and teachers, used questionnaires to collect personal responses, collected reports and self-assess-
ments written by students, project memos written by the librarian and teachers
etc. We use some of this data to complement the views in the discussion section.

Data analysis

The research assistants became familiar with the task by applying the codes to
a set of two articles (one in literature and one in history). The codes and coding
guidelines were revised on the basis of the problems encountered. Next, a consistency test was conducted by coding a new set of two articles. The overall
consistency reached 91-95 per cent. After the consistency tests each research
assistant coded the data of her/his course alone. The coding data was first collected into Excel tables and after error-checks and pre-processing transferred
into (the) SPSS software. All variables to be examined were categorical and
thus the data were organized into contingency tables. The chi-square ($\chi 2$)
measure was used to test the statistical significance of differences in the distri-
butions of column and row frequencies (see Siegel and Castellan 1988, 123-
124). We used $p<0.05$ as the critical level of statistical significance.

Summary of articles and sources

The summary of the characteristics of articles written by the student teams is
presented in Table 1. The average length of the articles was 100 sentences in
the history and 66 in the literature articles, but the number of sentences per
student was surprisingly similar: 25 sentences in the history and 23 sentences
in the literature class. The volume of texts analysed in the set of literature articles was smaller because we excluded from the analysis sections based on the
direct literary analysis of the novel (description of the plot and characters).

The fourth column of Table 1 reports in how many sentences the analyst was not able to identify the source of the sentence. The overall share of sentences where the search for sources failed was about six per cent for history articles and about ten per cent for literature articles. Thus the analysis covers about 90-94 per cent of the source-based text written by the students.

Team #	Sentences			Cited & Used Sources			Plagiarised Sources			All Sources Used			Cited Sources Not Used
	Written	Analysed	Source Unknown	Web	Printed	Subtotal	Web	Printed	Subtotal	Web	Printed	Total	
History Course													
H1	116	116	8	11	4	15	4	1	5	15	5	20	1
H2	125	125	11	10	4	14	1	0	1	11	4	15	0
H3	68	68	3	12	3	15	10	0	10	22	3	25	0
H4	74	74	2	7	1	8	1	0	1	8	1	9	0
H5	143	143	12	12	4	16	3	1	4	15	5	20	0
H6	59	59	1	5	1	6	3	1	4	8	2	10	11
H7	116	116	6	10	5	15	1	1	2	11	6	17	2
Sum	701	701	43	67	22	89	23	4	27	90	26	116	14
Average	100.1	100.1	6.1	9.6	3.1	12.7	3.3	0.6	3.9	12.9	3.7	16.6	2.0
STDev	32.6	32.6	4.4	2.6	1.6	4.0	3.2	0.5	3.1	4.9	1.8	5.7	4.0
Literature Course													
L1	87	46	0	6	3	9	0	0	0	6	3	9	2
L2	55	17	1	0	4	4	1	1	2	1	5	6	0
L3	36	18	1	1	3	4	0	0	0	1	3	4	0
L4	107	69	17	0	6	6	2	1	3	2	7	9	0
L5	77	36	0	4	6	10	1	0	1	5	6	11	1
L6	88	41	9	0	5	5	0	0	0	0	5	5	0
L7	83	48	5	0	4	4	2	0	2	2	4	6	1
L8	52	30	0	2	4	6	6	1	7	8	5	13	0
L9	38	23	3	0	3	3	0	0	0	0	3	3	0
L10	37	24	1	3	2	5	2	0	2	5	2	7	2
Sum	660	352	37	16	40	56	14	3	17	30	43	73	6
Average	66.0	35.2	3.7	1.6	4.0	5.6	1.4	0.3	1.7	3.0	4.3	7.3	0.6
STDev	25.5	16.3	5.5	2.1	1.3	2.3	1.8	0.5	2.2	2.8	1.6	3.2	0.8

Table 1: Summary of articles and sources used.

Findings

RQ1: Does a library visit affect students' choice of sources?

The numbers of printed and Web sources used in each article are presented in Table 1 (columns 5-13). The last column lists the numbers of sources cited but – according to our analysis – not used by the students.

The overall trend in the main study was that, on average, the students of both courses used about four printed sources per article. Web sources were used less in the literature class (about three per article) than in the history class (about thirteen per article). In practice, all printed sources were books. In very few cases students had used their textbooks or printed reference sources. None cited printed journals or similar sources. The spectrum of Web sources used was much wider, including journal and newspaper articles, Master's theses and PhD dissertations, materials from theme-related academic or governmental Web sites. The use of Wikipedia and teaching materials were also quite common. Two literature groups and four history groups plagiarised Wikipedia extensively (three or more sentences).

The effect of the library visit on the use of printed sources seems obvious. In the pilot study we observed that very few of the sources (4%) were printed (books). In the main study, the share of printed sources was about 59 per cent (3.0 out of 7.3) in the literature class and about 22 per cent (3.7 out of 16.6) in the history class. All groups used printed sources.

Table 1 also shows that in both groups about 23 per cent of the sources used were not included in the list of references (i.e. indications of plagiarism). Sometimes the plagiarism was accidental. For example, one student said in the last session when the articles were uploaded to the wiki that he was not aware of the strict deadline. He could not complete the list of references because all his materials were at home (!).

RQ2: How did students transform information from the sources?

The source-related characteristics of texts written by students in the history and literature classes are summarised in Table 2 (first three data columns).

Degree of paraphrasing. Overall, slightly more than half of sentences were written in paraphrased form and the share of copy-pasted text was nine per cent. Copy-pasting was equally common in both assignment groups (9%) but paraphrasing was more typical in the literature assignments (65%) than in the history assignments (49%). The articles of the history class contained more mechanically edited text (42% vs. 26%). The measured difference was statistically significant ($\chi2$ (2)=23.5; p=0.000).

Degree of synthesis. The results show that most sentences written (58%) were derived from a single sentence in the source. About one third of sentences (35%) summarised the content of a single source. Seven per cent of sentences synthesised contents from two or more sources. A small but statistically significant difference was observed between the groups ($\chi2$ (2)=10.8; p=0.004). The students of the literature course showed a tendency to summarise and synthesise slightly more actively.

Accuracy of citing. The overall result was that in 60 per cent of sentences the text citation was assigned to the sentence itself or the surrounding text paragraph. Further, in about a quarter of sentences (24%) the source was in the list of references. In 16 per cent of sentences the source was plagiarised (cheating included). The history group was more meticulous in marking text citations ($\chi2$ (2)=28.3; p=0.000). An interesting result was that plagiarism was equally common in both groups (16%).

Credibility of arguments. The results show that the students constructed their arguments well on the sources. In 85 per cent of sentences, we could not find even minor problems in the students' way of interpreting the content of the sources. The difference measured between courses was not statistically significant.

RQ3: Is information similarly transformed from printed and Web sources?

The characteristics of texts written on the basis of printed and Web sources are presented in Table 2 (three last data columns). Twenty-nine sentences synthesising information from both printed and Web sources were excluded decreasing the basic dataset to 916 sentences.

Degree of paraphrasing. The figures reveal that direct copy-pasting was more common with Web sources (14% vs. 5%) and paraphrasing in using printed sources (57% vs. 48%). Mechanical transformations were equally common (38%) in the use of both source types. The difference measured in copy-pasting and paraphrasing was statistically significant ($\chi2$ (2)=21.8; p=0.000). This result suggests that students exploit the technical easiness of copying Web sources at the cost of paraphrasing.

Degree of synthesis. Information was summarised and synthesised similarly from printed and Web sources ($\chi2$ (2)=0.125; p=0.939).

Accuracy of citing. The results corroborate the widespread experience that plagiarism is associated with the use of Web sources. Twenty-nine per cent of sentences based on a Web source were products of plagiarism while this was only five 5 per cent in texts relying on a printed source ($\chi2$ (2)=97.7; p=0.000). The most commonly plagiarised source was Wikipedia.

Credibility of arguments. No association was observed between source types and the credibility of arguments since the measured difference was not statistically significant ($\chi2$ (1)=0.747; p=0.388).

The aspect of source-based writing		Class			Source type		
		History (n= 653)	Literature (n= 292)	Total (n=945)	Printed sources (n=486)	Web sources (n=430)	Total (n=916)
Degree of paraphrasing	copy-paste	9 %	9 %	9 %	5 %	14 %	9 %
	near copy-paste	42 %	26 %	37 %	38 %	38 %	38 %
	paraphrased	49 %	65 %	54 %	57 %	48 %	53 %
Total		100 %	100 %	100 %	100 %	100 %	100 %
		$\chi^2 (2)=23.5; p=0.000$			$\chi^2 (2)=21.8; p=0.000$		
Degree of synthesis	sen-sen	61 %	53 %	58 %	60 %	60 %	60 %
	summary	34 %	37 %	35 %	36 %	37 %	36 %
	synthesis	5 %	10 %	7 %	4 %	3 %	4 %
Total		100,0 %	100,0 %	100,0 %	100 %	100 %	100 %
		$\chi^2 (2)=10.8; p=0.004$			$\chi^2 (2)=0.125; p=0.939$		
Accuracy of citing	close	65 %	49 %	60 %	67 %	51 %	60 %
	loose	19 %	34 %	24 %	28 %	20 %	24 %
	missing	16 %	16 %	16 %	5 %	29 %	16 %
Total		100 %	100 %	100 %	100 %	100 %	100 %
		$\chi^2 (2)=28.3; p=0.000$			$\chi^2 (2)=97.7; p=0.000$		
Credibility of arguments	no problem	87 %	82 %	85 %	86 %	84 %	85 %
	problem	13 %	18 %	15 %	14 %	16 %	15 %
Total		100 %	100 %	100 %	100 %	100 %	100 %
		$\chi^2 (1)=3.2; p=0.072$			$\chi^2 (1)=0.747; p=0.388$		

Table 2: Characteristics of sentences in articles written by students in a source-based writing assignment.

Discussion

RQ1: Does a library visit affect students' choice of sources?

The findings strongly suggest that the special session organised in the City Library activated students to exploit printed sources, especially books. In the interviews, the students reported with satisfaction that the librarian had collected some books in advance about each topic of the assignment for the students. In the literature class, the books offered seemed to meet the students' needs. The students of the history class were less satisfied and claimed that the books offered did not directly meet their needs. The librarian commented that in her view the books were relevant to the students' topics but many students were obviously too impatient to work with books requiring substantial reading effort.

The higher satisfaction in the literature class with the books offered by the librarian and their active use may relate to the type of assignment. Each assignment was anchored to a well-known classic novel and the librarian could easily point out general and specific sources relevant for that task. The students of the history class had difficulties in finding a focus for their inquiry (cf. Kuhlthau, 2004). Some of them were desperately searching for information in the Web very late in the process. This is typical of survival strategies, where students seek right answers from the sources rather than build their knowledge. (Limberg, Alexandersson, Lantz-Andersson and Folkesson, 2008)

RQ2: How did students transform information from the sources?

The answers to the second research question emphasise that students wrote and used sources differently in differently profiled assignments. In the literature class, the students were more active in paraphrasing and synthesising sources. The students of the history course cited more meticulously but were behind in all other areas of source-based writing. The building of arguments on sources was credible in both groups.

We can only draw some preliminary conclusions as to why the articles in the literature course were more advanced. The design of the literature assignment was more focused (the classic novel anchored the topic), the personal essay prepared the students for the task, the structure and content of the required end-product was specified more explicitly (a Wikipedia article of a particular type), and the progress of groups was controlled more intensively (check points, the students' "own" teacher present at all sessions). Earlier research suggests that keeping the contextual aspects of the assignment simple and fixed seems to help students to focus on the content of the assignment and to achieve better outcomes (Limberg et al, 2008; Hongisto and Sormunen, 2010).

RQ3: Is information similarly transformed from printed and Web sources?

The comparison of information transformed from printed and Web sources shows that 1) copy-pasting instead of paraphrasing and 2) plagiarism instead of acknowledging sources are more common in the use of Web sources. The findings corroborate the widely shared view that the Web has an obvious role in inappropriate practices of source-based writing (McGregor and Williamson, 2005).

Reflections by the teachers

The teachers perceived that the case courses necessitated a great deal of extra work by the teacher. Compiling Wiki instructions and searching background information about the topics as well as course management caused several hours of extra work. According to the history teacher, the groups of students had problems in collaboration. Writing references and finding relevant sources was also difficult. The course schedule was too tight for the introduction of a new learning method: the students learned only a little about the topics of the other groups. The teacher commented that she might use wiki again but only on a smaller scale assignment.

The literature teacher also noted that much of the course went on studying a fairly narrow topic area. On the other hand, the students learned other skills such as literature analysis, source criticism, information search, collaborative work, project management and writing skills. The literature teacher would use Wikipedia assignments again, but only if the students were already familiar with Wikipedia practices.

Overall, the teachers considered that understanding the importance of IL skills has grown during the past few years in Finland. IL-skills are mentioned in the national curriculum as a goal in almost every subject. In practice the teaching of IL skills and the teaching staff's own IL skills vary a lot. Training in IL skills for teachers is often linked to ICT training, which has worked quite well. ICT offers the tools and IL offers access to content. At the time of this study the *Tieto haltuun* project had not yet fully started to offer training for teachers, but this has changed since the spring 2012. The continuing education for the teaching staff has been made the main focus in the project.

Teachers want their continuing education to be practical and useful for their own teaching. It would be ideal to train only teachers of a specific subject and school level at the same time. Simple examples and models of how to implement IL skills in teaching are very important in order to bring the teaching of IL skills into practice. It would be ideal, if the teachers were given tools to follow the stream of news and discussions on the rapid change of the field.

Reflections by the librarian

The librarian engaged on the project concluded that in order to design and deliver successful training librarians should know about the aim and the content of a particular course and the students' assignments. This makes it possible for the librarian to seek the best material and choose the most useful content for the lesson. In order to give the students what they really need and can comprehend, librarians should have a realistic conception of an average student's IL skills.

The librarian needs to have education and experience in both information science and pedagogy. Since this is very rare, students of information sciences at university should have more opportunities for pedagogical studies. Librarians should also have a better understanding of an average student's IL skills and of everyday life in modern schools. It would be good to follow the discussion on education and schools. Close connection to the school is the key to developing successful collaboration between schools and libraries.

The librarian found she has a good opportunity to see the students seeking information, which gave her a better understanding of their IL skills. This experiment suggested that IL teaching in libraries works better when it is integrated into a course programme. This gives students an opportunity to start practising their IL skills immediately and also makes them more motivated listeners. The students on the Finnish literature course were more successful in finding relevant literature. They already had a good conception of the assignment when they came to the library, and were able to start seeking information more efficiently. In future it would be good to advise the teachers to prepare the class for the library course well.

Some aspects of the courses were found challenging both by the library and teaching staff. On the history course it was especially challenging to motivate the students to work for themselves. Some were eager to make the librarian do the searching for them. They had not thought out the assignment well enough to mount an efficient search. The assignments may also have been a little too challenging for them.

It became obvious to the librarian that many students did not know how to efficiently seek information from a book. Especially seeking from various books and combining facts proved to be too difficult (or bothersome) for some. The librarian had instructed the students to use indices or tables of contents, but this proved to be too little too late. The students tended to use books as they use the internet, browsing superficially and quickly discarding a source they thought non-promising. This is something that needs to be addressed in greater detail on future courses, possibly starting with younger students.

Conclusion

The analysis of the Wikipedia and wiki articles written by the students shows that a carefully planned library intervention can help to activate students to use printed materials in their source-based writing assignments. Our findings corroborate the generally held view that students tend to copy-paste and plagiarise, especially when exploiting Web sources. However, we do not conclude that students should be forced to use printed sources instead of Web sources. Rather, we see the problem relating to the poor design of source-based assignments. Established models for information literacy instruction to overcome the key problems are available (Kuhlthau, Maniote and Caspari, 2004; Eisenberg, 2008), but practising teachers do not apply them (Limberg et al., 2008).

The teachers felt that the learning objectives regarding subject content were not met, but that the students probably learned other useful skills. Further, they commented that if the students' wiki skills were better, they would consider using the tools again. Although the teachers talked about the wiki the comments also apply to the situation of IL instruction in general. It is difficult to find space for learning good IL practices in the school tradition emphasising subject-specific knowledge. Teachers are always busy in meeting the content requirements of the curriculum in the various subjects. Self-directed learning with sources is always a slow process. Similarly, advanced IL practices cannot be adopted if student-centred work methods are not integrated into the curricula at different levels of education. How to find enough time for both learning IL practices and subject contents is a fundamental dilemma in schools.

Acknowledgements

The paper reports a joint study of the KnowId and "Tieto haltuun" projects. The authors thank the teachers of the case courses in the City of Tampere. We are also grateful to Leeni Lehtiö and Teemu Mikkonen, who took care of the data collection during the case courses.

References

Achterman, D. (2005). Surviving Wikipedia – improving student search habits through information literacy and teacher collaboration. *Knowledge Quest,* 33(5), 38-40.

Eisenberg, M.B. (2008). Information literacy: essential skills for the information age. *Journal of Library & Information Technology,* 28(2), 39-47.

Harouni, H. (2009). High school research and critical literacy: social studies with and despite Wikipedia. *Harvard Educational Review,* 79(3), 473-494.

Head, A., & Eisenberg, M. (2010). How today's college students use Wikipedia for course related research. *First Monday,* 15(3-1). Retrieved from: http://firstmonday.org/htbin/cgiwrap/bin/ojs/index.php/fm/article/viewArticle/2830/2476.

Hongisto, H., & Sormunen, E. (2010). The challenges of the first research paper – observing students and the teacher in the secondary school classroom. In: A. Lloyd & S. Talja (Eds.), *Practising information literacy: bringing theories of learning, practice and information literacy together* (pp. 95-120). Wagga Wagga: Centre for Information Studies. Retrieved from: www12.uta.fi/blogs/knowid/files/2010/05/Hongisto_Sormunen_PIL2010.pdf

Huvila, I. (2010). Where does the information come from? Information source use patterns in Wikipedia. *Information Research,* 15(3), paper 433. Retrieved from: http://InformationR.net/ir/15-3/paper433.html.

Jennings, E. (2009). Using Wikipedia to teach information literacy. *College & Undergraduate Libraries,* 15(4), 432-437. Retrieved from: dx.doi.org/10.1080/10691310802554895

Julien, H. & Baker, S. (2009). How high-school students find and evaluate scientific information: a basis for information literacy skills development. *Library & Information Science Research,* 31(1), 12–17.

Kuhlthau, C.C. (2004). *Seeking meaning: a process approach to library and information services.* 2nd ed. Westport, Connecticut: Libraries Unlimited.

Kuhlthau, C.C., Maniotes, L.K., & Caspari, A.K. (2007). *Guided inquiry. Learning in the 21th century.* Westport: Libraries Unlimited.

Lim, S. (2009). How and why do college students use Wikipedia? *Journal of the American Society for Information Science and Technology,* 60(11), 2189-2202.

Limberg, L. (1999). Experiencing information seeking and learning. *Information Research,* 5(1) paper 68. Retrieved from: http://informationr.net/ir/5-1/paper68.html.

Limberg, L., Alexandersson, M., Lantz-Andersson, A., & Folkesson, L. (2008). What matters? Shaping meaningful learning through teaching information literacy. *Libri,* 58(2), 82–91.

McGregor, J. & Streitenberger, D. (2004). Do scribes learn? Copying and information use. In: M. K. Chelton and C. Cool (Eds.), *Youth information-seeking behavior: theories, models and issues(pp.*95-118). Lanham: Scarecrow Press.

McGregor, J., & K. Williamson. (2005). Appropriate use information at the secondary school level: understanding and avoiding plagiarism. *Library and Information Science Research,* 27(4): 496-512.

Siegel, S., & Castellan, N.J. (1988). *Nonparametric statistics for the behavioral sciences.* New York: McGrawHill.

Sormunen, E., & Lehtiö, L. (2011). Authoring Wikipedia articles as an information literacy assignment – copy-pasting or expressing new understanding in one's own words? *Information Research,* 16(4) paper 503. Available from: InformationR.net/ir/16-4/paper503.html .

Sormunen, E., Heinström, J., Romu, L., & Turunen, R. (2012). A method for the analysis of information use in source-based writing. Paper accepted for ISIC 2012 conference, Tokyo, Japan, Sept 4-7, 2012.

Sundin, O. (2011). Janitors of knowledge: constructing knowledge in the everyday life of Wikipedia editors. *Journal of Documentation,* 67(5), 840 – 862.

EFFECTIVE CONTINUING PROFESSIONAL DEVELOPMENT

From the Cradle to the Grave: Empowering Zimbabwean Librarians through Continuous Professional Development in the Information Age

Collence Chisita
Senior Lecturer, Harare Polytechnic School of Information Science, Zimbabwe
collins.chisita@afritechno.com

Abstract

The Library and Information Science environment is extremely vibrant necessitating the need for continuous professional development (CPD) so that one remains relevant and effervescent as a practitioner. It is out of this context that the writer intends to examine the challenges faced by library and information science professionals in accessing opportunities for continuous professional development for librarians in tertiary institutions in Harare, Zimbabwe. This paper will explore the extent to which the library and information science profession is tackling the challenges of re-skilling librarians with the information literacy skills relevant for the information economy so that they are able to remain relevant and vibrant in their capacity to assist their users with greater proficiency. It will also seek to find out the challenges that librarians in higher and tertiary education, with specific reference to technical and vocational institutions, face in trying to update their knowledge and skills through further training. The paper will explore the factors that contribute towards successful continuous development education. It will also seek to find out how continuous development education programmes add value to the library practitioners as well as the users of the library.

Introduction

> "Not to know is bad; not to wish to know is worse."
> West African proverb

Generally continuous professional education or development (CPD) has become an in-vogue trend, considering the rapid changes of Information and

Communication Technology (ICT) and its impact on Library and Information Science (LIS) as a profession. Internationally, professional development is viewed as a remedy for enhancing efficacy and efficiency in LIS as a professional practice. Johnson (1998) states that the growing recognition of ICT and of the value of information in every aspect of development has raised an awareness of the complexity of the nature and volume of modern information provision and its challenges with regards to acquisition of new knowledge and skills. Technology, digital and information divide and socio-economic challenges affecting developing countries in the global information order have forced librarians and libraries to adapt a survivalist strategy hinged upon re-branding, re-skilling and information/ digital literacy and competency among other issues. In the 21st century, a forceful LIS profession can only remain significant if it abandons the traditional amateurish, straight-jacketed and ad-hoc approach towards development and comes up with a formalized strategic plan whose key priority areas will integrate continuous professional education, information literacy and modern technology.

CPD and the dynamism of the library and information profession

The information society has contributed to the growing awareness of the role of information in all aspects of life in progressive economies of the world. This has also meant that the nature and volume of contemporary information provision presents new challenges to the information professional and hence the need for CPD. The proliferation of e-resources, open access, digital technology, e-licensing and e-inclusion among other issues, makes it imperative for academic libraries to prioritise CPD as the country advances into the knowledge age.

Chirukian (1997) notes that the challenges that academic librarians face in the information age should be viewed as a golden opportunity for innovation or renewal, because when challenges are viewed from a dialectical materialist perspective they provide an opportunity for creativity and innovation. The writer advocates for CPD as a solution to overcoming socio-cultural, financial and technological challenges being faced by academic libraries in Africa. The Zimbabwe University Library Consortium (ZULC) and the College and Research Library Consortium (CARLC) have put CPD as a key component in their strategic plan with regards to capacity building. Zimbabwean librarians have embraced CPD as a way to overcome professional stagnation, intellectual laziness and rusticity. The success of CPD programmes requires commitment on the part of the institution and the individual, provision of material and financial support, as well as discipline.

CPD and information literacy

O'Beirne (2006) notes that library workers at all levels need to accept that instead of working as guardians to their own diminishing collections of knowledge they must transform into guides and instructors. Tredinnick (2005) also echoed similar sentiments by stating that making information available was not the limit of responsibility for enabling access to information among socially disadvantaged groups. It is equally vital to take a pro-active role by engaging with wider information literacy provision. At the University of Zimbabwe, information literacy has become an integral component of the curriculum since it is an examinable subject in all disciplines. The progression from user education to information literacy reflects an adjustment to the demands of global technology driven education. The new millennium demands the full integration of information literacy in all aspects of education in Zimbabwe.

The provision of information /digital literacy, and other literacies of the digital age, are helping to reinstate and reinforce the educational or pedagogical role of academic librarians. Librarians have often been perceived as mere custodians of information but the adaptation of information literacy has helped to elevate their status in the realm of the academy. In Zimbabwean universities, information literacy programmes are delivered by librarians in consultation with faculty heads. Information literacy programmes help to develop competent and liberated learners who are capable and confidently able to solve problems and exploit the panoply of digital technology to receive, create, evaluate and share knowledge. The pervasive nature of information makes it essential to promote information literacy so that if citizens are equipped with multimodal literacy skills they can participate fully and effectively in the global information economy. O'Beirne (2006) notes that CILIP's definition of information literacy is quite broad as it transcends the formal learning environment with regards to issues of social engagement and citizenship in digital environments, although it caters for the informal learner: "Information literacy knows when and why you need information, where to find it, and how to evaluate, use and communicate it in an ethical manner".

The information/ knowledge society

The emerging information/knowledge society and the changing role of information professionals has become an issue of great concern the world over. There is urgent need to ensure that LIS professionals stay at the heart of the digital revolution and claim their space in the digital environments. Simmonds (2003) states that it is imperative that for one to remain energetic and significant in this forceful information driven environment; there is need for flexibility, adaptability and strategic positioning to effectively exploit the opportunities that emanate from change.

Development within the Library and Information profession requires individuals who keep in constant touch with current trends in the profession, developing existing skills, acquiring new skills and generally developing personally within the job. Broady-Preston (2009) noted that continuous professional development is necessary in a climate of rapid change since it leverages information professionals in keeping abreast of new skills and knowledge. An investment in continuous professional education and technology is worthwhile in revitalising library services in universities and colleges in higher and tertiary education to remain effervescent.

What is CPD?

Madden and Mitchell's (1993) definition of CPD highlights the critical role of the key stakeholder in the process – namely the employer. The Institute of Personnel and Development views CPD as "systematic, ongoing, self directed learning". Browell (2000) views it as a process concerned with constant updating of professional knowledge throughout an individual's working life which requires self direction, self management and responsiveness to opportunities. The concept of CPD permeates each and every profession because it provides opportunities for renewal and regeneration. For example, the International Pharmaceutical Federation defined CPD as the "....the responsibility of individual pharmacists for systematic maintenance, development and broadening of knowledge, skills and attitudes, to ensure continuity competence as a professional throughout their career…"

Stephens (2005) noted the extraordinary popularity of CPD and attributed this to the dynamic nature of the information profession which compels members to keep their fingers on the pulse of the changes shaping their professional destiny. Robinson and Glosiene (2007) view CPD and Professional Development as synonymous terms that imply a process through which those involved in LIS maintain competence throughout their career irrespective of the changes taking place in the profession. Ritchie (2005) views CPD as a broader term that encompasses Continuous Professional Education (CPE), cognizant that without education a profession is as good as dead. Overall, all the definitions imply the need for continuous learning as a way to create more opportunities for advancement.

Continuous professional development, whose responsibility?

Houle (1980) noted that funding for CPD can come from individual professionals, society at large (taxes and grants), companies that employ professionals and associations, commissions and other entities. The individual professional is the architect of his or her own success or failure.

In Zimbabwe, funding for CPD should come from all the above mentioned sources, but due to economic constraints the onus has rested on individual professionals. However in Zimbabwe academic librarians rely both on institutional and individual initiatives with regards to CPE. Government ministries have manpower development programmes which incorporate both academic and non-academic staff. The major constraints for CPD in Zimbabwe include funding, commitment of top management and lack of initiative within the individual or amongst professional associations. Professional associations and learning institutions, such as the Zimbabwe University Library Consortium (ZULC), Zimbabwe Evidence-based Policy Network (ZeipNet), Zimbabwe Library Association (ZIMLA), the Information Training and Outreach Center for Africa (ITOCA) and the National Library and Documentation Services (NLDS), provide training opportunities in various aspects of LIS work.

Simsova (2000) concurs with Houle (1980) that responsibility for CPD rests with the individual, employers and professional associations. Hare (1989) carried out studies on professional development in academic libraries in Southeastern USA and found out that 80% of library directors encouraged professional development. The barriers to CPD included funding, general ennui and low motivation. The author further notes that employers of professional staff are bound by duty and obligation to ensure that their staff will be able to pursue career paths which will result in "… a growth in knowledge, experience and potential for development. In practice this means support by means of payment of course fees, allowances of time off for study and recognition of new knowledge and skills acquired".

"… a major part of the real cost of continuing education falls upon the individual practitioner; the acceptance of this obligation is part of the price which he or she must pay to secure the status, privileges, and exemptions that the occupation promotes" (Houle, 1980).

Justification for CPD

Rouse (2004) states that the concept of CPD is based on a cycle in which individual practitioners reflect on practice and assess their knowledge and skills, identify learning needs, create and implement a personal learning plan, and evaluate effectiveness of the interventions of the learning in relation to the practice. Even though the writer was speaking on behalf of pharmacists, the concept is applicable to LIS professionals and any other progressive professions. CPD challenges the pre-ordained concept amongst some professionals or organisations that learning ends when one leaves college or university.

" The maintenance and enhancement of the knowledge, expertise and competence of professionals through-out their careers according to a plan formulated with regards to the needs of the professional, the employer, the profession and society..." (Madden and Mitchell, 1993)

CPD has become critical at a time when the world is advancing towards the digital era, whereby information literacy skills become a priority for survival. University libraries, such as the College of Health Sciences Library at the University of Zimbabwe, are providing information literacy skills to both undergraduates and postgraduate students, and staff, to enable them to effectively and intelligently make use of both print and online resources. The Prague Declaration of 2003 proposed that the development of an information society was key to socio-cultural development of nations and communities, institutions and individuals in an information-driven economy. It is in this context that the initiative that library and information professionals have taken to advance themselves professionally, either as individuals or as a collective, should be viewed as the beginning of a long journey towards CPD in line with the philosophy of lifelong learning.

Anunobi and Ukwoma (2009) noted that re-skilling through CPD is critical due to insufficient skills to operate in the digital era, with environmental changes, changes in users needs, the wider horizon of employment opportunity, competition and low budgetary allocation to information services. Dahl, Banerjee and Spalti (2006) warn that library and information centres that persist in the traditional service model in a world characterised by modern ICTs, flat budgets and rising costs of resources will find it difficult to survive. Anunobi and Ukwoma (2009) noted that Nigerian libraries should not be isolated from current developments taking place in the LIS world and strongly recommended re-skilling as the only option. Zimbabwean librarianship is no exception in the battle for reinvention and renewal through re-skilling and this is confirmed by the inclusion of CPD in all higher and tertiary education institutions' strategic plans.

Adanu (2007) noted that the impact of ICT, challenging user expectations, requirements of employers and managers of library and information organizations, and the information deluge, coupled with growing competition from information professionals in the broader information industry, compels institutions and professional associations to transform into learning organisations and provide opportunities for CPD. Illeris (2003), supports CPD as a strategy to counter retrogression in the face of technological change, saying that "...competence that is needed cannot be established and acquired through education in the more traditional sense because there is constant need for change and renewal and it has become vital to see the extent to which this learning and competence development can take place directly in working life in close association with the ongoing change and renewal".

It is assumed that the principal objective of library education is to produce new entrants to the profession who have depth and breadth with regards to professional issues and ability to apply such knowledge to realize organizational goals. The Association for Library Collections and Technical Services (ALCTS) has been providing online CPD courses, covering, preservation, collection development, fundamentals of electronic resources acquisitions and fundamentals of acquisitions among others. These are important courses but the content might be too advanced for local professionals because of technological differences between developed and developing countries. In a similar manner, library consortia in Zimbabwe have CPD programmes incorporating current trends in LIS.

It is interesting to note that higher and tertiary institutions have incorporated digitization as one of their key priority areas. This is reflected by the drive towards creating and developing e-inclusive learning environments, e-learning and institutional repositories. In such a society information and digital literacy become critical skills hence the need for CPD to avoid the pitfalls of sinking into professional oblivion. The World Summit on the Information Society (2005) prioritized social inclusivity through its main goal " ….to build a people-centered, inclusive and development–oriented information society, where everyone can create, access, utilize and share information and knowledge, enabling individual communities to achieve their full potential in promoting their sustainable development and improving their quality of life…"

Strategies for re-skilling

Okojie (2007) noted that the critical skills needed for library and information professionals in the new technology driven worlds included ICT skills, information/digital literacy, internet search skills, marketing, fundraising, advocacy, and intellectual property/copyright laws. ZULC has championed the provision of these critical skills through workshops. Anunobi and Ukwoma (2009) stated that the strategies for re-skilling in Nigeria included those at the professional, institutional, and individual level all meant to ensure continuity and relevance. In Zimbabwe, re-skilling is accomplished through both levels starting from the individual to the professional levels. Government is keen to support CPD through allowing employees in technical and vocational institutions to go for staff development and paying for workshop attendance. However provision of funding is subject to availability.

Workshops are held by national associations and institutions also provide opportunities for further training, self sponsored part-time training, training provided through donor agencies, and exchange programmes, among others. Benefits emanating from re-skilling include: improved worker skills resulting in improved services to patrons and increased use of services and improved performance by LIS professionals and new innovation and creativity in the area of ICTs. Adanu (2007), who researched on CPD in state-owned universities in Ghana, concurred with Anunobi, and Ukwoma (2009), whose research has a Nigerian context, in that both researchers agreed that CPD resulted in increased job satisfaction, competence and career development. In Zimbabwe, the grading system for librarians starts from National Certificate right up to Masters and this has forced many to invest more in professional education in order to enhance prospects for employment and climb the career hierarchy. Reskilling is also made possible through the knowledge transfer system which allows those who have reached a 'dead end' in their career to pass on their knowledge to young professionals.

Shaughnessy (1992) notes that individual choice, peer group and organisational culture are critical factors that influence professional development and emphasizes the need for the library to create a conducive environment for continuous learning. The library can play a crucial role through creating a functional committee that oversees issues relating to professional development. For example, libraries in the USA like Polytechnic University Kennedy Library, Oregon, Louisiana, Missouri and Chicago, among other institutions, use such committees to capacitate their members through further training. In Zimbabwe the situation is similar, because the decision to recommend members for CPD is a product of negotiations at committee level. However individuals might not need to wait for institutional support but can self fund for distant learning programmes.

Training and development strategies ought to be derived from the organisational and human resources strategy, with a human resources development programme helping to ensure that the organization has people with relevant knowledge and skills to realise its organisational strategy. Browell (2000) states that in modern day technology-driven organizations learning must be equal to or greater than the pace of change in order for organizations to succeed. Polytechnics, teachers colleges and universities in Zimbabwe fall in the category of learning organizations because of their abilities to anticipate, react and respond to change. It is commendable to note that CPD is considered a special vehicle in the process of knowledge generation, coordination and promotion in academic institutions. Pedlar, Burgoyne and Boydell (1991) define a learning organisation as a dynamic, flexible and innovative entity in the drive to facilitate the learning of its members to realise organisational objectives " ... continually transforms itself and... harnesses full brainpower, knowledge and experience available to it in order to evolve continually for the benefit of its members."

Figueroa and Gonzalez (2006) note that the efficient management of organisational learning is anchored on the use of previous knowledge as well as the creation of new knowledge within the structure of communities of learning. The drive towards creation and development of institutional repositories, electronic dissertations and thesis databases is a reflection of e-readiness. They further note that rapid developments in technology and the critical role of knowledge make it imperative for organisations to put in place systems to manage both physical and intellectual assets through communication and cooperation. Such systems should be characterized by a culture of CPD. A learning organisation is defined by Senge (1990) as "...a group of people continually enhancing their capacity to create what they want to create...", while Malhotra (1998) defines it as "an organisation with an ingrained philosophy for anticipating, reacting and responding to change".

Research study into CPD in Zimbabwe

A small scale research study was undertaken to find out the challenge, nature and opportunities for CPD in tertiary institutions in Harare. After also analysing factors affecting CPD in higher and tertiary institutions recommendations were identified with regards to CPD. The researcher used survey methodology which involved the selection of random samples to obtain empirical evidence with regards to CPD in higher and tertiary academic institutions in Harare. It allowed for generalisations to be made on the overall research population. The survey allowed the researcher to gather information regarding the target population without undertaking a complete enumeration. The researcher employed the use of questionnaire and interview as data collection techniques. This allowed for accurate descriptions of situations or relationships between research variables.

The researcher focused on Harare Province which hosts Harare Polytechnic, Belvedere Technical Teachers College and Seke Teachers College. The researcher however makes references to other institutions like universities because they all fall under the Ministry of Higher and Tertiary Education. Interview schedules and questionnaires were prepared for the Head Librarians of the Polytechnic and (two) teachers colleges. The researcher administered questionnaires to a group of twenty librarians drawn from the three institutions. The researcher also interviewed three Librarians to ascertain their views on continuous professional education.

It was found that both universities and polytechnics have a manpower development plan covering both academic and non-academic staff. This was the general situation in all state polytechnics. However this does not accommodate everyone or all those interested in long-term CPD programmes because the competition for manpower development slots is high amongst both the academic and non-academic staff. It was also found that most workshops for information professionals were provided by professional organisations like Zimbabwe Library Association, by library consortia such as Zimbabwe University Library Consortium and College and Research Libraries Consortium

(CARLC), International Network for the Availability of Serial Publications (INASP) and National Library and Documentation Services (NLDS). The Zimbabwe University Library Consortium (ZULC) through its partnership with EIFL conducted the following programmes as part of CPD for librarians in universities, as reflected by the following:

a. SubjectsPlus in Zimbabwe: helps users find e-resources 14 Feb 2011 SubjectsPlus will address one of the main challenges facing library users in the digital environment—how to locate high-quality, relevant e-resources both commercial and open access.
b. EIFL-FOSS first themed week is a success 28 Jan 2011 Demonstrating 'disability tools' that increase access 'Disability tools' was the topic of the EIFL-FOSS programme's first themed week. The week kicked off with a remote presentation attended by 25 people from Africa, Asia and Europe. They learned about the most commonly used and easy to install FOSS...
c. Disability Tools in Zimbabwe: new project for 2011 7 Jan 2011Following the EIFL-FOSS Call for Participation in October / November 2010, a number of projects are getting underway in a variety of areas. The first of these is a project in The University of Zimbabwe Library,
d. Evergreen ILS workshop, Chinhoyi, Zimbabwe 25 Oct 2010 as part of the EIFL-FOSS Skills and Tools workshop effort, the Zimbabwe University Libraries Consortium (ZULC) has organised a 3-day workshop on the installation and use of Evergreen, a FOSS integrated library system (ILS).

Other Workshops for librarians are held by Zimbabwe Library Association (ZIMLA), ZIBF, National Library and Documentation Services and Information Training and Outreach Centre for Africa (ITOCA) these afford professionals opportunities to network and learn from each other. The researcher found that due to lack of institutional funding individual librarians end up sacrificing their salaries to fund themselves to either enrol for conventional undergraduate or postgraduate degree programmes. 10% of the respondents had attended an Association of Library Collections and Technical Service Course (ALCTS) courtesy of a benevolent fund.

Out of the twenty respondents, two (10 %) have a Masters degree, six (30%) have first degrees, while eight (40%) have Higher and National Diplomas and the rest (20%) represent Certificate holders. The researcher found that the opportunities which were open for CPD included conventional and nonconventional degree courses offered by polytechnics and universities, workshops, conferences and seminars. There was no evidence of exchange programmes at a national level. The researcher also found that nearly 80% of the respondents who had either completed a certificate, diploma or degree had been rewarded through regarding or received a notch.

The researcher found out that ICT applications in libraries, e-learning and issues to do with free open access were high on the agenda as critical areas for CPD in tertiary institutions. Polytechnic graduates whose highest qualification was a Higher National Diploma felt that they needed opportunities to upgrade their qualifications to a degree level and the only opportunities were either joining local universities or crossing over the border to neighbouring South Africa or Namibia or other parts of the Commonwealth. There is a splintered approach to CPD reflected by the lack of a coordinating central body . The researcher also found out that 90% of the respondents were either involved in workshops, seminars, reading professional literature, research, online discussion forums, educational development and sharing information through online discussion groups as part of CPD. The most common CPD programmes were workshops, staff development and reading professional literature.

The following recommendations were made from this study:

1. Academic institutions should provide funding for CPD to empower librarians with current knowledge.
2. National professional associations and library consortia should adapt CPD schemes to encourage and compel members to keep abreast of current technological changes in the profession.
3. Professional associations should develop systems to monitor and control CPD programmes.
4. The national professional association should play an active role in CPD of librarians and should unveil an annual academic calendar of training workshops for librarians.
5. There is a need for a central body to coordinate CPD and formulate a national policy on how CPD can be promoted.
6. The development of a qualifications framework at the local and regional level would help in matching qualifications with knowledge, skills and competence. This would bring coherence to sub-systems of qualifications, such as higher education, technical and vocational credit transfer, maintenance of standards, opening up progression routes, facilitating flexibility for learners and making qualifications more relevant to local needs.
7. Job promotion should also be tied to CPD
8. CPD should be promoted through library consortia, such as College and Research Libraries Consortium (CARLC), or University Libraries Consortia.
9. Library Schools at both polytechnics and universities together with professional associations and other stakeholders (including employers and government) should come up with a job relevant CPD credit system that

includes technical, non-technical and professional aspects of library and information science.

Conclusion

CPD is critical in library and information science as it is a special vehicle to help informational professionals keep abreast of current trends and overcome academic and intellectual rusticity and redundancy. There are immense benefits that can be accrued from an investment in CPD such as enhancement of one's ability, job promotion, job satisfaction, future employability or job mobility, among other factors. CPD is an essential activity that goes beyond attending one-off courses but encompasses a variety of activities, including everyday experiences, results-based management, independent study, communities of practice, on-the-job training, writing papers and discussions, among other activities. It should be viewed as a key feature of a progressive learning organization. The information/knowledge age requires information professionals imbued with a progressive philosophy, anchored on well grounded psychological, praxeological, social and professional capabilities to be involved in CPD and withstand the challenges of the information /knowledge age. The absence of CPD programmes will ultimately translate to professional stagnation or inertia.

References

Adanu, T.S.A, (2007) Continuing professional development (CPD) in state owned university libraries in Ghana. *Library Management*, 28(6/7), 292–305.

Anunobi, C.V. & Ukwoma, S.C. (2009). Strategies for reskilling the library and information profession in Nigeria. In J.Varlejs & G. Walton (Eds.) *Strategies for regenerating the library and information professions* (pp 243-259). Munchen: Saur. [IFLA Publication 139].

Broady-Preston, J. (2009). Continuing professional development-its role in the changing educational and qualification landscape of the information profession: case of the United Kingdom. In J.Varlejs & G.Walton (Eds.) *Strategies for regenerating the library and information professions* (pp 265-272). Munchen: Saur. [IFLA Publication 139].

Browell, S. (2000). Staff development and professional education: a cooperative model. *Journal of Workplace Learning,* 12(2), 57–65.

Churukian, A.P. (1997). The academic librarian and scholarship: a vision for twenty first century. In P.L.Ward & E.D.Weingand (Eds). *Human development competencies for twenty first century: papers from the IFLA CPERT Third International Conference on Continuous Professional Development* (pp 278-293). Munchen: Saur.

Dahl, M., Banerjee, K., & Spalti, M. (2006). *Digital libraries: integrating content and systems*. Oxford: Chandos .

Figueroa, L.A., & Gonzalez, A.B. (2006). Management of knowledge, information and organizational learning in libraries. *Libri,* 56(3), 180-190.

Hare, A. (1989). Professional development in the 1980s in college libraries in the South East. *The Southeastern Librarian*, 39, 18-19.

Houle, C.O. (1980). *Continuing learning: the professions*. San Francisco: Jossey-Bass.

Illeris, K. (2003). Workplace learning and learning theory. *Journal of Workplace Learning*, 15(4), 167-178.

Institute of Personnel and Development (2008). *Continuing professional development, the IPD policy*. London : IPD.

Johnson, I.M. (1998) Challenges in developing professionals for "The Information society" and some responses by the British schools of librarianship and information studies. *Library Review*, 47 (3), 5-59.

Madden, C.A., & Mitchell, V.A. (1993). *Professions, standards and competence : a survey of continuing education for the profession*. Bristol: University of Bristol Department for Continuing Education.

Malhotra, Y. (1998). Knowledge management for the new world of business. *Journal for Quality and Participation*, 21 (4), 58-60.

O'Beirne, R. (2006). Raising the profile of information literacy in public libraries. *Update* 5(1/2), 42-45.

Okojie, V. (2007). Library and information science education in Nigeria. *Nigerian Library Association Newsletter*, 19(2), 2.

Pedlar, M., Burgoyne, J., & Boydell, T. (1991). *The learning company: a strategy for sustainable development*. Maidenhead: McGraw-Hill

Ritchie, A. (2005) Conference Opening Address. In: P.Genoni & G.Walton (Eds). *Continuing professional development-preparing for new roles in libraries: a voyage of discovery* (pp11-13). Munchen: Saur. [IFLA Publication 116].

Robinson, L., & Glosiene, A. (2007). Continuing professional development for library and information science: case study of a network of training centres. *ASLIB Proceedings*, 59(4/5), 462-474.

Rouse, M. (2004). Continuing professional development in pharmacy. *American Journal of Health Systems Pharmacy*, 61, 2069-2076.

Senge, P.M. (1990). *The fifth discipline: art and practice of the learning organization*. New York: Currency Doubleday.

Shaughnessy, T.W. (1992). Approaches to developing competencies in research libraries. *Library Trends*, 41, 282-298.

Simmonds, P. (2003). Continuing professional development and workplace learning 2: CPD and you – how CILIP is meeting the continuing professional development needs of its members. *Library Management,* 24(3), 169-170.

Simsova, S. (2000). *The concept of professional development in the information professions in Britain : a comparison of the use of professional development in the Library Association and the British Computer Society. Paper presented at the CASLIN 2000 conference.* Retrieved from Institute of Computing Science website: www.ics.muni.cz/caslin2000/simsova-e.html

Stephens, J. (2005). [Review of the book *Continuing Professional Development: a guide for information professionals*]. *Library Management*, 2(8/9), 806-808.

Tredinnick, L. (2005). The graduate of tomorrow. *Library + Information Update*, 4(9), 4.

World Summit on the Information Society. (2005). *Fostering information and communication for development: UNESCO's follow up to the World Summit on the Information Society*. Retrieved from the UNESCO website: http://unesdoc.unesco.org/images/0018/001849/184921e.pdf